Greek Tragedy

BLACKWELL INTRODUCTIONS TO THE CLASSICAL WORLD

This series will provide concise introductions to classical culture in the broadest sense. Written by the most distinguished scholars in the field, these books survey key authors, periods and topics for students and scholars alike.

Published

Greek Tragedy
Nancy Sorkin Rabinowitz

Roman Satire
Daniel Hooley

Ancient History
Charles W. Hedrick, Jr.

Homer, second edition
Barry B. Powell

Classical Literature
Richard Rutherford

Ancient Rhetoric and Oratory
Thomas Habinek

In Preparation

Ancient Comedy
Eric Csapo

Ancient Fiction
Gareth Schmeling

Augustan Poetry
Richard Thomas

Sophocles
William Allan

Euripides
Scott Scullion

Catullus
Julia Haig Gaisser

Cicero
Robert Cape

Roman Historiography
Andreas Mehl

Ovid
Katharina Volk

Greek Historiography
Thomas Scanlon

Greek Tragedy

Nancy Sorkin Rabinowitz

Blackwell
Publishing

BLACKWELL PUBLISHING
350 Main Street, Malden, MA 02148-5020, USA
9600 Garsington Road, Oxford OX4 2DQ, UK
550 Swanston Street, Carlton, Victoria 3053, Australia

First published 2008 by Blackwell Publishing Ltd

1   2008

Library of Congress Cataloging-in-Publication Data

Rabinowitz, Nancy Sorkin.
  Greek tragedy / Nancy Sorkin Rabinowitz.
      p.   cm. – (Blackwell introductions to the classical world)
  Includes bibliographical references and index.
  ISBN 978-1-4051-2160-6 (hardcover : alk. paper) – ISBN 978-1-4051-
2161-3 (pbk. : alk. paper)   1. Greek drama (Tragedy) – History and
criticism.   2. Theater–Greece–History–To 500.   I. Title.

  PA3131.R26 2008
  882'.0109 – dc22

                                                              2007036295

A catalogue record for this title is available from the British Library.

Set in 10.5 on 13 pt Galliard
by SNP Best-set Typesetter Ltd., Hong Kong
Printed and bound in Singapore
by C.O.S. Printers Pte Ltd

The publisher's policy is to use permanent paper from mills that operate a
sustainable forestry policy, and which has been manufactured from pulp
processed using acid-free and elementary chlorine-free practices. Furthermore,
the publisher ensures that the text paper and cover board used have met
acceptable environmental accreditation standards.

For further information on
Blackwell Publishing, visit our website at
www.blackwellpublishing.com

Dedicated to the memory of
Patricia Francis Cholakian and
Jonathan Walters,
with whom I shared so much,
and my beloved mother and editor extraordinaire,
Sophie Wax Sorkin

Contents

List of Figures	ix
Preface	x
Introduction	1
Part I Tragedy in Its Athenian Context	11
1 What Was Tragedy?	13
Definitions of Tragedy	13
What Did It Do?	16
Where Did It Come From?	18
How Were the Plays Performed?	20
2 Tragedy and the *Polis*	33
Democracy	36
Empire and Hegemony	39
Performance Setting	43
Rhetoric	47
Referentiality	48
Ideology	51
Nothing to Do with the City?	58
3 Tragedy and Greek Religion	60
Dionysos	60
Sacred Time and Space	65
Ritual Practices	67

Ritual Practice in Tragedy   73
Greek Gods and Mortals   76
Tragedy and Myth   79
Euripides' *Bacchai*   81

Part II   Thematic Approaches   **85**

4 War and Empire   **89**
Aeschylus' *Persians*   89
Aeschylus' *Oresteia*   95
Euripides' *Iphigeneia at Aulis*   108

5 Family Romance and Revenge in the House of Atreus   **116**
Euripides' *Elektra*   117
Sophocles' *Elektra*   122

6 Victims and Victimizers   **133**
Euripides' *Trojan Women*   133
Euripides' *Hekabe*   138
Euripides' *Medea*   146

7 The King and I   **155**
Sophocles' *Antigone*   155
Sophocles' *Oedipus Tyrannos*   166

8 Epilogue: Modern Performances (with Sue Blundell)   **180**

References   199
Index   205

List of Figures

---

1. Chorus of satyrs, with Dionysos, Ariadne, and Herakles.   12

2. Chorus of youths raising a figure from a tomb.   20

3. Plan of Athens.   22

4. Theater of Dionysos (photo).   23

5. Restored fifth-century theater of Dionysos (plan).   24

6. Pre-fifth-century deme theater at Thorikos.   25

7. Map of Greece.   41

Preface

Ever since I was first invited to write this book, I have been mulling over, not to say stewing over, the question of why we should bother with the Greeks. The answers will be different depending on your position and who you are. So teachers of theater return to Greek drama as the earliest example of a formal theater that was not ritual, though, as we will see, it was connected to ritual. Those of us who are trained as classicists may want to convey what fascinates us about this body of literature (or history and philosophy). My love affair with classics began in high school, with two factors especially prominent. One, my wonderful Latin teacher (Irving Kizner) generously introduced us to Greek on his lunch hour. Two, I read Aeschylus' *Oresteia* in English during my last year of high school. I have been drawn to tragedy since then because of the depth of meaning that one can find in the poetry and because the stories themselves address very contemporary issues of the family, sex, war, and the relationship of individual to society—to name a few. To say that tragedy raises questions that we still wrestle with does not mean that the ancient solution would be identical to our own (as if there were a single ancient or modern solution to such problems). Rather, these plays enact morally ambiguous situations in a complicated way, which makes them useful as a way of thinking through difficult scenarios in our own lives.

I have written this book with my students in mind, and I am grateful to the students in the Senior Seminar on "Theme and Variation" and "Tragedy: Then and Now"; their questions forced me to sharpen my insights. I have tried to make this book as accessible and as useful as possible; scholars often have a tendency to write as if their audience were all people exactly like themselves. Writing for a general audience has been liberating. At the same time it would be irresponsible to omit my debt to other scholars, so I have included suggestions for further reading at the ends of chapters, as well as a list of works cited.

Transliteration and translation are tricky issues. I have kept to Hellenic spellings for less common words and names, but where the Latinized version is well known, I have retained it (for instance, Kreon not Creon but Oedipus not Oidipous). Translations are my own; where I have used an existing translation, it is noted in the text after the line numbers, e.g., "(101–9, trans. Lattimore in Grene and Lattimore." In citing line numbers, which are given parenthetically in the text, I refer to the Oxford Classical Texts. For translations of the ancient authors, including the tragedies, consult the volumes in the Loeb Classical Library series for individual authors and texts (e.g., Aristotle, *Rhetoric*), which offer Greek texts with facing translations (Cambridge, MA: Harvard University Press). Dates referring to ancient authors and texts are b.c.e. (before the common era).

Thanks to the estate of Muriel Rukeyser for permission to reprint the poem "Myth" in its entirety.

Prefaces are the place to express one's debts; I have many people to thank, and I am grateful for this opportunity to do so. Two of the major influences on my thinking, Pierre Vidal-Naquet and Jean-Pierre Vernant, died while I was completing this book; I owe them an enormous debt of gratitude, though I never studied with either of them. They were activists in their lives and impeccable scholars in their work and set a standard that will be difficult for the rest of us to live up to.

I would like to thank my colleagues in Classics at Hamilton College and Colgate University for stimulating conversations about Greek tragedy; on issues of performance, I have benefited from the perspectives of Mary-Kay Gamel, Craig Latrell, Peter Meineck, Nick Rudall, and Yana Sistovari. Carole Bellini-Sharp, Sue Blundell, Barbara Gold, Richard Seaford, and Nancy Warren graciously read drafts of chapters (some more than once), as did my wonderful students Rachel Bennek, Katie Berlent, and Lindsay Martin. Research was facilitated by supportive deans at Hamilton College: David Paris, Kirk Pillow, and Joe Urgo. It was made pleasant and productive by the library staff at the Institute of Classical Studies in London, the Centre Louis Gernet in Paris, the American School of Classical Studies in Athens, and the reference librarians at Hamilton College's Burke Library, in particular Kristin Strohmeyer and Lynn Mayo. Research assistants over the years—Keturah Brown, Katie Cameron, Cassie Sullivan, Tim Van der Voort—deserve a special vote of thanks for bibliographical assistance, line checking, and bringing order out of chaos. The editors and staff at Blackwell (Al Bertrand, Justin Dyer, Sophie Gibson, Ben Thatcher) have been unfailingly cooperative and attentive, and the readers of the manuscript gave it thorough attention from which I benefited greatly. Thanks to Clifton Ng for his careful and insightful work on the index. Norman Rosenberg provided a foundation for reading Greek tragedy in the context of other traditions. With all those thanks comes the proverbial reminder that any errors that remain are my own.

Finally, Peter J. Rabinowitz read and reread every word with a critical eye, gave moral support, and in general continued to make life possible while this book was in process. For all that and more, I am, as usual, in his debt.

Introduction

There is no dearth of books on Greek, or, to be more precise, Attic, tragedy, some intended for experts and some for novices, some for those who read Greek and some for those who do not. This book is not only written with students and general readers in mind, but it is also written from the perspective of certain challenges and questions that have been raised more generally by educators in the recent past. This is done deliberately, for it is my strong conviction that tragedy is not just an object from the past that we study, but that it is also re-created in the present through the active involvement of reader, spectator, actor, and director. The original context for tragedy is central to this book, but that is not its only important context.

In 2002, Simon Goldhill published a book entitled *Who Needs Greek?* You can read those words with a dismissive intonation (as my son once did)—meaning "no one," or at least "not me." Do we need Greek? The answer to that question has long since ceased to be an obvious yes. Classics, derived as it was from the Latin word *classicus*, meaning "top rank, the best," used to connote just that, and, practically speaking, familiarity with the classics was required for success; its study, therefore, needed no explanation or defense. But in the U.S. and U.K., and indeed elsewhere in Europe as well, Classics as a discipline has increasingly lost that status as a signifier of class and culture. This process began with the move from Greek to Latin almost 100 years ago but has been exacerbated recently.

The academy as a whole has been involved in a large-scale dispute often called the "culture wars." From the late sixties on, there have been basically two camps regarding the curriculum, and this division has affected the study of Classics. One camp, made up of what we might call the educational conservatives, argues that students must know about (and honor) western civilization. Former U.S. Secretary of Education and director of the National Endowment for the Humanities, William Bennett, gave three reasons—it is our past, it is good, and the west is under attack. Lynne Cheney, head of the National Endowment of the Humanities under Republican Presidents Reagan and Bush, Sr. from 1986 to 1993, summed it up this way:

> The key questions are thought to be about gender, race, and class. . . . but focusing on political issues to the exclusion of all others does not bring students to an understanding of how Milton or Shakespeare speaks to the deepest concerns we all have as human beings. . . . Should students be required to know about the Old Testament and New, about the classical works of Greece and Rome . . .? Since Western civilization forms the basis for our society's laws and institutions, it might seem obvious that education should ground the upcoming generation in the Western tradition. (12)

Such claims for the foundational importance of Greek civilization are made routinely: for instance, as I was standing on the Akropolis, I heard tour guide after tour guide assert the direct connection between ancient Greece and modern western culture, and at a conference in Havana, Cuba, the same link was affirmed for Cuban culture. One of the important arguments for the continued study of the humanities is that it can help "humanity" find its future, and Attic tragedy is one of the most privileged sites for humanistic learning. As a teacher educated and steeped in Greek literature, I, of course, find this moral centrality very attractive.

These brave assertions are often based on unexamined assumptions about the existence of a transcendent human subject, which are debatable given cultural diversity, global changes, and postmodern theory. When someone argues that we study Greek literature "to keep our past live to us," we must analyze whose past it is. In identifying this particular heritage as "our" past, we actually create that "we" by placing ourselves in a certain lineage, but worldwide immigration debates reveal that that lineage is in the process of being defined and redefined and therefore cannot simply be taken for granted.

Bennett and Cheney were defending canonical education against attacks that had been levied in the U.S. by experts in the growing fields of Latino Studies, Black Studies, Women's Studies, and, somewhat later, Cultural Studies and Gay and Lesbian Studies. These scholars debated Bennett's underlying assumptions and constitute my "second camp." They asked what makes the history of Europe "our" history for non-European men, or for women of any race? Moreover, the name "Classics" for the study of Greek and Latin implies that there was only one classical period, when in fact many cultures might be said to have their own. Were students also well educated if they didn't know anything about Latin America, Africa, and Asia? What about Islam? Racial and ethnic diversity is increasing across Europe and within the U.S., and educational resources are scarce. These critics asked educators to justify teaching Greek literature, which comes from a society that used slave labor and marginalized women, to the exclusion of other literatures.

Part of what had made knowledge of Greek culture essential was the myth of "the Greek Miracle," which credited the Greeks (and more particularly the Athenians) with creating drama, philosophy, lyric poetry, and history as we know them from nothing and with no outside influence. But Afrocentrists have questioned the pride of place given to Greece, with its corresponding devaluation of Africa. Even a moderate position today would concede that there were outside influences on Hellenic culture, as Greek myth and the evidence of trade routes attest.

One extreme position ("throw the old texts out") is more or less a straw person; although there was (and is, though more ironically these days) much talk about "dead white men," few scholars, and of course no classicists, seriously entertained getting rid of the whole tradition. Nor do we need to accept the other extreme position—that tragedy is essential reading because it is a crucial part of western civilization, the best that has been thought and written—to see interest and value in the plays. Tragedy and Greek philosophy have, after all, been part of the European/Euro-American intellectual and cultural traditions. The references to these texts make information about them necessary for much academic work. Moreover, the Greeks were asking questions that we continue to ask, not perhaps because every person or every culture has the same questions, but because we have been formed in a culture that has studied Greek literature and philosophy.

There are, however, many approaches to the study of tragedy. Until quite recently, tragedy was viewed primarily as text. Classical philologists of the nineteenth and early twentieth centuries produced texts and commentaries, establishing what the Greek actually was, what it meant, and how to translate given words and lines. Any critic of tragedy must depend on the monumental labor of these scholars. One continuing strand of criticism treats the texts that these scholars established as great works of literature; the dense language of the plays rewards that approach. New Criticism in the 1950s and 1960s, a method of close reading that stressed the coherence and interpretation of the text itself to the exclusion of everything else, built on earlier forms of humanism that made tragedy accessible to the modern reader by emphasizing its universality. It focused on elements that were familiar and comfortable, such as character, themes, and images.

Close reading of the text itself, however, offers a limited perspective; so, for instance, a study of fire imagery in Sophocles' *Women of Trachis* benefits from attention to Greek myth that might or might not be mentioned in the play but would have been understood by the original audience. The study of tragedy in larger contexts has come to predominate more recently, overlapping with rather than superseding the more strictly linguistic and literary approaches. Structuralism, which is based in anthropology and related to Saussurean linguistics, has been very productive in Classics. The name most prominently associated with structuralism is that of Claude Lévi-Strauss; he developed a method for analyzing myths and other phenomena as part of universal structures that underlie and organize cultures, by analogy to the structure of language. Focusing on a matrix of binary oppositions (the raw and the cooked, famously), he sought the logic behind seemingly disparate elements. Though Lévi-Strauss was not a literary scholar, he studied the Oedipus myth, interpreting all the variants, as part of the system of endogamy/exogamy. His work and that of Louis Gernet have led to a great deal of further work on these oppositions as they appear in Greek tragedy and society. For instance, Euripides' *Hippolytos* shows a young man who is a hunter and associated with the wild; he resists the domesticated and political realms of the city. In general, tragedy is seen to challenge order by revealing tensions between the elements in the various binaries before ultimately resolving them. The binary oppositions remain a fruitful way of approaching the plays, as we will see in Part II.

Psychological criticism has attended to a different set of deep structures, those taken to reside not in the culture *per se* but in the human psyche. Looking at the plays in this way at its most general takes character (more than poetic form or cultural concepts) as central; more specifically, critics have followed psychoanalytic theory, seeing evidence of the Freudian model of human psychological development in the tragedies. Freud found in Greek myth evidence for the universality of the stages and structures he had discovered (especially his Oedipus and Electra complexes); narcissism is named for Narcissus, a mythic figure who was in love with his own reflection. While Freud's claims are extravagant and challenged on many grounds, particularly in view of the gendered nature of his analysis and the great variety in cultures, his theories have nonetheless been useful in looking at tragedy. The same Hippolytos, for example, can be seen through a psychological lens, which would give his resistance to sexuality a different flavor and emphasis. Other psychoanalytic theories, e.g., Jungian and Lacanian, have also used Greek myth and been used to some extent in reading tragedy. Jung studied the archetypes for human behavior and found them in Greco-Roman myth, while Lacan built on and departed from Freud's analytic model. He is best known for his concepts of the mirror stage and the symbolic, both of which can be used to decode tragedy.

Jacques Lacan makes up part of the poststructuralist movement, which, though much less expansive than structuralism in its effect on classical studies, has nonetheless had an impact. Jacques Derrida's *Of Grammatology*, a foundational text for deconstructive criticism, works closely with Plato. Though it is daring to sum this school up in a phrase or two for an introduction to tragedy, I will risk it. Where structuralism emphasizes the binary oppositions and the ways in which they are mediated in culture, deconstruction emphasizes the ways in which the supposed hierarchy of terms is not really stable. Its effects in discussions of tragedy can be seen most readily in the places where closure is deferred and questioning is celebrated.

At the same time that these ways of reading Greek tragedy in relation to other fields have found acceptance, there has also been heightened attention to the political and ritual contexts of the original productions. These approaches will be taken up in detail in Chapters 1 to 3, but let me say a few words here. The attention to ancient context is helpful in that it may offer a middle ground between the two camps identified earlier. If we seek to understand tragedy as a creation of the democracy of Athens, which was both extremely radical and at the same time based on fundamental exclusions, we can not only celebrate its achievements (as Bennett and Cheney would have us do) but also turn our attention to the elements that were excluded in order to create the system (a practice that Cheney, however, laments). Thus, we can look at the class, race/ethnic, and/or gender constructions within the body of literature. The modern investigation of the relationship between inside and outside is prefigured in the Greek/Persian conflict (configured as west and east), and the issues of class and gender that have led some critics to want to displace Classics from the curriculum are also prominent in these very texts. Modern feminist criticism, Marxist criticism, and multicultural criticism have challenged the status of these so-called classics; as the rest of the book will make clear, we can employ those frameworks to enrich our readings of the plays. At the same time, we can examine what they can tell us about the problems that plague us in those arenas. We can look at the ways in which tragedy enabled Athenians to face their contradictions as a way for us to think about how we will face our own. In looking at ancient Greece not with nostalgia for the good old days but with recognition of the price that was paid for the affluence of Athens, we can focus on similarities as well as differences between us and them. I will develop these topics, as well as the relations between mortals and immortals, in Part II.

As part of the stress on the ancient context, there has also been a deepening emphasis on the performance of the plays, with critics approaching them as drama (from a Greek word for doing) or theater (from a Greek word for watching). Taking seriously the element of performance in antiquity has in turn led scholars to a consideration of contemporary performances, which can give us new insight into the past as well as the present. When a tragedy is staged, directors and actors have to find a way to reach the contemporary audience; watching these productions or reading about them can reveal elements in the play that you hadn't thought about before. Thus, the modern production can illuminate what the original might have meant. At the same time, adaptations and productions must articulate what they find of continuing significance in these ancient plays. Whenever we are at war, for instance, we seem to turn to Greek tragedy. In these cases, production choices can also inform the audience about its own time.

Can there be modern tragedy? Some writers, arguing that tragedy is dead, point out that there is no longer a controlling religious frame of reference; with the loss of the gods and the concept of fate, they say, we have lost the capacity for creating tragedy. It seems premature, however, to talk about the death of religion. In fact, fundamentalist religious groups (from whatever faith) seem to be very much at the forefront in the early twenty-first century. Tragedy's religious resonance can be used to broaden contemporary secularism: it suggests that not everything is knowable by humans, nor can everything be controlled by humans. Another view of the death of tragedy maintains that in antiquity tragedy centered on those with elevated stature, and we don't have that mythic structure today. But the poor, the oppressed, the victims of injustice, are in a privileged position for understanding tragedy and for living it; they know well that there are constraints on them that might constitute fate, and that they are not totally free agents. Indeed, in what are called contemporary tragedies, economic or political forces often replace the divine/mythic level.

The larger-than-life characters, the elevated language, and the mythic plots make Athenian tragedy distant to today's students. Can it still stir our emotions? In speaking about the Oedipus complex, Freud argued that the ancient play could move us only because it touched on a universal desire. Marx too wondered why Greek art still gives us pleasure; he found the answer in history, arguing that it represents our own childhood. In other words, we are nostalgic for the past. In either case, viewing tragedy is not simply an intellectual or political exercise. The plays raise questions of life and death, of family dynamics and their relationship to the political realm, and they do so with awe-inspiring intensity. To return to contemporary adaptations, modern writers and directors often respond to the affective element of drama. Charles Mee, a contemporary playwright and one of the great creative spirits of the present, goes back to antiquity for inspiration. Here is what he says about the relationship:

> I've been inspired a lot by the Greeks. I love the Greeks because their plays so often begin with matricide and fratricide, with a man murdering his nephews and serving the boys to their father for dinner. That is to say, the Greeks take no easy problems, no little misunderstanding that is going to be resolved before the final commercial break at the top of the hour, no tragedy that will be resolved with good will, acceptance of a childhood hurt, and a little bit of healing. They take deep anguish and hatred and disability and rage and homicidal mania and confusion and aspiration and a longing for the purest beauty and they say: here is not an easy problem; take all this and make a civilization of it. (2002: 93–4)

Mee adds material from newspapers, popular songs, and the like. At the beginning of *The Trojan Women a Love Story*, Mee writes:

The Trojan Women a Love Story, based on the works of Euripides and Berlioz, was developed with Greg Gunter as dramaturg and incorporates shards of our contemporary world, to lie, as in a bed of ruins, within the frame of the classical world. It uses texts by the survivors of Hiroshima and of the Holocaust, by Slavenka Drakulic, Zlatko Dizdarevic, Georges Bataille, Sei Shonagon, Elaine Scarry, Hannah Arendt, the Kama Sutra, Amy Vanderbilt and the Geraldo show. (1998: 160)

The family and world history, feeling and thinking, are intermingled in his view.

Part I will develop the ancient performance, political, and ritual contexts I have mentioned here. In Part II, we will look at a group of the plays selected in part because they are so often read and taught, but also for their relationship to the themes and methods set out here. In that section I will emphasize issues of interpretation, in antiquity as well as today. The book concludes with a consideration of some significant modern performances.

Suggestions for further reading

On the culture wars, see Allan Bloom, *The Closing of the American Mind* (New York: Simon and Schuster, 1987); Victor Davis Hanson and John Heath, *Who Killed Homer? The Demise of Classical Education and the Recovery of Greek Wisdom* (New York: Free Press, 1998).

On Afrocentrism and classics, see Martin Bernal, *Black Athena: The Afro-Asiatic Roots of Classical Civilization* (Brunswick, NJ: Rutgers University Press, 1987), *Black Athena Writes Back: Martin Bernal Responds to His Critics* (Durham, NC: Duke University Press, 2001); for an opposing view, see Mary Lefkowitz and Guy McLean, *Black Athena Revisited* (Chapel Hill: University of North Carolina Press, 1996).

For an example of formalism, see H. D. F. Kitto, *Form and Meaning in Drama* (London: Methuen, 1956). For structural anthropology, see Claude Lévi-Strauss, *Structural Anthropology* (New York: Basic Books, 1963) and *The Elementary Structures of Kinship* (Boston: Beacon Press, 1969).

Following from Louis Gernet, most important is the Paris school of Jean-Pierre Vernant and Pierre Vidal-Naquet, especially *Myth and Tragedy in Ancient Greece*, 2 vols. (New York: Zone Books, 1988); the work of Charles Segal, e.g., *Tragedy and Civilization: An Interpretation of Sophocles* (Cambridge, MA: Harvard University Press, 1981) and *Interpreting Greek Tragedy: Myth, Poetry, Text* (Ithaca, NY: Cornell University Press, 1986), exemplifies this school in the U.S.

For an early psychoanalytic perspective, see Philip Slater, *The Glory of Hera* (Boston: Beacon Press, 1968). Other examples are George Devereux, *Dreams in Greek Tragedy: An Ethno-Psycho-Analytical Study* (Oxford: Oxford University Press, 1976) and Bennett Simon, *Mind and Madness in Ancient Greece: The Classical Roots of Modern Psychiatry* (Ithaca, NY: Cornell University Press, 1978). Charles Segal's work *Dionysiac Poetics and Euripides' Bacchae* (Princeton: Princeton University Press, 1982) is in part a psychoanalytic approach to that text.

For an early Marxist analysis of drama and specifically the *Oresteia*, see George Thomson, *Aeschylus and Athens: A Study in the Origins of Drama* (London: Lawrence and Wishart, 1946). More recently, see Peter Rose, *Sons of the Gods, Children of Earth: Ideology and Literary Form in Ancient Greece* (Ithaca, NY: Cornell University Press, 1992).

Feminist criticism or work on gender in tragedy is vast and still emerging; a recent collection of essays by Vanda Zajko and Miriam Leonard, *Laughing with Medusa: Classical Myth and Feminist Thought* (Oxford: Oxford University Press, 2006), has interesting material on tragedy; on the question of women's speech in general, see Laura McClure, *Spoken Like a Woman: Speech and Gender in Athenian Drama* (Princeton: Princeton University Press, 1999) and Helene Foley, *Female Acts in Greek Tragedy* (Princeton: Princeton University Press, 2001). Other suggestions will follow other chapters.

Part I

Tragedy in Its Athenian Context

In the next three chapters, we will be speaking of Greek or Attic tragedy, defined by its function: that group of plays performed in the contest at the festival in the city, or *polis*, of Athens (in the state of Attica) called the Great or City Dionysia, in honor of the god Dionysos Eleuthereus. In the summer before the festival, which took place in late March, one of the city magistrates, the eponymous archon (so-called because the year was named after him), would grant each of three tragic poets the right to produce plays in the contest. There were many playwrights in antiquity, and we have the names of some of these from lists of contestants, as well as fragments of their plays from references in later authors, but the only three whose plays survive are Aeschylus (525/4?–456/5), Sophocles (497/6?–406), and Euripides (485/4–406?). We have seven plays each from Aeschylus and Sophocles (in collected editions from the Byzantine period) and more than twice that number by Euripides, due to the vagaries of manuscript transmission, but each of these playwrights wrote many more plays (approximately eighty in the case of Aeschylus, 120 for Sophocles, and ninety by Euripides). While we can assume that these writers were considered to be very good, others whose work is missing or exists only in fragments also won prizes and sometimes even won the prize over one of our three.

The archon also assigned the playwright three actors and a *chorêgos*, who would train and pay for the chorus. Each tragedian put on three tragedies and a satyr drama, which was more playful and provided a contrast with the mood of the serious drama. The form is named after its chorus of mythical figures, who were costumed with animal tail, a phallos, and a mask with pointed ears and snub nose (characteristic features of satyrs who followed Dionysos) (see Figure 1). Unfortu-

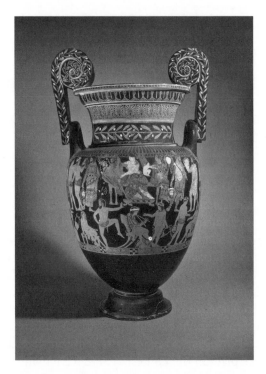

Figure 1. Attic red-figure volute-krater with a chorus of satyrs, Dionysos and Ariadne (center), Herakles (upper right). c. 400. Pronomos vase. (Museo Nazionale Archeologico, Naples. Inv. 3240. Photo: akg-images/Nimatallah.)

nately, we have only one complete example (Euripides' *Cyclops*) and one fragmentary example of which about half survives (Sophocles' *Ichneutai*). In the early years, all four plays were thematically related and formed a tetralogy, but Sophocles and Euripides later adopted a single-play format. We only possess one trilogy (Aeschylus' *Oresteia* [458]), and even in that case, we are missing the related satyr drama (*Proteus*). Other events at the festival make it clear that it was an emotionally and culturally wide-ranging event: comedies were produced on a separate day; a thousand men and boys (fifty men and fifty boys from each of ten tribes) also competed in singing the dithyramb, which was a choral form dedicated to Dionysos.

In the following chapters of Part I we will examine these elements in greater depth. Chapter 1 asks the question of what Greek tragedy was, emphasizing debates about its function and ancient performance practices. Chapter 2 looks at tragedy as a civic art form, while Chapter 3 looks at it from the perspective of religion.

I

What Was Tragedy?

Definitions of Tragedy

When we use the word "tragedy" in ordinary conversation ("What a tragedy," or "how tragic!"), we may be referring to something that is merely sad. On reflection, however, most of us would agree that the word should be reserved at least for situations of great suffering; when it is used to speak of a death, that death should be early or exhibit "tragic waste." My students thought it was tragic when drunk driving led to the deaths of four students in one car at a nearby college; similarly, when five young people from one town in Maine died in a car crash, the community felt it was a tragedy.

In the course of our lives we often encounter grievous events, and we mourn them, using the word tragedy. We typically label terrifying acts of nature a tragedy: for instance, when a tsunami struck in Southeast Asia, it was widely called a tragedy. And six months later, not only were the events seen as a "most vivid manifestation of the globalisation of tragedy," but the reaction of the world was even called a *katharsis*, which, as we shall see, alludes to tragedy as well (*New Straits Times Press* [Malaysia] Berhad, June 26, 2005). War and other political events, such as the 2001 attacks on the World Trade Center, frequently summon up the word. And sometimes nature and political reactions combine to create a disaster of tragic proportions; in the case of Hurricane Katrina in 2005, the winds and flooding caused the initial physical devastation, but the political and economic conditions led to more death and destruction and to the continued suffering of the storm's victims.

Scholars typically distinguish this ordinary-language use of tragedy from the artistic form, locating tragedy not in such events but in their structuring into art, and in the audience response to that structure. Historically, tragedy has virtually boiled down to any serious drama—it is not comedy, although Chekhov confuses the issue when he calls his very serious and pessimistic plays "comedies." Many people, including most of my students, assume that a tragedy is a play that ends badly, and most often with death. Or, with more detail, they take tragedy to be the fall of an important person from a high place because of a flaw. The flaw is often interpreted as a deep error of character, generally pride.

Most elements of the basic definition my students look for (the fall of a person from a high place because of a flaw) come from slight misreadings of Aristotle's *Poetics*, a very brief and fragmentary treatise dating to the 330s. Although Aristotle was not contemporary with fifth-century tragedy, he had a great deal more evidence at his disposal than we do; at the same time, he also had his own philosophical perspective and cannot be taken as giving an objective or authoritative verdict on the subject. According to Aristotle, a tragedy is "an imitation of an action that is serious, complete, and of a certain magnitude; in language embellished with each kind of artistic ornament, the several kinds being found in separate parts of the play; in the form of action, not of narrative; through pity and fear effecting the proper purgation of those emotions" (6.2, trans. Butcher). Aristotle begins by contrasting tragedy with epic poetry, in which a single rhapsode, or singer, narrates a story rather than enacting it, but likens the two forms in that they both make men better than they are (in contrast to comedy) (1–3). Aristotle adds later that since tragedy imitates an action, there have to be actors (6.5), and they should imitate someone better, not worse, than the audience. For Aristotle, then, Greek tragedy centers on the story; the characters are there for the sake of the action, not vice versa. He further emphasizes two elements of the plot that make for tragedy: overturn or change in fortune and recognition (*peripeteia* and *anagnórisis*, 6.13), which dominate much later discussion of individual plays. Recognition is essential but painful in such plays as Sophocles' *Oedipus Tyrannos*, where Oedipus blinds himself when he realizes who he is.

Crucially, in terms of common mis-understandings, tragedy does not have to have an unhappy ending to be successful for Aristotle, or for the Athenians in general: it is enough if something terrible almost happens, but does not. The change or overturn can theoretically go in either direction—from bad to good, from good to bad fortune (though Aristotle acknowledges that it makes better drama in the latter case). Aeschylus' *Oresteia* ends with harmony, as his other trilogies might have done, though we don't know for certain because we have only single plays from the others. In the case of the plays written to stand alone, two of Sophocles' seven end well for some of the characters at least; and many tragedies by Euripides end well. His *Ion* depends on a recognition for the happy ending: a mother almost kills Ion but does not because she finds out that he is the baby she had born to the god Apollo, now grown up and working at the god's temple. In *Ion*, then, there is a positive *peripeteia* based on the *anagnôrisis* of the child's identity.

While Aristotle never says that the tragedy *must* involve a fall, he implies it when he says that in the best tragedies the tragic action should come about through some mistake of the character's own (10–11, 13.4). He uses *hamartia*, which comes from a word that also means missing the mark in archery; thus it is an error, not a character flaw and certainly not pride. Some small mistake that you make unleashes catastrophic consequences, and in some tragedies the mis-recognition of a family member is that mistake. Modern students and critics writing in the wake of Shakespearean drama often see pride as the error, and they look for evidence in Greek tragedy; people also mistakenly assume that the Greek concept *hubris* against the gods is the ancient equivalent for a modern (and Christian) notion of pride. For the Greeks *hubris* was problematic, but it was typically externalized in an arrogant or violent action and was not simply an attitude. Pride within bounds, not humility, was appropriate for the aristocratic Greek male in the heroic age who was the subject of tragedy; therefore, we have to be wary of importing Christian values into pagan times. We will discuss this further in the chapter on Greek religion and when we come to discuss Oedipus and his drama.

Aristotle's definition is for the most part formal, not emotional or political. However, he further points out that the best tragedies are based on a few families because they have done or suffered something terrible (13.5) and, contradicting his earlier theoretical position, says that they do end unhappily (13.6). Through the emphasis on myth and "purgation" (*katharsis*) of pity and fear, he opens the way to a discussion of the emotions in tragedy.

What Did It Do?

What was the function of tragedy—to teach or entertain or both? Aristotle's view was undoubtedly developed as part of a conversation with his teacher Plato. Plato is dismissive of artists in general on the grounds that they simply imitate physical reality; his philosophy of the "forms" holds that these "ideal" versions are "real," while everyday reality is an imitation of these abstractions. Art, then, is an imitation of an imitation, and consequently worthless, or even pernicious. Plato argues that the arts are not educational, as they were generally thought to be; he attacks poetry, in particular, because it represents the gods as quarreling, and is thus misleading. He goes further in his attack on tragedy: it encourages self-pity by leading its audience to feel pity for the characters, and makes the actors womanish (*Republic* 3.395D–E). His point is that society should not nurture such behaviors (*Republic* 10.606b). The citizens and especially the leaders of a city should be trained to be strong and reasonable, not emotional; since the arts in general and tragedy in particular create a pernicious emotional response, they should be banned. To sum up Plato's view: poetry (epic or tragic) does not give access to the truth; thus, it has nothing to teach and does not deserve its reputation and high status. The poets may be inspired, but they are not teachers. Plato grants that we learn by imitation, but he argues that tragedy does not provide good models for the audience to imitate.

Plato's philosophy of education and art is countered by Aristotle in the *Poetics;* by asserting that tragedy is the imitation of an action, he avoids the suggestion that the plays are merely third-rate (compared to reality and the ineffable forms). For Aristotle, tragedy as mimesis is a reenactment, not a bad copy of something else. The reenactment can be positive, because the action imitated is a serious or weighty matter; thus, it is important. The experience of watching a play is educational because people instinctually imitate and learn by imitating. Aristotle argues that tragedy is also pleasurable because human beings by nature take pleasure in works of imitation (4.2). Furthermore, he claims a philosophical status for tragedy. It points out general truths, the sort of thing that might happen (9.1–4), and is thus more philosophical than history.

The tragic emotions that Aristotle names are pity and fear. He counters Plato's claim about the destructiveness of the emotions (especially pity) by asserting that the audience is not left with those emotions raging in its breasts because tragedy effects their *katharsis* (6.2, 14.2–3). *Katharsis* is a much-debated term, and we are not sure what it means in this context. While its dictionary definition is "purification," it can refer to physical (a purgative) as well as spiritual cleansing. If there is no implication that the audience requires ritual purification, perhaps we can think of this as the stimulating of emotion and the emptying out of it. The audience, then, would be "wrung out" by watching tragedy, leaving the theater not in the heightened state of the crisis but in the calm that follows. We can envision this process as analogous to the difference between actual suffering in life and the artistic representation of suffering in which we can learn from someone else's pain instead of going through it. Aristotle no more than Plato holds that the emotion is good in and of itself, but the experience of *katharsis* means that tragedy can produce the rational citizen Plato maintains is desirable for the state. We feel pity and fear for the characters in the story, but because of the universal nature of tragedy, and because we understand that the actors are like ourselves, we understand that what happens to them might happen to us (on pity and fear, see also Aristotle, *Rhetoric* II.5.1382b25, II.8.386a). The Aeschylean phrase "learning through suffering" (*pathei mathos*, *Agamemnon* 177) can therefore be taken to apply to Greek tragedy as a whole.

For both Aristotle and Plato, tragedy is an aesthetic object that has as its goal the arousal of emotion, but they differ in that for Aristotle tragedy is also educational. In *Frogs* (405), the comic playwright Aristophanes shows clearly the dominant view that tragedy is both instructive and entertaining, though of course everything in a comedy is potentially being played for laughs. In the play, Dionysos is starved for good poetry; as a result, he has gone down to the realm of the dead (Hades) to bring Euripides back to life. While in Hades he is asked to judge a contest between Euripides and Aeschylus to determine who is the best writer (Sophocles declines to participate because he is content where he is). Aristophanes' Chorus links Euripides' cleverness to that of Socrates, and contrasts it to the "high serious matter of tragic art." After much repartee, which highlights Aeschylus' impenetrable verse and Euripides' novelty and excessively democratic tendencies, Dionysos chooses Aeschylus because he has done the poet's duty—injected virtue into the people—and has the wisdom necessary to save the state. On the one hand, tragedy seems to be visceral; it fills a need as food or sex does since Dionysos was hungry for it, and the play opens with jokes about food and sex. But, on the other hand, the tragic poet's function is to educate the citizens. It remains to be seen whether or in what ways both these things are true. How do our emotions and our intellect interact in the experience of spectatorship or reading?

Where Did It Come From?

Classics is not, as the name would seem to imply, a fixed and static field but one in which practically everything is debated, especially when it comes to the origins of tragedy. Even the meaning of the word *tragôidia*, which gives us tragedy, is the subject of disagreements: it has something to do with a goat (*tragos*) and song (*oidos*), but how the two parts are connected is not clear. It might have been a song sung over the sacrifice of a goat, or a song for a goat prize, or the singing of a goat chorus. Whatever is said about the origins of tragedy is conjectural. Aristotle gives many bits of "information" in the *Poetics*; he first states that the Dorians claimed that tragedy developed in their regions, the Peloponnese, citing as evidence the fact that the word "drama" has its origins in their word for doing, *dran* (3.3). He also says that tragedy came from those who "led off" the dithyramb (4.12), but he later mentions that tragedy was initially "satyr-like," or satiric, and not elevated in tone (4.14). Both satyr drama and dithyramb remained elements of the festival in historical times, and Aristotle might have been hypothesizing as to why, not simply giving us the facts.

We have references to tragic performances in the sixth century, with Arion, a Corinthian named by Herodotus, and Thespis, named by Aristotle as the first to separate himself from the chorus and deliver a prologue and a set speech. One tradition dates Thespis to 534, in what would be the earliest contest, but it is increasingly popular to take a later date, 502, for the beginning of the competition (see also Chapter 2). In any event, the earliest play that we have is Aeschylus' *Persians* (472).

The texts that have come down to us are also less than secure. Just to give you some idea of the difficulties: our earliest manuscripts date from the tenth or eleventh century, though we can with other sources get reasonably close to what would have been texts from the third century. However, it is not at all clear that those texts represent what was actually performed in the fifth-century contests. In the early years of tragedy, Greek society was in a transition between an oral and written culture; books were not widely available until the end of the fifth century. People, including the actors, learned through memorization. The importance of memory in education continued into late antiquity; students learned poems and speeches by heart, and it is said that Alexander the Great could recite whole speeches from Euripides' plays. In a story that is not necessarily accurate but that is nonetheless significant about the power of tragedy, Athenians taken prisoner after their failed attempt to conquer Sicily gained their freedom by reciting Euripides (Plutarch, *Nicias* 29).

The festivals continued into the fourth century; while new plays were written, tragedies by Aeschylus, Sophocles, and Euripides were also produced as "revivals," which made it almost inevitable that there would be changes to the plays as a result of actors' interpolations, for example. The texts were not firmly established until around 330, when Lykurgus, an Athenian politician, passed a law that required the preparation of an official version for re-performance; these texts were, however, based on what was already an amalgam of written and oral material. And even those manuscripts had to be recopied, since they were written on papyrus and thus were highly perishable; as a result, the process of unintentional change continued until the invention of paper.

To make matters more difficult, the original manuscripts did not have divisions between words, and there were no assignments of lines to one speaker or another; these issues would have been resolved by the actors and directors in performance, and analyzing the texts to see what was original and what was added later has been the work of philologists since antiquity. The ancient scholars left notes in the margin (called *scholia*) which form the basis of much critical debate. The plays themselves did not necessarily have titles affixed to them by the playwright: how would it change our view if *Agamemnon* were called *Clytemnestra*? When we read a text, especially in translation, all of these questions will have been answered for us, and unless there are ample footnotes, we don't even realize the work of scholarly production by philologists that has gone into the book we hold in our hands. And of course, each editorial decision is also an act of interpretation, as this passage from an ancient commentary on Sophocles' *Ajax* 354 makes clear: "for in places where the roles are unclear, one should guess at the character, and make a distinction accordingly" (Csapo and Slater 31).

How Were the Plays Performed?

Despite Aristotle's claims that the spectacle is the least important aspect of the tragedies, and that even hearing the story should elicit the tragic emotions of pity and fear, Greek tragedy was written to be performed. To state the most important points: it had a conventional, not realistic, aesthetic. There were at the most three actors, all men, who performed in masks; they were accompanied by a chorus of twelve to fifteen men who sang and danced, also masked (see Figure 2). The set had only the most basic markers of place. The audience, then, was

Figure 2. Attic red-figure column-krater with a chorus of youths raising a figure from a tomb. (Antikenmuseum Basel und Sammlung Ludwig, Inv. BS 415. Photo: Andreas F. Voegelin.)

accustomed to using its imagination and to reading the codes of mask and gesture.

Performances began at dawn; in some of the plays, such as Aeschylus' *Agamemnon*, the dawn is remarked upon, and it would have been real; similarly Sophocles' *Antigone* and *Ajax* speak of what has happened the night before. People might have started arriving during the night if they came from far away in Attica. We might think of lining up for tickets to a rock concert, or for some festival without reserved seating. The festival lasted for five days, and each was a massive all-day affair; people in the audience typically ate and drank during the performances. Therefore, we should not imagine a hushed space. The audience was an active participant, not a passive one.

The plays were first performed outdoors, in daylight, for a large audience (estimates vary, between 6,000 and 14,000). The backdrop was the city of Athens (Figures 3 and 4). Unfortunately, not much can be said with assurance about the physical fifth-century theater because of subsequent changes (see Figure 5); many images that we have in our minds come from the theater at Epidauros, which is from the fourth century. The Greek word *theatron*, from which we get our "theater," has as its primary significance "seeing," and the audience members were spectators. Yet, as some argue, the voice of the actors was more useful for audience comprehension because of the distance between actors and audience. The importance of sound is evident in Aristophanes, as well as in Plato's and Aristotle's discussions of tragedy; and we hear that Sophocles gave up acting his own plays because his voice was not strong enough (*Life* 4). Even if this story is not literally true, it does indicate that the ancients believed a powerful voice to be crucial.

We have only a few stones left from the original theater on the Akropolis. We know that there was a space for dancing (called the orchestra) and a building (called the *skênê*, from which we get our "scene") in front of which details of location could be indicated, and into which actors could go in order to change costume (or role), or simply to indicate that they were going indoors. Sophocles is also credited with beginning the practicing of painting on the *skênê*. We do not know if there was any form of stage, although if there was one, it was not the high version we are familiar with in the western theater today. The first theater for the purposes of play production was built of wood in 500. Though recent arguments from archaeology favor a roughly rectangular shape for the orchestra and auditorium, as it was

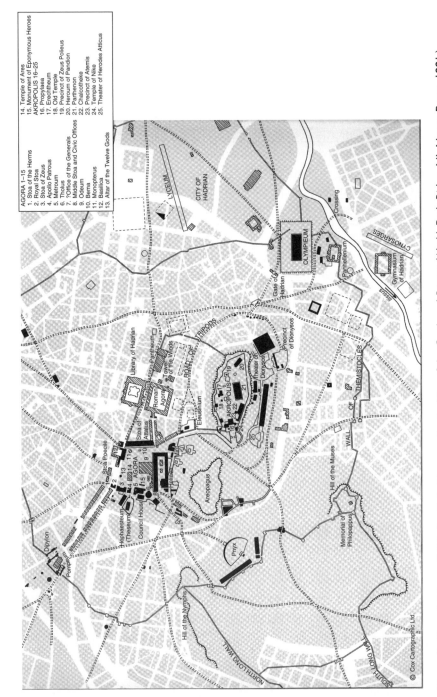

AGORA 1–15
1. Stoa of the Herms
2. Royal Stoa
3. Stoa of Zeus
4. Apollo Patrous
5. Metroum
6. Tholus
7. ?Office of the Generals
8. Middle Stoa and Civic Offices
9. Odeum
10. Bema
11. Monopterus
12. Basilica
13. Altar of the Twelve Gods
14. Temple of Ares
15. Monument of Eponymous Heroes
AKROPOLIS 16–25
16. Propylaea
17. Erechtheum
18. Old Temple
19. Precinct of Zeus Polieus
20. Heroum of Pandion
21. Parthenon
22. Chalcotheke
23. Precinct of Artemis
24. Temple of Nike
25. Theater of Herodes Atticus

Figure 3. Plan of Athens. (Nicholas G. L. Hammond, ed., *Atlas of the Greek and Roman World*, Park Ridge, NJ: Noyes Press, 1981.)

Figure 4. Theater of Dionysos (© Michael Palis/istockphoto.com.)

in the deme theater of Thorikos (Figure 6), others think it was circular, as it was in the later theater at Athens (Figure 5). Like the question of origins, this issue has ideological significance. For instance, if we emphasize the chorus and hypothesize a circular playing area, we can retain "the traditional idea of a democratic Athenian community gathered in a circle in order to contemplate itself in relation to the fictive world of the play" (Wiles 1997: 52). The circle theory sees corroboration in the notion of a round threshing floor, as well as from lines in the *Iliad* (18.590ff.); thus, it is related to assumptions about the connection between harvest and dance, between dance and chorus, between chorus and tragedy, as an evolved form. This way of thinking emphasizes the fact that the audience looks at one another, not on some individual leader; the shape of the auditorium is related to democracy, not tyranny. Other writers, however, disagree with one element or another of this correlation.

Entrances came either by way of the aisles leading in and around the stage building or from the stage building. The character coming on through one of these external entryways was visible to the audience for some time, which accounts for some of the less naturalistic lines of tragedy—entrances are announced by those on stage as the charac-

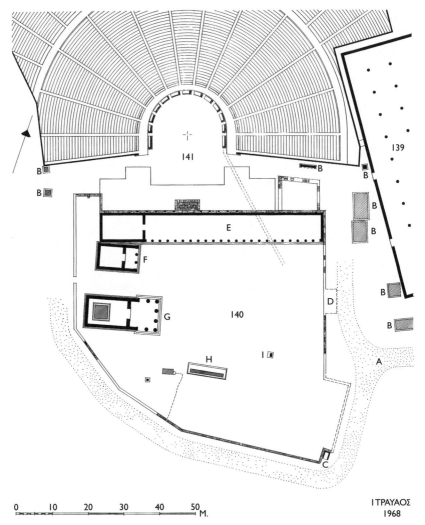

ΙΤΡΑΥΑΟΣ
1968

139. Odeion of Perikles – 140. Shrine of Dionysos – 141. Theater of Dionysos –
A. Street of the Tripods – B. Choregic monuments – C. Poros naiskos – D. Probable
site of the propylon – E. Doric stoa – F. Earlier temple of Dionysos – G. Later
temple of Dionysos – H. Great altar – I. Small altar.

Figure 5. Restored plan of the fifth-century theater of Dionysos. (John Travlos, *A Pictorial Dictonary of Ancient Athens*, New York: Praeger Publishers, 1971; p. 541.)

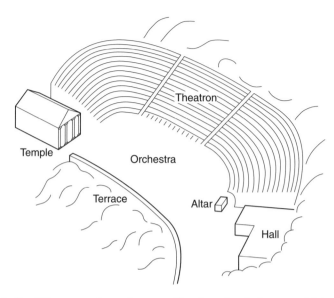

Figure 6. Pre-fifth-century deme theater at Thorikos. (Ian C. Storey and Arlene Allan, *A Guide to Ancient Greek Drama*, Oxford: Blackwell, 2004; p. 37.)

ter is walking on. The characters coming out of the stage building were imagined as coming out from the household or shrine. Other elements of stagecraft include the famous *ekkyklêma*, a wheeled platform, which allowed what had transpired inside to be shown to the audience and other characters. For instance, in Aeschylus' *Agamemnon*, the Queen, Clytemnestra, kills her husband, Agamemnon, and his lover, Kassandra, inside, but then they are rolled out, so that she can gloat over the bodies to the Chorus (and to the theater audience); in the second play of the trilogy, her son Orestes kills her and her lover, and their bodies are similarly revealed. The use of this technical device allows the playwright to make an explicit parallel between mother and son. Actors also used the stage building and could stand on it; there was a crane-like machine that could hoist them up (the *mêchanê*). We presume that it was used to reveal the gods who often end plays, thus the Latin phrase *deus ex machina*. Euripides uses this machine for the entrance of his eponymous heroine at the end of his play *Medea*, thereby emphasizing her divine origins.

It is very important to remember that this art form, like other poetry of the period that was written for a festival setting, was not individual but collective. To the best of our knowledge, tragedy developed out of a choral performance, not with the actors. Aristotle says in the *Poetics* that tragedy began with a satyr chorus that danced (see Figure 1). Moreover, the poets who won the honor of producing plays at the Athenian festival of the god Dionysos were said to have been "granted a chorus." Similarly, the prize for director/author went to the "teacher of the chorus." The choral odes dominated in early tragedy. Aeschylus' *Oresteia* is largely choral, and he made the chorus the center in other plays, e.g., his *Suppliants*. Choral songs remained important even in Euripides, though they were less integrally related to the action in his later tragedies.

In many plays, the choral songs are metrically matched, so that a pair of stanzas would balance one another (sometimes denoted by the terms strophe and antistrophe); the poetic meter would have set a rhythm for the choral dance. Each pair of stanzas might end with an epode, metrically different from the strophic pairs but related to the other epodes. Strophic pairs may relate to one another not only in meter but also in terms of meaning, providing the reader with a guide to interpretation. But as with any general statement, we must be sensitive to nuance; different playwrights used these techniques differently. Euripides especially contributed many stylistic innovations, and, as I have mentioned, in his plays the odes are often less tightly connected to the overall meaning of the tragedy.

Because the meter varied, it could be expressive of mood, speeding up to indicate anxiety or lengthening syllables to imitate mourning and lament, for instance. The music and dance, integral parts of the performance tradition, have been almost entirely lost (we have fragments of music from two of Euripides' plays, but we don't know what the notes sounded like). We think that the chorus probably mimed what it was singing, which would have undoubtedly increased the intensity of the experience for the audience. They danced to the music of pipes, which would have added another register to the voices, perhaps making it possible to represent women's tonality. In addition, the importance of music and dance throughout the culture would have provided a point of contact for the original audience, who would most likely have participated in choruses at some point in their lives. The men would have been accustomed to the role of song in military activity—for instance, pipes also kept the beat for the crews on warships. Moreover, the pipes had strong associations with lamentation as well, making them particularly suitable for tragedy. Finally, for the Greeks, music (not the lyrics) was seen to have ethical coloring and to move its listeners. Participation in these and other choruses was educational. Thus music was part of the pedagogical force of the plays, not a contradiction to that effect.

Students sometimes assume that the chorus gives "background information," and it may, but that is not a generalization that holds good for all Greek tragedy. In fact, the chorus fulfills multiple purposes; it could both articulate general truths of the culture and take on an individualized character. In each play, the chorus has a personality and position of its own and a role to play in the action, though it differs in importance from play to play. For instance, in Aeschylus' *Agamemnon* there is a chorus of elders; perhaps as a result of their age, they possess great knowledge and connect the action to significant cultural themes, but they are specifically portrayed as *impotent* old men. Therefore, they are incapable of intervening and preventing the murder of the king.

The choral songs typically punctuate the action, separating episodes where the actors dominate, but the chorus could also interact with the actors. It may comment on the action, and its reactions must be taken into consideration as we try to understand what the ancient audience would have thought. But we must be cautious in assuming that the chorus is representative of the audience since it is typically not enacting Athenians. Then, too, the chorus may participate in a sustained scene with the actors. In Aeschylus' *Libation Bearers* the Chorus prays with Elektra to the dead Agamemnon in what is known as a *kommos* (a word that also means lament or dirge).

The Greek word for actor (*hypokritês*) literally means the one who responds, answers, or interprets, that is, he answers the questions of the chorus or perhaps interprets the myths. As I said at the outset, there were never more than three actors with speaking parts in tragedy, and the actors were all men, as were the choristers. One consequence of this convention or rule is that an individual actor had to be prepared to represent more than one character, and often more than one gender, in any given play and certainly in the course of the festival. As a result of the use of male actors, cross-dressing is thus a central part of Greek drama (tragedy, comedy, and satyr drama). Recent work on theater has emphasized the importance of transvestism as a crucial aspect of the imaginative work of performance; playing the "other" gender is the essence of mimesis. As we will discuss further (Chapter 3), there is ritual significance in this gender-fluidity of tragedy. There is considerable debate as to how much the actor strove for an accurate imitation and remaining in character, and how much he strove to be recognizable as himself. As some emphasize, there was a version of a star system in effect: after 449 there was a prize established for the best actor, and therefore perhaps a premium for the actor in being seen through the role. We do not know what made an actor the best, however, and recognizability might not have been an essential ingredient. Aristophanes' comedy *Women of the Thesmophoria* makes it explicit that a male actor would try to imitate a woman's voice, and, therefore, not sound like himself.

The actors' language was no more ordinary speech than the chorus', but it was in a meter that was more similar to the rhythms of everyday language. We expect naturalistic or realistic patterns of conversation in our film and theater. In Greek tragedy, there are either long speeches in which one character responds to another (*Medea* is a very good example of this kind of presentation), which become contests between the characters in some plays, or there are sections in which the characters rapidly exchange lines (*stichomythia*). No one interrupts, no one loses his or her train of thought, and only very rarely do characters contradict themselves. In the last third of the fifth century, more singing was required of the actors, another element of loosening the constraints as tragedy developed.

Given the size and outdoor setting of the theater, audibility and visibility would have been critical concerns. The physical setting and masking would have consequences for the style of acting, which would have been very different from the intimacy, say, of film, where we can catch the slightest whisper. Speakers would tend to face front or risk losing the audience. Gestures would have to be clear since small gestures would be missed by an audience at a distance. We can find many hints about the action in the language, which seems to have cued the audience as to what it was supposed to be seeing. It is clear that there was a shared code of behavior in life that could be utilized in a play: bowing the head in mourning or touching the chin or the knees in supplication.

It is often noted that there is no violence enacted in Greek tragedy, and in general violent actions did take place out of sight. As a result, in order to inform the audience of what has happened, we have the ubiquitous messenger speech. The disaster that has struck the Greek army returning from Troy is reported by a messenger in Aeschylus' *Agamemnon*, and similarly, in Sophocles' *Women of Trachis*, a messenger tells the heroine, Deianeira, what is happening elsewhere.

The messenger can be deceitful, as in the latter case, or can be reluctant to articulate such horrors as he has seen (*Oresteia, Medea*). The messenger, as an outsider looking on at the violence, may to some extent model the audience's response. Thus, Talthybios in Euripides' *Trojan Women* has tears in his eyes at the death of Astyanax, the last remaining Trojan male. The convention enables the playwright to have his cake and eat it too: the physical violence is eliminated, but the emotional reaction is enacted (assuming that the messenger mimes as well as reports). However, it is also possible that the music and dance of the choral portions were in fact violent. For instance, in Aeschylus' *Suppliants*, there are fifty women who are almost raped by fifty men. The language of the chorus would have been sung with accompanying actions and would have been very exciting indeed.

The aesthetic as a whole was non-realistic and conventional, as we can see from the emphasis on the chorus, the limited number of actors, staging practices, etc. The masks are an important part of that formalism. They don't seem to have had exaggerated features, though the mouth had to be open enough to allow for the projection of audible voice; the human mouth would have been visible behind the mask. But they represented a typology of characters and were not individualized (so, young/old female, young/old male, barbarian/Greek). Thus Kreon in *Antigone*, Oedipus in *Oedipus*, and Theseus in *Hippolytos* share common tendencies toward arrogance, symptomatic of the fifth-century view of the tyrant. The rulers might have been represented by similar masks. In keeping with the masked dimension, introspection and psychological motives are not characteristic of the plays, but this does not mean that we give up all concern for consistency of character. A modern tendency toward psychological interpretation must be moderated in dealing with ancient plays; we are, however, encouraged to psychologize in some cases—for instance, the Chorus of the *Agamemnon* announces the change in Agamemnon (218), and Clytemnestra in Euripides' *Iphigeneia at Aulis* remarks that her daughter was always "father-loving" (638).

Costume reveals a salient feature of tragedy, its combination of antiquated and what was then contemporary. The scenes on the Pronomos vase show actors, some from a satyr drama, but the detail is revealing. We see that the actors' costumes (Figure 1) are highly decorated but are more or less like fifth-century attire; they would not have seemed unfamiliar to the audience. Their long sleeves might have been a way of disguising male arms in female characters. In keeping with tragedy's high tone, aristocratic characters are lavishly attired, leading Aristophanes to mock Euripides for his habit of bringing on ragged heroes (in his *Elektra* the heroine repeatedly complains about her déclassé clothing). In modern times, directors have to decide how they will approach this problem—which "now" will be represented. Will the dress be modern, or if ancient, what setting will be adopted? In 2004, Peter Meineck staged a version of *Agamemnon* neither in the present nor in the distant past but in the fifties, so that World War II would be in the background and women's roles would have been more constrained than they were in 2004. Clytemnestra's dress was an important element in conveying that flavor.

In stressing that the aesthetic of tragedy was "conventional," I am not saying that it did not maintain an illusion of reality that the audience shared. The audience was only infrequently (if at all) made aware of the author behind the actor, and we have reason to believe that the actions and objects were realistic, not strictly symbolic; nonetheless the maintenance of the illusion did not require the imitation of everyday life. Moreover, the conventions were not rigid rules; the number of actors and the use of mythic subjects were not absolutes and should not be seen as too tightly controlling the playwrights. Tragedy changed over time—for instance, the number of actors grew from one to three. There were different versions of many of the myths, and the playwrights were free to modify them (as we will see in more detail in Part II). It is more productive to ask how the tragedians used these conventions rather than assuming that they could not deviate from them or manipulate them creatively.

So far we have amplified certain basics: Greek tragedy was presented outdoors in daylight as part of a competition in an Athenian festival honoring the god Dionysos; the plays, usually on a mythic subject, were enacted by choruses who sang and danced and three (at most) actors who spoke in verse. All the participants were men, and all wore masks which emphasized the role not the individual character. The current experience of going to the theater is radically different in practically every respect: we go inside, sit in a darkened auditorium, and look at a stage; in our dominant realistic aesthetic, we expect to see costumes and sets that represent the time and place of the action, and the actors represent the characters' "psychological truth." The Greeks combined music, dance, high art, and popular appeal into one art form, whereas in our own day these elements are divided. We have to turn to musicals and opera to give us the sense of the formal multiplicity of tragedy, to rock concerts or sporting events to give us the sense of mass appeal and the outdoor experience. The form of Greek tragedy is what was most distinctive about it, yet it is for the stories that we return to the plays over and over again; we shall focus on that dimension in the next chapters, but most extensively in Part II. In order to better understand the ancient performances, in the next two chapters we will look in greater detail at the political and religious contexts shaping them.

Suggestions for further reading

For a recent consideration of tragedy in general and the dilemmas modern liberals face, see Terry Eagleton, *Sweet Violence* (Oxford: Blackwell, 2003). George Steiner's *The Death of Tragedy* (London: Faber and Faber, 1961) is a classic consideration of modern tragedy.

On Aristotle and Plato, see Gerald Else, *Plato and Aristotle on Poetry* (Chapel Hill: University of North Carolina Press, 1986); John Jones, *On Aristotle and Greek Tragedy* (New York: Oxford University Press, 1968); Walter Kaufmann, *Tragedy and Philosophy* (Garden City, NY: Doubleday, 1968; Anchor, 1969); and M. S. Silk, *Tragedy and the Tragic: Greek Theatre and Beyond* (Oxford: Oxford University Press, 1996).

For the sources on performance and history, see Arthur Pickard-Cambridge, *Dramatic Festivals of Athens,* revised edition (Oxford: Clarendon Press, 1968) and Eric Csapo and William J. Slater, *The Context of Ancient Drama* (Ann Arbor: University of Michigan Press, 1995).

On the shape of the theater, see, in addition to David Wiles, *Tragedy in Athens: Performance Space and Theatrical Meaning* (Cambridge: Cambridge University Press, 1997), Rush Rehm, *The Play of Space: Spatial Transformation in Greek Tragedy* (Princeton: Princeton University Press, 2002). The arguments are well summarized by Scott Scullion, *Three Studies in Athenian Dramaturgy* (Stuttgart and Leipzig: Teubner, 1994); see also his contribution to *A Companion to Greek Tragedy*, ed. Justina Gregory (Oxford: Blackwell, 2005).

On performance and internal stage directions, see Oliver Taplin, *Greek Tragedy in Action* (Berkeley and Los Angeles: University of California Press, 1978); Wiles (*Tragedy in Athens*) offers a contrasting view.

On "The Historical Moment" of tragedy, between myth and contemporary Athens, see the chapter by Jean-Pierre Vernant in his co-authored book with Pierre Vidal-Naquet, *Myth and Tragedy in Ancient Greece* (New York: Zone Books, 1988), pp. 23–8.

On the actor, see Paulette Ghiron-Bistagne, *Recherches sur les acteurs dans la Grèce antique* (Paris: Les Belles Lettres, 1976); in English, there is a recent collection of essays, P. E. Easterling and Edith Hall, eds., *Greek and Roman Actors: Aspects of an Ancient Profession* (Cambridge: Cambridge University Press, 2002).

On music, see Martin L. West, *Ancient Greek Music* (Oxford: Oxford University Press, 1992) and Andrew Barker, ed., *Greek Musical Writings*, 2 vols. (Cambridge: Cambridge University Press, 1984–9).

2

Tragedy and the *Polis*

The move from a literary, "great books," or textual emphasis to a historical emphasis has become more or less mainstream (though it is also opposed in some quarters). As we will discuss in more detail later, the tragic performances were produced in Athens as part of the City Dionysia, or Great Dionysia, a festival in honor of the god Dionysos; thus, they were offered as part of a ritual celebration and were strongly affected by the ritual context (see Chapter 3), but they were also political, in that they were sponsored by the *polis*, or city-state, of Athens-Attica. The school of thought that has grown up around the work of Jean-Pierre Vernant and the Centre Louis Gernet, in particular, has focused on tragedy and the mentality of the society producing it: the "preconceptions, presuppositions that compose as it were the framework of everyday life in the civilization for which they are one form of expression" (Vernant and Vidal-Naquet 10). These scholars emphasize the relationship between tragedy and its historical moment—which largely coincides with the period of the development of democracy in Athens (472–404 are the dates of the extant tragedies; *Rhesus*, often attributed to Euripides, probably actually comes from the fourth century, after his death).

What caused this heightened interest is perhaps the predilection of our own times. First, much of the recent attention to ancient democracy coincided with the anniversaries of democracy in the U.S. and France and was explicitly concerned with what we could learn from the past in our current multicultural postcolonialist present. Issues of democracy and citizenship are certainly not safely set in the past. An obituary in 2006 for a distinguished classicist, Pierre Vidal-Naquet, who was an activist involved in struggles against French colonialism in Algeria, highlighted the fact that this generation of scholars made connections between the history of ancient Greece and the history of the struggles of the recent past. Similarly, Jean-Pierre Vernant was a member of the Resistance during World War II; writing in Paris (at the center of France as Athens was at the center of Attica, and Greece) in a democracy that had until very recently been an empire, he saw similarities to Athens, also both democracy and empire. He wondered what could be learned from Athens. His writing addresses the general question of "how myth led to rational thought," but he is also clear that he was interested in how the ancient Greeks dealt with the "other," with issues of inclusion and exclusion; he admired what he saw as the Greeks' tolerance (Vernant 1996: 77). Likewise, American writers at the end of the twentieth century looked back to Athens when thinking about the democratic empire of the U.S. As we will see shortly, the demands for participation in ancient Athens made its democracy very different from contemporary representative democracies, but the claim for the importance of Athens to modernity is, nonetheless, based in large part on that democracy. Second, feminist theory and Marxist analysis have burgeoned and increased attention to women and slaves in antiquity. Finally, contemporary literary theory has had an effect on our ways of reading tragedy; its predisposition to see openness and ambiguity has led to the discovery of such openness in tragedy, not necessarily because Athenians always and in all circumstances valued openness and ambiguity.

There are many ways in which the relationship between tragedy and its social setting can be seen. The very conventions of tragedy relate to the *polis*, for, as we have seen, the centrality of the chorus emphasizes collectivity. At one end of the spectrum of opinion, David Wiles (2002) and John Winkler have argued that the citizens who made up the chorus were young men who were essentially learning a war dance. Vernant more moderately claimed that the chorus stands for the city, in contrast to the heroic characters (Vernant and Vidal-Naquet 24). The chorus members, however, almost never represent Athenian men of citizen age; indeed, they are mostly women and outsiders. The dynamic of individual and group is, nonetheless, emphasized through the relationship of actor to chorus; moreover, as mentioned in Chapter 1, the chorus provides an internal audience, and can be taken to instruct the actual audience in one way to respond to the action. In that case, the connection between chorus and actor is analogous to that between the spectators and the action.

Others take tragedy more generally still as a form "consolidating the social identity, maintaining the cohesion of the community" (Longo 14). This view fits with what we know of the role of choral singing and dancing, as well as the reading of poetry, in the education of both Athenian and Spartan citizens—which was heavily based on the values of the culture. Therefore, the ancient Greeks were accustomed to seeing artistic works not as only individual creations but also as cultural productions, meaning that they were aware that art was value-laden, or ideological. We will return to this point later.

Recent work more specifically stresses the link between the tragic festival and democracy, taking the festival proceedings and the activity of the audience of tragedy as preparation for mass meetings, jury service, and participation in self-government (Cartledge 19). Plato (*Laws* 701b) makes the connection between the dominance of the many in the audience and disrespect for the laws in general, and he calls this "theatocracy," rule of the audience. Before delving more deeply into this particular context for tragedy, we have to address the fact that traditionally tragic performances have been thought to pre-date the democracy. In particular, Thespis, the legendary first trage-dian, is reported to have won the first prize for tragedy in 534 under the rule of Peisistratus, a "tyrant" (simply meaning non-hereditary king). What do scholars making the connection to democracy do with this "fact"? First, this reference might indicate only that tragedy was developing in those years before the full institution of democracy. Second, there are also strong arguments that this traditional early date is based on a reading of one piece of evidence that is badly preserved, and that, even if the date is accepted, Thespis might have won his prize at one of the rural festivals, not at the City Dionysia. If we thus dis-count or explain the early date, the Festival may be taken to celebrate the incorporation of the god Dionysos Eleuthereus into Athens in 502 and Athenian freedom from tyranny (since *eleutheria* means freedom in Greek) (Connor). Those who accept the 534 date often argue against the connection being made between tragedy and democracy, but in any event, the plays that *we have* definitely come from Athens in the period of the democracy, even though the form was as definitely evolving in different cities and throughout the sixth century (see Chapter 1).

Democracy

Let us look at the history of democracy in Athens, and then at the concepts associated with that form of government. In the pre-democratic periods, rule was typically invested in kings, and there-after in leaders chosen from the ranks of a few leading families. Sometimes an outsider, called a tyrant, would seize power or attempt to do so; backed by a faction, the tyrants sometimes became well established as rulers, leaving power to their heirs. Though the preconditions for democracy, for instance an emerging focus on the virtues of those of "middling" status, are visible in the eighth century, the democratization of Athens really begins in the early sixth century with the reforms of Solon, a legendary lawgiver often considered the founder of democracy, which literally means rule by the people, or *dêmos*. Most of our information is late, however, and may well be biased since democracy was a highly contentious subject; indeed Aristotle, one of our most complete sources, opposed the later radical democracy.

Solon, traditionally renowned as a man of wisdom, came to power in a time of intense factional fighting between the wealthy classes and the people. Until his time, political power rested completely in the hands of men from a small group of aristocratic families who con-trolled the Areopagus, a governing body that consisted of all the former *archontes* (leaders, or magistrates). Solon began to make changes. According to Aristotle, Solon divided the citizens into four wealth classes and established a council of 400 men based on that division (*Constitution of the Athenians* 8.4; Plutarch, *Solon* 19.1–2). Members of the lowest class (*thêtes*) did not have the power to vote, but they could attend the Assembly and serve on juries. Solon relieved debtors from imprisonment, and although he did not redistribute land, he claimed to have made laws that were applied equally to all (Fragment 24.18–20). He made numerous other rules for the conduct of everyday life, including inheritance practices, clothing, and, most significantly for tragedy, mourning for the dead. The latter affected women especially. For instance, Solon decreed that women under 60 could not attend the laying out of the body and that no woman could follow the procession to burial; women were also limited in what they could do or say in mourning.

After Solon, there was another period of factional dispute, until the rule ended up in the hands of the tyrant Peisistratus, mentioned above in conjunction with Thespis; his sons, Hippias and Hipparchos, inherited his position. The ending of the tyranny was a complicated process. Although the Athenians celebrated Harmodios and Aristogeiton, a pair of lovers who killed Hipparchos, as tyrannicides, they actually failed to kill Hippias. The latter, indeed, became more severe as a result of the attempted coup, killing and exiling many thought to have been part of the conspiracy. In the end, Spartan assistance was required to rid Athens of the tyranny.

After the democracy was established, there was a series of expansions of the power of the *dêmos*. Kleisthenes took power and made many changes, including a new way of organizing the populace into tribes and demes in order to undercut traditional familial loyalties and power. The power of the Assembly increased, and it was now open to all the classes as voting members. The role of the Areopagos, which the upper classes still led, gradually declined. Although aristocratic influence diminished, established families continued to provide some leaders, in particular the elected generals; Perikles' standing came from being repeatedly elected general. The Athenians depended on the drawing of lots to fill other positions in order to avoid the concentration of influence in any family. Ostracism was a procedure that enabled citizens, by casting lots, to exile any citizen temporarily; it was another method of limiting the accumulation of too much power in the hands of any individual. Athenian fear of the effects of wealth and influence on government seems justified in the modern world, where elections in the U.S., for instance, are so expensive that the very rich wield inordinate influence.

As I mentioned earlier, a crucial difference between ancient and modern democracy is in the level of participation of the average citizen. Participation in politics was expected: our word "idiot" comes from the Greek *idiôtes*, meaning private; for Athenian men, there was no life without public activity. Solon even made it a law that individuals had to take sides in disputes or they would lose citizenship (Aristotle, *Constitution of the Athenians* 8). One final note about Kleisthenes: democracy and theater went hand in hand in his changes. As I said earlier, he instituted the practice of having choruses of fifty men and fifty boys from each of the ten new tribes sing songs in honor of the god Dionysos. He also initiated the building of a theater of Dionysos at the base of the hill of the Akropolis (literally, the high place in the city), which contained the temples to the gods, the Parthenon of Athena among others. Dionysos' temple was near the theater (see Figure 3).

The full flowering of democracy came in 461/2 with the reforms of Ephialtes, which stripped the Areopagus of most of its remaining functions (crucially for Aeschylus' *Oresteia*, it retained jurisdiction over murder cases). The Assembly was now the ruling body, and all citizens could participate in its deliberations. There was a 500-man *boulê*, or council, and in addition the courts had enormous juries on which citizens sat. Still later, stipends for service were put into place so that administrative duty no longer required independent wealth; in the late fifth or fourth century Assembly service was paid, and a fund was even established to subsidize attending the theater.

As you can see from this brief history, power was vested in an ever greater number of citizens: rule by the wealthy yielded to rule by those who had at least enough money to buy a full suit of armor (the hoplite class), to rule by the poorest citizens (the rowers of the ships) later in the fifth century when the navy was responsible for the defense of Athens. The wealthy sometimes even complained that the masses had more power than they, who were responsible for paying for the ships through a system of public works (*leitourgiai*). Not everyone approved of the democracy, and there was some debate about definition of terms as well. For instance, the *dêmos* could refer to all the people in the city, or it could refer to the lower classes. There was an oligarchic party (a faction believing in government by a small group) that despised the *dêmos* and saw it as little more than a mob. They agreed that freedom was essential to democracy, but thought that those who were truly free, those who did not have to work, should be in charge. Moreover, there were contradictions: though voting in the Assembly was egalitarian, the old and wealthy families still wielded considerable political *influence*, and although the change to a navy to fight Persia increased the power of the less wealthy (Herodotus 7.144), it was paid for through the development of silver mines, which in turn were worked by slaves.

In short, though it was radically participatory for citizens, Athenian democracy did not mean rule by all the people: slaves, foreigners, and, notably, women were not citizens and did not participate in the political activity of the city. Women were not called citizens of Athens, though they were called women of the city (*astoi*). They did not attend the Assembly, nor did they serve on juries, those characteristic activities of the democracy. Indeed they could not appear in court on their own behalf, and respectable women were not even named in the proceedings but were spoken of in terms of their relationship to male citizens.

Moreover, in Athens they had very limited money at their disposal, although they did have a dowry that had to be returned with them to their natal family in the case of a divorce. It is arguable that women were better off in the aristocratic past than they were in the democracy; in the representations of women in Homer, they seem to have been consulted on matters of importance and to have been present at banquets. Women were, nonetheless, important as residents of the city, and a citizenship law promulgated under Perikles (451–50) required that an Athenian citizen had to be born from two Athenian parents. As we shall see in more detail later, the role of the tragic festival as a site of democracy has relevance to the ambiguous status of women, and vice versa.

Empire and Hegemony

In our attention to democracy, we must not overlook Athenians' widening sphere of influence. The changes in the constitution and the economic resources of those making the decisions in Athens were taking place while Athens was fighting the Persians, who invaded twice in ten years (490 and 480–79), then establishing an empire, and finally fighting with Sparta to maintain hegemony. The development of democracy (and the navy) and the defeat of Persia were contemporaneous events, and in the city's idea of itself there was a causal connection between the defeat of an empire under an autocratic ruler and the Athenian democracy. The defeat of Persia was, moreover, a source of great pride. The victories at Marathon in the first Persian War, and Salamis in the second, were decisive for the Greek and Athenian sense of self. Persia, however, retained its influence during the fifth century, even intervening in local politics—for instance, when Darius invaded, he brought the deposed tyrant Hippias back with him. Those who attacked democracy and made up the oligarchic party were often suspected of having Persian aid and connections (e.g., Thucydides 1.116, 1.134–9; Hall 1989: 58–9). All of this was very live to Aeschylus and Sophocles, who reportedly had strong associations with the key battles of the Persian Wars: Aeschylus fought at Marathon, and Sophocles is said to have danced in the chorus during the victory celebrations after Salamis.

The cultural life of Athens and the glorification project begun under Peisistratus and continued under Perikles were based in part on making distinctions between the Greeks and barbarian others. The Trojans, who were not noticeably ethnically different from the Hellenes in Homer, were rendered "orientals" in the fifth-century Parthenon sculptures. The concept of the Persians as the opposite of the Greeks developed in the context of the Persian Wars and the very real danger they posed to democracy. The Persian Wars were assimilated to the other great "civilizing" battles of the Greeks against the Amazons, centaurs, and giants and became an example of a higher order of reality (Hall 1996: 9, citing Conacher 143). While one of these struggles was clearly a historical event, it was seen to share attributes with the others (Hall 1996: 10). The whole of Greek mythology came in time to be seen as a struggle with the East. Self and other were organized around Greek and Persian.

The word *barbaros*, from which we get barbarian, comes from the sound "bar bar," meaning that to the Greeks the speech of foreigners sounded like nonsense. It does not have the connotations of lack of civilization, however, so much as lack of freedom. For the Greeks the categories of *barbaros* and the slave were mapped onto one another: the Persians bowed down before their rulers, while the Greeks were free; non-Greeks were therefore suitable slaves. Other stereotypes of the barbarian "other" were their luxury, tendency to incest, and effeminacy (see Chapter 4 on *Persians*).

There are two notions of slavery in Aristotle, the best-known ancient philosopher on the subject. While Aristotle recognizes that there was a contingent form of slavery (slavery as a result of piracy or war), he focuses his attention on what he calls the natural slave: there are "some who are by nature free, so others are by nature slaves, and for these latter the condition of slavery is both beneficial and just" (*Politics* 1.5.11). He also mentions that the line between the two kinds of slavery is drawn as a matter of preference; speaking of prisoners of war, he says: "Greeks do not like to call such persons slaves, but prefer to confine the term to barbarians" (1.6.6). Importantly, to Aristotle, Asians seem particularly well suited to slavery (1.2.4; 1.6.6; 7.7.1–3). As we can see, the category of the natural slave overlaps with the Athenian notion of the other.

The existence of slavery has been downplayed in the literature perhaps because it was difficult for scholars to acknowledge that the Greeks were slaveholders given that their popularity with modern readers was based in part on their invention of democracy. Nonetheless the truth is that a great deal of Athenian wealth in the fifth century came from the empire (based on the tribute of the members of the Delian League) or from the mines of Laurion, which were worked with slave labor. Even ordinary households would have one or two slaves. The Athenians idealized liberty as freedom from work; thus, their very conception of themselves was based on the presence of others to do that work for them.

For the last third of the fifth century, and the period when many of the extant plays of Sophocles and Euripides were written, Athens was involved in the Peloponnesian War (431–404) with Sparta (see Figure 7). Thucydides' *The Peloponnesian War* interweaves the threads between the democracy, the Persian Wars, and the current war with Sparta into a seamless tapestry:

Figure 7. Map of Greece. (Ian C. Storey and Arlene Allan, *A Guide to Ancient Greek Drama*, Oxford: Blackwell, 2004, p. xvi.)

The actions of the Hellenes against each other and against foreign Powers . . . all took place in a period of about fifty years between the retreat of Xerxes and the beginning of this present war. In these years the Athenians made their empire more and more strong, and greatly added to their own power at home. (1.9.120, trans. Warner)

In the debates about trading rights for the city of Megara, Thucydides represents Perikles as making an explicit argument by comparing the present war against Sparta to the Persian Wars:

We must realize, too, that, both for cities and for individuals, it is from the greatest dangers that the greatest glory is to be won. When our fathers stood against the Persians they had no such resources as we have now; indeed they abandoned even what they had, and then it was by wisdom rather than by good fortune, by daring rather than by material power, that they drove back the foreign invasion and made our city what it is today. We must live up to the standard they set: we must resist our enemies in any and every way, and try to leave to those who come after us an Athens that is as great as ever. (1.11.144)

Furthermore, the victory over the Persians grounded the Athenian claim to leadership in the Delian League, originally a loose collection of independent city-states based on the island of Delos; the Athenians argued that they were entitled to loyalty from their allies because they had led the fight for freedom against Persia and suffered so much for it. The treasury was moved to Athens, and the "allies" devolved into subjects and were forced to present tribute to the Athenians (at the City Dionysia). Though the Athenians claimed to be spreading democracy, that was strictly on the domestic level: a democratic constitution was consistent with subjection to Athens in international affairs (we might think of how, in the early twenty-first century, President Bush and Prime Minister Blair sought to spread democracy in the Middle East through military intervention).

This historical coincidence of democracy and empire reveals a tension in the ideology: at the same time that Athens founded the democracy on the power of the *dêmos*, the freedom of the *dêmos*, it was establishing a claim to rule others. Athens would not see itself as a tyrant but as bringing freedom to its allies, who then gave tribute in recompense for the freedom received. The Persian enemy was essential to this self-perception of the Athenians. After the Persian Wars, Athens and Sparta had a peace agreement, but the parties in favor of war often picked fights about whether the colonies of each power were free to choose a constitution that suited them (Thucydides I.11.140–4). In the Peloponnesian War, Sparta also represented itself as attacking Athens as the tyrant city and claimed to be bringing freedom to those colonies that resisted Athenian dominance.

The Peloponnesian War was protracted and exhausting for Athenians; they had taken Perikles' and Themistokles' advice and developed a strong navy, but the Spartans were strong on land and repeatedly destroyed the crops in Attica. A devastating plague, which killed Perikles, added to the suffering. Despite an ill-conceived and ill-fated expedition to Sicily (415–413), in which the Athenians were defeated and the fleet destroyed, they regained their strength, and the war continued with brief intervals of truce; in 406 Athens rejected the proposals of Sparta for peace, having won victory at Arginusae. But in the end, Sparta developed a navy as well, which enabled them to stop food from reaching Athens. When they simultaneously attacked by land, the Athenians were defeated. The democracy at Athens was replaced briefly by a Spartan-style oligarchy, though democracy was restored and continued through the fourth century—ending with the conquest by Philip of Macedon.

This history—with its tension between inclusivity and exclusivity, between freedom for some and servitude for others—will be seen in tragedy's performance setting, both physical and social, in the ways that texts refer to specific events, as well as in the ways in which texts relate to ideology more broadly construed.

Performance Setting

The physical space of the performances reveals the similarities (and differences) between tragedy and the other institutions of the city. Before the theater proper was built, it is said that plays had been produced in the Agora (a marketplace with temples to the gods, monuments to heroes, and political buildings), though this view is based on late evidence. The Council continued to meet in the Agora, below the Akropolis, and the Assembly met on the Pnyx, a hill like that of the Akropolis and facing it. Sitting in the theater below the Akropolis, you would have the view of the other hill (Figure 3). Like the Agora and Pnyx, the theater of Dionysos was a distinctive location of the democracy. In the theatrical spectacle, the audience was also on display: since the performances took place outside in broad daylight, and in an amphitheater, one's fellow audience members would have been visible. The natural environs (which were economic, too, since they provided Attica's honey and marble, for instance) would also have been in plain sight. If you imagine concerts taking place in an outdoor amphitheater in Washington D.C., say, where you looked out on the Pentagon and the Potomac River at the same time, or in London in sight of the Houses of Parliament and the Thames, you might get the flavor.

State organization was reflected in the physical arrangements of the audience as well: late evidence suggests that spectators were seated by tribes, and that the front rows were reserved for the generals as well as the priest of Dionysos. The young men of age for military service (*epheboi*) had permanent seats. Democracy's inclusions and exclusions are notable here. Scholars debate whether women attended at all, or were seated in a section in the rear. If the latter were the case, we might compare this situation to the segregated theaters of the American South under Jim Crow rules, or the separate stairways for those who sat up in the peanut gallery in older theaters and opera houses. Women's marginal position in the city is reflected in the ambiguity of the evidence regarding their attendance.

The festival included two processions that connected the plays to the city. In one the god's statue was taken away and brought back for the start of the festival proper. Another procession led the audience through the city, past the Agora and along a street lined with monuments commemorating theatrical victories, to the theater. This latter procession was finely calibrated politically; so, for instance, the non-citizen residents (metics) wore red or purple robes that identified them as a group, and the *choregoi* (who funded the events) wore gold and carried crowns on their heads. Women were basket-bearers at the front of the procession. Thus, the various constituencies participated in ways that reaffirmed collective, not individual, identities.

In describing spectatorship and processing we have already entered the realm of the sociopolitical setting; the festival was explicitly political in that it was sponsored and funded in part by the city of Athens. It is as if the state arts organizations were the major source of theatrical entertainment in our own day. The eponymous archon was in charge of the festival; he selected the poets who were going to compete; he also assigned the actors (and arranged for their payment, later in the century). The prizes for writer/director, *choregos*, and best actor were paid for by the city, as were the extensive animal sacrifices that began the festival, and of course the city built and maintained the theater.

At some point later in the fifth or fourth century, the city established a fund to help pay for tickets for poorer citizens. The stipend, like that for attending the Assembly and sitting on a jury, indicates the importance of the activity for the citizens' identity; it simultaneously links the theater to the Assembly and law courts. Indeed Plutarch (*Perikles* 9) specifically mentions the festival fund and payment for public service as two of Perikles' democratic policies. The audiences of tragedy were compared to the audiences in the law courts, both said to be mob-like from time to time. Moreover, some audience members would be chosen by lot to be the judges of the performances—another parallel to the law courts. Elitist critics like Plato (*Laws* 701b) and Aristotle took exception to the dominance of the people, whose taste they did not respect: "Just as in the theater the actors are now more important than the poets, so it is in the political contests, because of the degeneracy of the citizens" (*Rhetoric* 1403b31–5). Here artistic and political decline are correlated. It is not surprising, then, that modern critics sometimes consider the theater a training ground for those who would be involved in more formal political actions.

The archon also designated the *chorēgoi*—the wealthy citizens who paid for equipping, housing, feeding, and training the choruses. Men who took on this expense were fulfilling a civic duty (*leitourgia*) comparable in expense to outfitting a ship for the navy; one *chorēgos* claims to have spent 3,000 drachmas, compared to 5,143 for running a warship for a year (Csapo and Slater 140–1). The importance of the *chorēgia* as one form of contribution to the city makes clear the elevated position of the drama. It also points to a potentially antidemocratic element of the democracy since the wealthy, prominent citizens could use their sponsorship of public events as a way of enhancing their status and influence. And as always when speaking of tragedy, we must remember that all the major participants were men and, with few exceptions, of the citizen class. Thus both the inclusivity and exclusivity that I have been pointing out are evident here.

The political nature of the festival is apparent in other ways, too: prisoners were freed temporarily so that they could attend the Dionysia; no debts could be incurred; law courts did not sit; and it seems possible that no Assemblies were held during the festival. Obviously attendance at this festival trumped other civic responsibilities.

After the festival, an Assembly was held in the theater to assess the conduct of the archon and the behavior of the audience. The power of Athens was embodied in the presence of the military at the festival. Not only did the generals have preferred seating, they also made the liquid offering to Dionysos. In addition, Athens maintained at state expense the orphans of citizens who had died for the city-state; at the festival, these young men marched in full armor and swore an oath to defend the city, as had their fathers.

The theater was also the place to honor those who had conferred benefits on Athens. The fourth-century orator Demosthenes defends the practice with these words:

> But by the gods are you so stupid and insensitive, Aiskhines, that you are unable to perceive that the crown gives the same joy to the person crowned wherever it is proclaimed, but that *the proclamation is made in the theater for the benefit of those who confer it? This is because all the audience is encouraged to do service to the city, and they applaud the gratitude of the giver more than the receiver. This is why the city made this law.*" (*On the Crown* 120, emphasis added)

Clearly, from his point of view, the theater was an important location for Athens' positive self-presentation, so that making the awards there would encourage citizens to serve. But Aiskhines thinks it makes for rivalry and is a stupid idea (*Against Ktesiphon* 153–4). What if at the opening of a Broadway musical, awards were given to those who had served New York State, or if the Queen awarded knighthoods in the theater?

The festival was also used to promote the empire. It took place in early spring when the seas were navigable, and it was an international affair (in contrast to the comic festival or the more local deme events); as a result it was also an occasion for the city to display its power to the members of the Hellenic world, who came to the festival, though it is unclear in what numbers. The allies in the Delian League presented their tribute at the festival, and it was stored in the Akropolis immediately above the playing space. The economic value of the empire was enacted, or performed, at the Dionysia.

Performances are not univocal, however, and spectators might have differed in their responses. For instance, when the war orphans marched in their regalia, they exemplified Athenian military might, and its costs. At the same time that they might have inspired a patriotic glow, consolidating loyalty to the city, they might have had another effect on the wives and mothers who had lost their loved ones, or even the men who would perhaps be lost in the next campaign. One might think in this regard of the many meanings attached to Memorial Day parades, for example, in our own day, in the context of a war. These celebrations can be a time for political resistance to the war, as well as for patriotic speeches.

Rhetoric

The audience in the theater was, as I have said, like those in the Assembly and courts. The plays' extensive use of set speeches would have been recognizable from those arenas—they were all sites where the active citizens would listen to addresses, and in some cases make decisions as a consequence of what they had heard. The parallel goes both ways: the dialogue was a popular device outside of drama in philosophy, and in tragedy we see frequent trials or contests between speakers. There is an actual trial in Aeschylus' *Eumenides*, the third play in his *Oresteia*. In the first play, you will remember, King Agamemnon returns from the Trojan War with his prize, Kassandra; his wife Clytemnestra kills them both and assumes rule with her consort, Aigisthos. In the second play, her son, Orestes, kills her at the order of the god Apollo; he runs from the scene, pursued by the avenging spirits (Furies) of his mother. Athena sets up a court to judge him in *Eumenides*. The audience of that play would in all likelihood have been directly addressed by the goddess Athena when she instructs the jury she is empanelling to consider the case of matricide. Both chorus and audience would then be in the position of judging. In Euripides' later treatment of the same topic in *Orestes*, there is also a legal debate, though it is recounted not enacted.

Athenians took pride in their sophistication in rhetoric, but, at least in the late fifth century, they were simultaneously suspicious of overly clever speakers and of the moral relativism associated with such men as Protagoras, who had the ability to make the worse argument appear the better. Aristophanes' mockery of Socrates and the sophists in the *Clouds* reflects this concern, as do many passages in tragedy. For instance, Jason in Euripides' *Medea* says that he has to be a good orator to answer her charges against him. Kreon in the same play is afraid that Medea's "cleverness" will harm him; in the end, it is poison that kills him and his daughter, but Medea's skill as a speaker puts her in a position to inflict that damage. In many plays characters win by deceptive rhetoric (for instance, Clytemnestra in Aeschylus' *Agamemnon*) and draw attention to the fact that they have lied to get their way. Euripides seems most attentive to the power of rhetoric: in his play *Hekabe* the fallen Trojan queen makes a special prayer for persuasion so that she can convince Agamemnon (816), and Iphigeneia wishes for the tongue of Orpheus so that she could persuade her father not to murder her (*Iphigeneia at Aulis*). Euripides' other plays also feature prominent debates, which seem somewhat analogous to courtroom scenes. The references to problematic speech, as well as the predominance of argument, may be signs of Athenian awareness of the ambiguity of language in general, as postmodernists hold, but they can also be related to tragedy's concern with the issues of its own day.

Referentiality

The connections between tragedy and the democratic city of Athens that we have been making on the basis of the physical and social setting may seem to be contradicted by the plays themselves. As has already been mentioned, most of the tragedies are set in the mythic past, not the democratic present, and they take place in locations outside of Athens. Some plays, however, are set there or nearby: Aeschylus' *Eumenides*, Euripides' *Suppliants* and *Children of Herakles*, and Sophocles' *Oedipus at Kolonos*. Euripides' *Medea* and *Ion* project Athens as the site in which the future action will take place, even though the plays are set elsewhere (Corinth and Delphi, respectively).

While comedy more than tragedy depended on the political situation of the day, it is also possible to find references in tragedy to contemporary events, and to Athens in particular. Aeschylus' *Eumenides* is the text that responds best to this methodology, a play to which we have referred already for its political content. Athena says that the charges are too grave for any human or even herself to judge, so she sets up a court to judge murder for all time (470–84); she later describes exactly the Council of the Areopagus, which Ephialtes' reforms had recently reduced to simply judging murder cases. This is a reference that would have been understood by the audience of Athenians. It is not clear, however, what it means—in particular, we don't know whether Athena/Aeschylus support the democratic changes that have taken place since the founding of the Council. As we read the play, however, it is important to recognize that this reform is in the background and that Aeschylus has not imagined this court but modeled it on one he and his audience knew.

Furthermore, in the same play, Orestes pledges that Argos will help Athens; the Athenian alliance with Argos was significant in the fifth century, but again, it is not made explicit how that alliance is deployed here. The conflicted relationship with Argos may be alluded to in other plays. For instance, Euripides' *Suppliants* is set in Athens, and the mothers of the fallen Argive warriors have come to ask Athens' aid in regaining their bodies; Theseus, the king, agrees and reminds them always to honor Athens. Athena comes and exacts an oath, to make sure that the cities won't fight with one another in the future.

During much of the time that Sophocles and Euripides were writing, the Athenians were at war with Sparta. We might ask, then, whether that war influenced how people received plays about the Trojan War, and/or whether the plays influenced how the Athenians thought about their own actions in the Peloponnesian War. How should you treat your enemy? We know something about this delicate topic from Thucydides' history, for he recounts two debates that are particularly relevant: first, the Athenians meeting in assembly decided to kill the men and enslave the women and children of Mytilene (3.3.36), but they later changed their minds (37); second, the Athenians similarly decided to kill the men and enslave the population of Melos, but this time they executed their decision (5.7.116). The Melian massacre took place in the year that Euripides' *Trojan Women* was produced (415). The play is set in the aftermath of the Trojan War; the Greeks have won, and the Trojan women are waiting to hear where they will be sent as slaves. All the men are already dead, but in the course of the play, the Greeks kill Astyanax, the last remaining male member of the royal family because, as the son of Hektor, the great Trojan hero, he might in the future pose a threat to Greek security. The connection to the Peloponnesian War dilemma seems obvious, with the exception that there the combatants were all Greeks; indeed, many modern productions of *Trojan Women* mention Melos in their program notes, as if it were certainly referred to by Euripides. That is unlikely to be the case since the archon appointed the playwrights some time during the summer before the campaign, and would presumably have seen the plays or at least parts of them before making his decision. Evidence also suggests that the chorus was in rehearsal for months. But up-to-date allusions could have been added at the last minute, if they were small in scale. Surely, it is equally unlikely that the audience, seeing the play after the Melian debate took place, would not have thought of its own situation. This would be especially true of the citizens, who sat as a body in the Assembly and, though they might not have spoken, participated in the decision-making process. That does not mean that all citizen members of the audience responded in the same way; we know that there was debate in the Assembly and therefore division on the issues, as we might have imagined even without Thucydides' evidence. If the play encourages the audience to sympathize with the Trojans, did it also encourage them to sympathize with Athens' present-day enemies? Modern readers often assume that because he points out the horrors of war Euripides must be anti-war, but that value judgment does not necessarily follow from his observations, as we will discuss more fully in Chapter 6.

In any case, the audience might respond one way to the play and another way to the events in their own lives, as is attested to by a fascinating speech written by an orator known as Andokides called "Against Alkibiades." He accuses the Athenians of turning a blind eye to those "who flagrantly commit acts of violence." His example is Alkibiades, a member of Socrates' circle and a very problematic person in Athens, who, "after recommending that the Melians be sold into slavery, purchased a woman from among the captives and has had a child by her—a child whose birth is more transgressive than Aigisthos', since his parents are each other's bitterest enemies and his family is divided between those who have committed and those who have suffered the most extreme wrongs" (23). "Andokides" goes on to point out that, "When you watch such things in tragedies you regard them with horror, but when you see them taking place in the *polis* you think nothing of them" (Wilson 81). The incident in question is the Melian episode, but his argument reminds us that it is perfectly possible that even if the play were taken as a reference to contemporary events, the audience members might have responded more vigorously to the tragedy than they did to events in their everyday life.

As we have seen, certain elements might have reminded the audience of their own lives; these similarities, even if not political, would still have had the effect of bringing the action closer to home. To take a famous example from Sophocles, the plague at the beginning of *Oedipus Tyrannos*, in which the people come to Oedipus seeking aid in healing the city, must have resonated with an audience that had recently experienced a plague, as Athens had (Thucydides 2.5.47–58). Perikles seems similar to Oedipus, a confident leader bested by disease. It is not necessary for it to be an intentional reference, and it could also refer to other literary plagues (in Book I of the *Iliad*, Apollo has sent a plague that initiates the action). Moreover, not every member of the audience will get the same set of allusions, nor will they respond to them in the same way. Let us look at a modern example: How do audiences at the movie *Rent* understand references to the source opera, *La Bohème*, or to the AIDS epidemic? *Rent* began as a radical play in 1996, while *La Bohème* is one of the canonical works in the operatic repertory (hardly a radical genre). Audiences familiar with the opera will hear its echoes and may find the film wanting, or may enjoy the updating. Audiences who loved the play may resent the film version. How does the availability of AIDS treatments change the audience response? The actual audience will have different experiences with the disease, some intimately aware of its effects, some unfamiliar with it. Because we cannot know what any author intended, nor can we generalize about the actual audience, critics often speak of the "notional audience" or the authorial audience to get at the idea that we can think about what the author had in mind for the audience on the basis of evidence in the text.

Ideology

The most general way in which tragedy is taken to reflect its social and political context is through recourse to the concept of ideology, but that word has many different meanings and can be used in a very slippery way. Some years ago Terry Eagleton defined the term thus: "it signifies the way men [*sic*] live out their roles in class-society, the values, ideas and images which tie them to their social functions and so prevent them from a true knowledge of society as a whole" (1976: 16–17). In a more recent book, *Ideology* (1991), he lists six uses of the word (winnowed down from sixteen), pointing out that they don't always mesh with one another. In discussions of tragedy, the meaning is often unclear. Ideology may mean something as general as world view, or Vernant's notion of "mentality," but it does have a historical relationship to Marxist criticism which gives it a little more of an edge. For Marx, the economic explanations were the real ones, but they were masked, parading as our ideals. In the Vietnam era, there were frequent debates about what the reasons were for the war—to support democracy or to keep a U.S. presence in Asia?—as there have been more recently about Iraq. Did the U.S. and Britain go to war with Iraq because of Saddam Hussein's weapons of mass destruction, to bring democracy to the region, to fight terrorism, or for oil? Cultural artifacts like tragedy cannot be expected to intervene in such debates in a straightforward manner. They may support or subvert the values of the dominant class, or may even subvert some elements while supporting others.

Tragedy most obviously acts as an element supporting Athenian ideology in those few plays where characters incongruously praise Athens and highlight elements central to its self-conception as a democracy. For instance, the Trojan women in Euripides' play seem to know about Athens and hope to be taken there (207–8); in Aeschylus' *Persians*, the Queen gratuitously asks about the city of Athens, and the city is lavishly praised in Euripides' *Medea* and Sophocles' *Oedipus at Kolonos*. When Medea is planning her revenge, she receives a promise of asylum from the Athenian King Aigeus; the members of the Chorus respond to her plan to murder her children by asking how the noble city of Athens could welcome her if she did it. They describe Athens as holy and unconquered (825–6) and associate it with Harmony, Aphrodite (the goddess of love), Wisdom, and the Muses, who through Desire assist "every kind of excellence" (845). *Oedipus at Kolonos*, too, presents an opportunity for the praise of Athens. Kreon has come to Athens to take Oedipus back to Thebes, having exiled him years ago. Theseus vows to protect him and says:

> You come to a city-state that practices justice,
> A state that rules nothing without law;
> And yet you cast aside her authority, take what you please, and worse, by violence,
> As if you thought there were no men among us,
> Or only slaves; and as if I were nobody.
> (913–18, trans. Fitzgerald in Grene and Lattimore)

This speech and these plays connect Athens' hospitality to outsiders (guests and suppliants) to its rule of law. In Euripides' *Suppliants*, the primary situation concerns, as we saw above, the bodies of the dead Argive heroes; the Athenians pride themselves on their defense of the powerless, in this case the aged mothers. But the play also presents a long and quite unnecessary debate between the Theban Herald and the King about the merits of democracy, in a city that is presumably a monarchy since it has a king. The anachronism is handled in quite an interesting manner: the Herald asks for the man in charge, using the word *tyrannos*. Theseus says that this is a "free city-state, not ruled by one man. The people rule in annual succession in their turn, not giving most power to the rich, but rather the poor share it equally" (404–8). Theseus may be viewed in this play as a constitutional monarch; he says that he must consult the people, though he also has no doubt they will do what he wants (350). Similarly in *Oedipus at Kolonos*, though King Theseus rules, it is up to the people to make decisions (79–80). This is not the way it was in fifth-century Athens: the Assembly made all the decisions, though Perikles advised them (Thucydides 1.140.1). But the values are fifth-century Athenian values. Sophie Mills points out that the character of Theseus "comes to represent the idealized imperial Athens, the city of justice and mercy that is familiar from a substantial body of Athenian writing about Athens" (2). Importantly, Theseus wants to hear from the people; whoever has something good to say can put it "in the middle" (perhaps an equivalent to our "on the table"); that way you get the best results (*Suppliants* 439). The positive features of his rule include equality before the law (433–4) and selection by lot—both of which were elements of Athenian democracy. The Herald makes the arguments associated with the oligarchic parties in Athens: a working man can't rule because he can't look out for the common good; if one person is in charge, there is less chance that rhetoric will rule by swaying the mob (411).

Suppliants refers to two other important elements of Athenian democratic ideology—freedom from tyranny and freedom of speech—and other plays make similar allusions. The Athenians took pride in their self-definition as a free people, not dominated by a tyrant. As Aristotle says, under democratic constitutions, the people can do what they want (as children still say in the U.S.: "you can't make me; it's a free country"). That freedom was epitomized in their freedom of speech (*parrhēsia*); *isēgoria*, the equal right of all citizens to speak in the Assembly, was essential to the definition of democracy in Greek writers.

Tragedy is, as I mentioned earlier, rarely set in Athens. What is the meaning of that foreign setting? What are the consequences? The Athenians might be forced temporarily to identify with the other who takes center stage, or, conversely, they might distance themselves from them, thinking "that's their [Theban, Trojan, Argive] problem, not ours." Both of these audience reactions are possible, even within the same play. Froma Zeitlin (1990b) argues that Thebes becomes an "anti-Athens," a vehicle through which the Athenians could safely confront themes too dangerous to be set at home. The plays may be seen to mediate between self and other, present and past; as a result the Athenians, like current audiences, had to be able to see both what was strange and what was familiar about the world of the play. The slightly distant setting, as well as the non-realistic elements of the production, prevented total identification, while the anachronisms could act as a small shock leading to recognition of the situation's applicability to the audience's present. What is most important to stress is that tragedy does not simply glorify Athens and the Greeks compared to the Trojans and Persians. Even if we take tragedy as an ideological institution, it is not propaganda.

The claim that a work of art is ideological has traditionally been tantamount to assuming that it supports the dominant class in a society or the dominant point of view. However, the school most concerned with Athens' relationship to tragedy often takes Athenian ideology (and therefore the support of it) to be radical. As I mentioned above, Vernant emphasizes the particular moment in which tragedy came into being, its "tensions and ambiguities," and its relationship to the city which turns itself into theater (Vernant and Vidal-Naquet 185). According to Vernant and others who follow him, the world of the city is called into question, not simply reaffirmed, by tragedy, and the plays remain open (Vernant and Vidal-Naquet 33). Others, most notably Simon Goldhill (1990), understand tragedy both to re-present the city and to challenge it; they argue that the city values the ambiguity of tragedy.

We could say that tragedy supports the status quo, in that the festival is clearly an arm of the city-state and one way in which it praises and maintains itself, but at the same time that the content of the plays may challenge the status quo. Mikhail Bakhtin's theories are fruitful here, in particular his observation that texts have many voices (heteroglossia) not one, and that there are centripetal and centrifugal forces at work at the same time (esp. 272), though one voice may be enforced and empowered. The idea of competing voices enables us to accommodate the seeming contradiction between the festival—an ideological institution of the democracy—and the plays—which seem to question most received opinions. The dialogic quality that Bakhtin isolates in narrative is essential to drama. In the plays, women, slaves, and "others" are given voice that they would not otherwise have had in civic society.

The many individual challenges might well, nonetheless, have been brought back under control in the orderly process of ritual or festival. As modern theories of ritual point out, festivals may embrace conflict temporarily, but they ultimately reintegrate participants into the body politic. The riotous carnival may function as a release valve and not have lasting resistance effects; similarly, in initiation ceremonies the youth being initiated is incorporated into the city as an adult, having experienced its opposite in the border lands or wild zone (see Chapter 3 on initiation). A scholar like Richard Seaford sees closure, not openness, in the plays; he argues that the city is restored after the eruption of conflict caused by the actions of individuals. Many of the protagonists of tragedy suffer because they abuse their legitimate power—from Xerxes in Aeschylus' *Persians*, to Agamemnon and Aigisthos in his *Oresteia*, to Theseus in Euripides' *Hippolytos*, or even Pentheus in his *Bacchai*. The memory of the tyrants was still live, and the isolated individual was seen as a threat in tragedy though a threat that was dealt with in the end.

The focus on tragedy's openness to questioning and challenge may tend to idealize Athens in a new way, leaving aside the rifts and inequities within the *polis*, and Athens' role as tyrant to its subjected allies. In fact, the institution of tragedy had a complex relationship to those excluded from the democracy. The pre-play rituals give the clearest evidence of the role of the city, and they seem to have included women, metics (non-citizen residents), and colonial subjects, albeit in roles consistent with their positions; all presumably shared in the feast. In contrast, the enactment of the plays underscores the limitations of the democracy: the actors, writers/producers, directors, chorus members, and judges were men, and for the most part citizens.

It is common to offer no explanation for the exclusion of physical women from the stage, as if it went without saying. Of course, women could not appear in public with men. For more than one hundred years, the orthodox position was that women were virtual slaves, ill-educated and confined to the women's quarters; since marriage was primarily for the purpose of producing children and especially for continuing the male line, men had their significant affectionate and sexual relationships with other men and *hetairai* (high-class prostitutes). Quotations from Medea's speech to Corinthian women (which we will discuss below) and fragments from the lost Sophoclean *Tereus* give evidence for this perspective; the orators of the fourth century offer further documentation.

But Athenian women were not strictly sequestered indoors; they regularly participated in funerals and in other ritual events, in particular the worship of Dionysos. As the city took over the previously religious functions of lamentation and the celebration of Dionysos in the dramatic festivals, women were edged out. There are many possible explanations of this change. We could say that by eliminating women, men took on whatever power women did have by playing their roles; they had the opportunity to experience emotions to which they would not otherwise have had access (Zeitlin 1990a; Loraux). That would have been true for the male audience as well. The transvestism of Dionysos' worship and the transvestism of initiation (see Chapter 3) indicate that experiencing the other was part of what was required for the development of a sense of self for the ancient Greek male; tragedy would then act as a form of sacrifice or initiation, where the sacrificer takes on the power of the animal, and the initiand is transformed. Alternatively the practice might have been a protection from the danger of the feelings women were held to express. There was always the threat that emotion would be out of control, a central theme in Dionysos' myth; the festival context restrains and controls, but it might have been even more problematic to have biological women expressing these feelings.

The evidence about the audience is more complex. As we saw earlier in the section on the audience at the festival, one line of thought compares the audience at the tragic performances to audiences at civic performances in the Assembly and courts. The Athenian citizenry made up only about 15% of the entire city population, and non-citizens did attend, so when we speculate about the effect of the plays on the spectators, we have to bear in mind that even in antiquity it was not only the city's insiders who were listening, even though insiders might have been the predominant addressees. We are left guessing about whether slaves attended, for the evidence is inconclusive, at best (they are left in "conceptual invisibility," Csapo and Slater 287 with sources). Plato refers to slaves and women as well as children in the audience, but he is speaking of performance more generally (*Gorgias* 502d; *Laws* 658c–d).

As I mentioned earlier, it is still vigorously debated as to whether women were in the audience. How we answer the question depends in part on our view of women's lives, and on whether we see the occasion as primarily a political site (where women were typically absent) or a religious site (where women were typically present). It is telling that the very same lines from Aristophanes are taken both to confirm and to disconfirm women's presence. There are potential consequences for each of these positions. If women did not attend but were there for the procession, it would make the production of the plays even more fully a representation of Athens as a men's club. If they attended in diminished numbers and/or if they sat in the back, that fact would constitute a visual reminder of their status during the watching of the plays. If the spectators were all men, or even mostly, how would they have reacted to the prominence of the female characters? Why would they have been interested in Clytemnestra, Medea, Phaedra, Antigone, to name only the most notable?

There are questions of interpretation for individual plays attendant on all of these ambiguities, and we will address these in more detail in Part II. Briefly, tragedy's representation of foreigners and their stereotyping has led critics to see its response to the Persian Wars as contributing to Athenian xenophobia. But how would the foreigners or slaves in the audience have responded? Clearly, Athens was a class-based culture; freedom from work was highly valued. For Aristotle, only if things could do the work themselves would there be no need for slaves (*Politics* 12541; duBois 97). Does tragedy support slavery and the implicit assumptions of Athenian culture, the ideology, on which it rested? It is possible that tragedy participated in naturalizing slavery by the ways in which it does and does not represent slaves. In the plays, for instance, the subjectivity of slaves is either ignored or made to support their owners.

When we come back to women, we are at the crux of much recent work on gender in antiquity and in tragedy. While women did not make tragedy, fund it, judge it, or perhaps even watch it, the plays seem to focus on female characters. Critics have wrestled with the ways in which the tension between performance practice and text might be interpreted. Froma Zeitlin (1990a, 1996), for instance, has argued that the female characters are really there to enable men to work out their subjectivity, while I have argued that Euripides uses the predominance of female characters to support the patriarchal values of Athens

(Rabinowitz). Recent critics, however, have seen women's speaking parts in tragedy as a form of action and as a subversion of the norm of women's silence; that is, they take the women on stage as countering the restrictiveness of the performance practice (Foley 2001).

Nothing to Do with the City?

The positions that I have discussed here represent, as I said, the main stream of current interpretation, but they are nonetheless challenged by others. This entire mode of study, and most especially the attention to the democracy, is seen as a political act. "Whatever happened to great literature?," some critics of this approach may ask. Critics who would deny the pedagogic efficacy of theater separate education from pleasure and argue that the school of "collectivists" (Griffin 1998, 1999) removes the aesthetic pleasure from reading tragedy. Indeed the pleasure in the language, music, and dance that made up a crucial part of the spectacle, as we saw in Chapter 1, ought not to be overlooked. Thucydides has Perikles point out that the Athenians specialized in festivals, and they were notorious theater-goers. As a teacher, I refuse to accept that there is a necessary division between the pedagogic and the pleasurable; after all, classes that do not keep the students' attention are not going to be effective as education.

One way to integrate the ideological and aesthetic strands is through ethical criticism. Tragedy aimed at an emotional response from the audience. If readers or viewers have the appropriate reaction, then something will have happened to them; they will be changed, if only temporarily. The transformation may be longer lasting if it coincides with what is going on in one's own life. So, for instance, if you are reading or seeing *Antigone* when you are being called upon to make an ethical decision, her story may have a sharpened impact on the choices you make. If you are in the opposition, you may gain perspective on your situation by gaining an increased understanding of Kreon and Antigone. In addition, something happens to the audience as a group by their having shared an emotional experience together, as we are aware if we go to an event with friends, for instance, instead of alone. Finally, no performance medium, especially not a highly conventional form such as Attic tragedy, reflects reality straightforwardly, and it may even change reality or challenge it—by changing the audience. When thinking in this way, one can ask not only how society shaped the work in front of us but also how the play helped shape the society.

In the end, any view of tragedy must take into account the fact that it has had and continues to have appeal far beyond its original geographical and social location. Indeed the historical or social approach is a testament to the continuing interest of these works. The fact that there are cultural or ideological reasons for the rise of this particular way of looking at the plays now does not invalidate its findings. It should lead us to ask what will be next, and I hope this book leads students of tragedy to think that they too might make a contribution to setting the future agenda with their questions and interests.

Suggestions for further reading

On tragedy and ancient sociopolitical environment, see essays in P. E. Easterling, ed., *Cambridge Companion to Greek Tragedy* (Cambridge: Cambridge University Press, 1997), and Justina Gregory, ed., *A Companion to Greek Tragedy* (Oxford: Blackwell, 2005); John J. Winkler and Froma Zeitlin, eds., *Nothing to Do with Dionysos?* (Princeton: Princeton University Press, 1990). For ancient materials and (abridged) essays, see Eric Robinson, *Ancient Greek Democracy: Readings and Sources* (Oxford: Blackwell, 2004). The following collections of essays and monographs are but a sample of what is available: Deborah Boedeker and Kurt Raaflaub, eds., *Democracy, Empire, and the Arts in Fifth-Century Athens* (Cambridge, MA: Harvard University Press, 1998); Moses Finley, *Democracy Ancient and Modern* (New Brunswick: Rutgers University Press, 1973); Barbara Goff, *Tragedy, History, Theory* (Austin: University of Texas Press, 1995); Christopher Pelling, *Greek Tragedy and the Historian* (Oxford: Clarendon Press, 1997); A. J. Podlecki, *The Political Background of Aeschylean Tragedy* (Ann Arbor: University of Michigan Press, 1966).

On women attending the theater, see Simon Goldhill, "Representing Democracy: Women at the Great Dionysia," in Robin Osborne and Simon Hornblower, eds., *Ritual, Finance, Politics* (Oxford: Oxford University Press, 1994), 347–69; A. J. Podlecki, "Could Women Attend the Theater in Ancient Athens?," *Ancient World* 21 (1990): 27–43.

On performance culture, see Simon Goldhill and Robin Osborne, eds., *Performance Culture and Athenian Democracy* (Cambridge: Cambridge University Press, 1999).

3

Tragedy and Greek Religion

To study tragedy in its Athenian context is, of course, not necessarily to study it only as political or democratic drama. While Chapter 2 grows out of one prominent school of contemporary thought, another influential way to look at the Athenian context of tragedy is through ritual and myth. Remember that the tragedies were performed at "The City Dionysia," an Athenian festival in honor of Dionysos Eleuthereus. Just as the relationship between tragedy and democracy is not simple, but the city's control over some aspects of the setting seems clear, so the relationship between tragedy and the divine is complex, but the cult aspect is clear. In this chapter, I will emphasize the ritual aspects of the events, some of which have already been mentioned in the earlier chapters on performance and the city. We will then look at the god's relationship to tragedy more generally, eventually expanding our view to other elements of Greek ritual and myth that are relevant to the plays, and then return to examine Euripides' *Bacchai* in some detail.

Dionysos

City Dionysia

The festival's two processions center on the statue of Dionysos—its removal and restoration—and his sanctuaries. Sacrifices and hymns were probably also offered at an altar outside the city before the statue was returned to Athens. The removal and restoration of the god's image imitates the mythic introduction of Dionysos to Athens. According to legend, Pegasos brought the god's statue from Eleutherea to Athens; the Athenian men resisted the worship of the god and were afflicted with an illness in their genitals (probably continual erection). They were freed from their suffering when they promised to worship the god by making and carrying *phalloi* (scholion to Aristophanes, *Acharnians* 243).

In the second procession, called the *pompê*, groups of men also carried phalloi as they marched singing hymns. It also seems that some colonies sent a phallos to the City Dionysia for use in the procession. The *pompê* was essentially a religious procession. A bull was led in a place of honor, and other sacrificial offerings were carried by members of the community. It culminated, like other festivals, in a feast in the sanctuary. Sacrifices to the god were extensive: in one year, testimony indicates that hundreds of bulls were killed. Not only did the sacrifices and processions take place in a theater adjacent to the god's sanctuary, but an altar to him was in the center of the playing space in the orchestra, and a seat dedicated to his priest is visible in the extant theater.

The dramatic portion of the competition began with the purification of the theater by the offering of a pig and the pouring of libations; the space and the events to take place there were thus rendered appropriate to the god. The competition itself was, as I have mentioned, preceded by men and boys from the ten tribes performing Dionysos' sacred song, the dithyramb (Archilochus fragment 120). Moreover, remember that according to Aristotle (*Poetics* 1449a2–25), dithyramb was the origin of tragedy. He also says that at first tragedy was somehow satyr-like; as we saw earlier, the fourth play offered by each tragedian was called a satyr drama. And satyrs, along with maenads (mortal female followers of Dionysos), are directly related to Dionysiac cult (for satyr costumes, see Figure 1). In short, tragedy is fittingly part of the god's festival.

Other festivals of Dionysos

Dionysos' other cults also included dramatic contests, or had aspects that resonate with the City Dionysia. Plays were performed in thirteen of the local celebrations of the Lesser, or Rural, Dionysia, as distinct from the Great, or City, Dionysia. Starting in the mid-fifth century, there was also a contest in comedy (and to a lesser extent tragedy) at the Lenaia, in the month of Gamelion (January). The Lenaia was named after the *lênai*, another name for maenads; thus the festival underscores Dionysos' association with women. We know very little more about what actually transpired at these secret rites, but a series of vases that show ecstatic women surrounding a column with the mask of the god mounted on it might refer to the ritual. Those images significantly connect the god to masking, an important feature of Greek drama.

The Anthesteria was a celebration of the "flowering Dionysos" in the month of Anthesterion (February–March); it lasted for three days, and late in its history, plays were added on the last day. In part, the holiday celebrated the association of Dionysos with wine; on the first day large vessels called *pithoi*, used for storing wine, were opened, and the wine was taken to the shrine of "Dionysos of the Marshes." His sanctuary in the marshes was only open that one day, and the sanctuaries of all the other gods were closed that day. The ritual was also related to Orestes, since Athenians poured a libation to him at the festival. According to myth, Orestes drank in silence before he was ritually purified for killing his mother; in commemoration, celebrants of the Anthesteria take part in a silent drinking contest. Other events that made up the three-day celebration are significant as evidence about Dionysos' other associations. For instance, the procession on the second day and vases showing Hermes and Dionysos in carts seem to indicate that the Anthesteria shares the theme of arrival we saw in the City Dionysia (Parke 107–20). The placement in the marshes reflects Dionysos' aspect as a creature of borders and his fluidity; it also has links to the behavior of maenads who left the city to worship the god. The maenads were in a way like young people undergoing rites of passage; they too went away from the civilized world in order to return as adults (as we will see below, both male and female Athenians had such experiences). The liminal quality of the events continued into the last day, on which ghosts were free to roam; thus, in the Anthesteria, Dionysos is connected to death. The freeing of ghosts that makes up part of the festival might have been drawn on in tragedy's consideration of mortality.

But Dionysos was not just a creature of the margins; he was also central to the city. At the sanctuary, choruses of honored older women (*gerarai*) made sacrifice under the direction of the Basilinna (wife of the King archon); there was also a holy marriage between Dionysos and the Basilinna. As in the City Dionysia, there was a civic nature to the ritual: the Basilinna is permitted to see what outsiders cannot and was empowered to make sacrifices on behalf of the city. The Basilinna had to be both Athenian-born and virgin in order to fill the role in this ritual drama. The marriage celebrates her rite of passage to womanhood, but also underlines the civic aspect of the festival: it took place in the center of the city, at the Boukoleion near the Prytaneion, though it began in the marshy region.

Dionysiac myth and legend

The cult practices are not always consistent with the myths about Dionysos, which tend to be more violent and show the god's dangerous side. Dionysos was famously twice-born. In one story, he is the son of the chief Olympian god, Zeus, and a mortal woman named Semele; Zeus smites Semele with his thunderbolt when she is pregnant, but he rescues Dionysos from her uterus, placing him in his own thigh. Dionysos is then born from his father. In another legend, Dionysos was hidden away from a jealous Hera in a cave in Crete; he was found by the Titans, who pulled him apart and ate him. He was later reborn and reconstituted. Dionysos is the only Olympian god who dies and is reborn. Both these myths of his birth have been taken as having initiatory significance for mortals, who imitate Dionysos and are reborn in the process. Dionysos also manifests himself as various animals, notably the bull and lion. Transformation could be a model for acting. His followers, the maenads, tear animals apart and eat raw flesh (*sparagmos* and *ōmophagia*). These practices might then be ways in which the worshippers imitate the god and take elements of the god into themselves, as do the actors.

Some aspects of Dionysos' mythology have already come out in the discussion of ritual: Dionysos was often resisted, as he was at Athens initially. The Anthesteria also has a myth associated with it that reveals a pattern of mortal hostility to the god: Ikarios received Dionysos well and was then given wine, which he gave to his guests. The effects of the wine led them to think that they were bewitched; as a result, they killed their host. When Ikarios' daughter found him dead, she hanged herself. The effects of wine similarly led to murder in the case of the Aetolians and Athenians: the Aetolians gave wine to the Athenians, who were unused to it and keeled over; their relatives thought they had been poisoned, so they killed the Aetolians. As a result of their crime, they were rendered infertile; they were told by the oracle to establish the festival of the Choes (part of the Anthesteria) to celebrate having learned the proper way to drink wine (the Greeks drank their wine mixed with water). In another legend that Homer reports, Lykurgus attacked Dionysos and the nurses of the god, driving them into the sea. He was blinded in punishment (*Iliad* 6.130ff.); later authors say that he went mad and killed his own son (Apollodorus 3.5.7). The thread of resistance to the god or of the effects of wine and killing is here tied to kin-killing, which predominates in stories in which Dionysos maddens women (the daughters of Minyas and Proetus). In those cases, child-killing often results.

Tragedy and Dionysos

The most overt connection between tragedy and Dionysos is through the ritual of the City Dionysia, as we have already seen. Can we say anything more? Of course, there does not have to be anything particularly Dionysian about the plays—athletic and poetic contests were used to celebrate Zeus and Athena, and there is no intrinsic connection between those contests and the divinities in question. The Greeks even had a saying "nothing to do with Dionysos" (Plutarch, *Moralia* 612e, 671e) that gave rise to an adjective used to indicate that something was irrelevant (*aprosdionusos*). The proverb suggests that, at least in later times, the plays did not seem to refer to the god. This phrase has caught on in recent scholarship and has been turned into a significant question. Is there a deeper connection to the god than that suggested by the pre-play rituals?

There are many ways in which tragedy has been found fitting to Dionysos, and vice versa. Friedrich Nietzsche's *The Birth of Tragedy: Genealogy of Morals* (1872) famously imagined tragedy as double, both Dionysian and Apollonian, a view which is consistent with the gods' shared worship at the oracle of Delphi (Dionysos in the winter, Apollo the rest of the year). Nietzsche saw Dionysos as standing for the fearful loss of self in the other, a process of merging, and Apollo for the rationality of individuation; the Apollonian element dominates in performance and makes that fearful experience accessible to mortals without their having literally to go through the dissolution that the characters experience. So, one god stands for disintegration, the other for articulation; one for passion, the other for reason (see esp. 19–28, 35–6). In non-Nietzschean terms, we could say that tragic drama makes it possible for the audience to have terrifying experiences vicariously; in this controlled setting spectators remain safely in their seats and yet benefit from the wisdom set forth. As in Aristotle's theory of *katharsis*, the audience does not wallow in its suffering but is purified by the time it leaves the theater. Similarly, in terms of gender, the male actors get to play female roles and therefore have temporary access to women's experience.

Other views also seek to understand the relationship of the god and theater. Jean-Pierre Vernant sees the appropriateness of Dionysos in his association with illusion; he emphasizes the role of the mask, as can be seen in the vase paintings mentioned above where the god's image sits atop a column, surrounded by his worshippers (Vernant and Vidal-Naquet 189–206; 381–412). Simon Goldhill sees the tension between the ideological setting and the tragic contest as reflective of Dionysos, the god of "illusion and change, paradox and ambiguity, release and transgression" (1990: 128). Cross-dressing in ritual, and in particular in regard to Dionysos, may have left its trace in the theater and may explain the power of the male actor of female roles.

While many would not go beyond these associations, Richard Seaford has argued persuasively that tragedy continued to be intrinsically Dionysiac in the plots of the plays, which derive from the pattern of his myth: kin-killing followed by the establishment of the cult. He takes the god to be the destroyer of the individualistic hero, who poses a problem to the community, but the savior of the city (255), basing this claim in part on the many rituals that show Dionysos leaving and returning to the city. Other aspects of the god that Seaford argues are relevant to tragedy and its narratives include the importance of women and their rituals, liminality, and arrival or border crossing. The main character is destructive of culture, while the rituals that end many tragedies reestablish civic order. Christiane Sourvinou-Inwood's work parallels that of Seaford. If the whole festival repeated Dionysos' arrival in the city, and expiated the poor welcome he was originally given, the religious aspect of tragedy can be taken as instructional: it is only by surrendering control to Dionysos that we can regain control (Sourvinou-Inwood 2003: 153). Seaford and Sourvinou-Inwood put the myth of Dionysos at the center of the drama, and while their analyses don't work equally well for all the plays, they do make it clear that Dionysos is not irrelevant to the plays that honored him.

Sacred Time and Space

Having participated in the procession, watched the sacrifice and the libations, and shared in the feast, the audience would have put the performance in a ritual context—then the resemblance to other rituals would have encouraged the audience to relate the drama to similar events in their lives. For instance, Zeus and Athena were also honored with contests (the Olympic games and the Panathenaiac festival). Epebes, young men about to come of age for military service, led the bulls for sacrifice at both Panathenaia and City Dionysia; the metics dressed similarly in red robes for each; and contributions were made to the city's treasury on both occasions (Seaford 249; Thomson 295). Thomson believes that at the end of Aeschylus' *Oresteia* the playwright "invited his audience to rise from their seats and carry on the drama from the point where he has left it" (297), in part because it was so close to their experience of the Panathenaia.

The Athenian ancient calendar was full of holidays, for men, women, or both. First set out under Solon, the ritual calendar was inscribed publicly in Athens; feast days, including both the annual and monthly events, accounted for about one-third of the year, just to give you some idea of the extent of it. These festivities punctuated life as festivals or feast days do for modern religious people; in our multicultural societies, however, not everyone is on the same religious calendar, whereas they were to a great extent in ancient Athens. The rhythm of life was regulated by the ritual calendar.

There was a *polis* dimension to many ancient Athenian religious practices (that is, they were state-organized) and a religious dimension to politics. For example, there was a public hearth dedicated to the goddess Hestia in the center of Athens, and prayers and sacrifices opened meetings of the Assembly and the law courts. Moreover, the civic dimension of religious life can be seen in the fact that the public treasury financed some cult observances, and that wealthy citizens were responsible for funding certain festivals as part of their contribution to the public good, as was discussed earlier. Given the civic dimension and the distribution of meat in some instances, most of the festivals enjoyed widespread participation. They constituted common experiences that would have provided a context within which the original audience would have responded to tragedy, since it too was part of a festival.

Rituals were also performed in the family—each household had its hearth dedicated to Hestia. The axes of power were reaffirmed through participation since the slaves, women, children, and male heads of household each occupied their appropriate place in the proceedings. The Olympian Zeus was a household deity, through his role as guardian of the fence (Herkeios) and hospitality (Xenios); as such, he received cult honors in the home. As Zeus Xenios he took the side of Menelaus and Agamemnon against Paris, who stole (or seduced) Helen away in defiance of rules of hospitality and thus started the Trojan War. Guest-friendship, or *xenia*, was the set of practices that linked men of aristocratic families to one another in the epics; it guaranteed safety and a place to stay for the traveler by forging relationships between families. *Xenia* transformed the stranger (and potential enemy) into a friend and was important in tragedy.

The demes and tribes established by Kleisthenes were also religious organisms, since they were responsible for some cult activity. There were many forms of religious associations in addition to these; heroes and heroines as well as gods received cult honors. It can be said then that the world of the Greeks was experienced spatially and temporally as an encounter with the divine.

Ritual Practices

Ritual practices more than any one coherent set of beliefs dominated ancient Greek religion. Rituals can be defined as actions that individuals or groups perform repeatedly in order to organize reality for themselves; the ancient Greeks used ritual to define relations between mortals and immortals, but also among humans, and between humans and animals.

Sacrifice

One of the most important rituals for the ancient Greeks involved giving to the gods. The City Dionysia opened with sacrificial offerings, and sacrifices play a major role in the plays. There were many forms of gift, notably the liquid offerings known as libations (*spondai*), which regularly marked the signing of treaties; they were also poured at graves. Hair was cut and left at graves, as well as in other rituals marking transitions (see below). Dedication to the gods was a significant part of Greek life; women and men might pay for statues that would be inscribed to a god or goddess and bear the mortal's name; smaller items like mirrors might similarly be left at a temple and inscribed with the donor's name. Girls offered their toys to Artemis when they reached puberty and the age for marriage. One of the most important offerings for the Athenian audience would have been the robe that was begun by young girls as a part of ritual service to Athena (see below on *arrêphoroi*) and woven by Athenian women to be given to the goddess at the Panathenaia.

A central aspect of ritual giving was animal sacrifice—a burnt offering (*thusia*) at an altar. Animal sacrifice was very carefully orchestrated. First the victim had to be a domestic beast that was perfect and unblemished and that had not been subjected to hard labor; those officiating had similarly to be pure. Second, the animal, adorned with garlands, was led by similarly garlanded attendants to the altar, and accompanied by pipe music. Third, the animal had to be willing and give a sign of consent—although consent could be manufactured by placing food near the animal's head, causing it to nod, or by putting something on its head that the animal would want to shake off, and thus make it seem actively to agree.

These sacrifices served to establish and reinforce proper relationships between several layers of existence—the animal world, the human world, and the divine world. As structuralist theory emphasizes, the ritual can be analyzed along horizontal and vertical axes. On the horizontal plane, sacrifice creates ties between the individuals who share the meat; thus through the enactment of sacrifice, the social group is organized, but with explicit hierarchies in place: in Greece insiders and male citizens ate more than women and children. Moving between the higher and the lower form, animal sacrifice connected and separated the human and the beast (as sacrificer and victim), as well as the human and the divine. Domesticated livestock were potentially too similar to humans to be eaten (since they were part of the household); thus, they were not consumed except in a ritual setting. Through this structured meat eating, the human distinguished itself from the domestic animal that was killed: the animal eats raw meat, the human does not. The most obvious purpose of the sacrifice, however, was to communicate with the gods—to thank them, request help from them, or honor them in the hopes of gaining (or keeping) their goodwill. The gods, unlike humans and animals, didn't need meat to sustain life; they were conceived to be spirit and to live on the smoke that rose up from the burnt offering.

There was an element of exchange between the human and the divine, however, because the gods were thought to need mortals to populate the world and to worship them because they liked honor (and presents) as much as mortals do. We can see this belief at work in Euripides' *Hippolytos*, where the hero is punished for snubbing the goddess Aphrodite. He ignores his tutor's warning that the gods are like humans in their desire for respect (88–107). The course of the play shows the power of the goddess to make Hippolytos pay for his mistake. Given divine greed, myth needed to explain why humans don't burn the best part of the offering but roast and eat it: the story of the first sacrifice tells us that Prometheus deceived Zeus, the supreme Olympian god, covering a pile of bones with fat to make it look attractive so that the god chose that portion for his offering, while humans share the meat among themselves (Hesiod, *Theogony* 507–616).

The prayers, the smoke, and the offering itself reached the god, who in turn spoke to the worshippers through a prophet who interpreted the inner organs of the animal. If the sacrifice were at the start of an expedition, the reading would predict its outcome. Alternatively, natural elements would be taken as "significant," that is, as signifying something about the event to take place. At the beginning of Aeschylus' *Agamemnon*, the Chorus sings about the setting out for Troy. The prophet Kalkhas has seen two eagles eating a pregnant hare; it appears on the right side (116), making it a favorable omen. He interprets the birds as the sons of Atreus (king of birds, kings of men); he further interprets the action as both positive for the Greeks (they will conquer Troy—equating the city with the rabbit full of young) and negative (Artemis protects the young and may demand another sacrifice—that of Agamemnon's daughter, Iphigeneia).

At the heart of sacrifice is typically a violent act: ritual practices transform murder into sacrifice instead (Vernant 1991: 293; Vidal-Naquet 2–3). Similarly, violence is at the heart of many of the tragedies and at the heart of the worship of Dionysos. Tragedy as a genre tends to deal with social crises; sacrifice in general offers a helpful code for playwrights to use in representing them. Since there is such a strongly delineated right way to sacrifice, deviations can point out what is wrong in a culture; then, the ritual gone wrong may be corrected, reinforcing the values of the culture.

It is no surprise that sacrifice is taken to be at the heart of tragedy by some. Walter Burkert and others who follow him define the very word "tragedy," from the Greek *tragôidia*, which, as noted in Chapter 1, combines goat and song, as referring to songs at the goat sacrifice to Dionysos (92–3). Thus, for him, the "memory of sacrifice stands in the center of the Dionysiac performance" (102). René Girard speculates that the sacrifice is controlled violence; it prevents vengeance, the interminable cycle of killing. The tragic festival, analogously, provides the reintegration of the community and allows it to deal with the violence that it fears will proliferate (120, 134). Sourvinou-Inwood argues, more plausibly I would say, that sacrifice was "important, for, being an important part of religion and life, it was a privileged locus for articulating order and disorder, which are central concerns in tragedy; but I do not think that sacrifice was the ritual core out of which tragedy was generated" (1994: 288–9).

The Greeks in the historic period did not perform human sacrifice, yet many legends recount such practices; in general a (female) virgin is required (as is consistent with the demand that the sacrificial animal be pure and without blemish). Such sacrifices (*Iphigeneia at Aulis, Agamemnon, Trojan Women, Hekabe, Children of Herakles, Phoenician Women*) are relatively common in tragedy; Menoeceus (*Phoenician Women*) is the only male sacrificed, and he kills himself. The demand for such a sacrifice has the power to throw the values of the culture into high relief, since it bluntly asks what the sacrificer and the victim are willing to give up, and in what circumstances. The requirement of consent simultaneously highlights the element of individual choice and the limits on it. Scholars differ on the historicity of the ritual—some hold that there were such rituals in the past, while others maintain that the myths stand for ritual not literal deaths and that the victims are models for what transpires for ordinary women in other ways (Foley 1985; Burkert). In the latter reading, the sacrifice is a symbolic death. The myth of sacrifice of a virgin may stand for the end of the old way of life and the beginning of a new stage of existence: the girl is now marriageable.

Rites of passage

The notion of symbolic death puts these stories of human sacrifice into the context of another important set of rituals, called rites of passage. Life consists of a series of moments that may be conceived of as dangerous and difficult transitions; many cultures construct practices designed to ease the passage between the stages. These transitional rites may share features with one another: for instance, in ancient Greece sacrifice, marriage, and death utilize rites of purification, garlanding, offering of locks of hair, and feasting. As a result, we sometimes see the conflation of marriage and death, or the image of the dead young woman as the Bride of Hades. The ritual sacrifice and marriage perform parallel functions in that they both strengthen community ties; Jean-Pierre Vernant links meat, grain, and marriage:

> At the same time that it is necessary, for survival, to eat the cooked flesh of the domestic beast sacrificed according to the rules, it is also necessary to nourish oneself with grain, with the cooked cereals of domestic plants cultivated by rule, and in order to survive oneself, to engender a son by union with a woman whom marriage has taken from savagery in order to domesticate by placing her in the conjugal hearth. (1980: 13)

(Like much functionalist and structuralist analysis, this formulation takes for granted the masculinity of the subject.)

Thinking about rites of passage is indebted to early work by Arnold van Gennep, who pointed out that "The life of an individual in any society is a series of passages from one age to another and from one occupation to another" (2–3). He argued that rites of passage consist of three stages—separation, transition, and reintegration into society (11). But the rites are not always performed in the same way, and the stages may not all be present to the same extent. Athenian girls participated in several actions that seem to have prepared them for marriage and motherhood, and when the members of the Chorus in Aristophanes' *Lysistrata* list the roles that they have played, they seem to outline the stages. First, at age 7, they were *arrêphoroi* to Athena Polias. Next, at age 10, they were corngrinders to Archegetis (another name for Artemis). Then, they tell us that they "shed [their] robe for Artemis at the Brauronia"; finally, they were basket-bearers (*kanêphoros*), possibly at the Panathenaia, although we cannot know for sure since many processions had basket-bearers as leaders or participants, including the City Dionysia *pompê*. We also do not know if all Athenian girls went through these rites, or whether a few elite girls enacted them for the age group. There were only two *arrêphoroi*, for instance, and they were selected for the role. They were clearly in a stage of separation since they lived apart in the sanctuary of Athena, but were being prepared for their lives as mature women as they learned about sexuality (their name refers to the fact that they carry "unmentionables") and weaving. The festival at Brauron marked the end of another period of separation from the life of the city. In that cult of Artemis, the girls spent time serving the goddess Artemis in her precinct; they are also said to "play the bear." In the service to the goddess and the distance from the family, being a bear was similar to being an *arrê-phoros*. At a similar cult of Artemis at Munichia the accidental killing of a bear necessitated the sacrifice of a girl, who was then replaced by an animal at the last minute. Significantly for the Iphigeneia story in tragedy, these myths blur the boundaries of human and animal, showing the identification between the two. They assuage the fear that underlies sacrifice with a beneficent promise, since the goddess often intervenes on the mortal's behalf (cf. Bloch 26).

There was no rite of incorporation into the adult group for women until marriage, a separate rite of transition in and of itself—and the transition to full womanhood was only accomplished still later with successful childbirth. Van Gennep's system works better for boys, who also went through initiations in ancient Greece, though they varied from city to city, and there is considerable debate about the evidence. The Athenian Apatouria was a three-day affair in which male infants were registered in the Phratry (a paternal kinship group); boys were reintroduced to it at puberty. The last day of the festival was called Koureotis, named after either the cutting of hair (which the youths did) or the similar word for youth (*kouros*). The whole festival was reputedly named after an act of deception (*apatê*) by a warrior called Melanthus; his use of a trick in a borderland struggle marks him as an ephebe, a male on the point of coming of age, a youth who had not yet become a full-fledged hoplite (a heavily armed foot soldier) and did not follow the very strict forms of warfare that hoplites swore to uphold. It is possible that young Athenian men served two years on the borders (and perhaps like Melanthus engaged in unheroic practices); the Apatouria would have marked their reintegration into the city after having lived on the margins of the city for that time. Spartan practices in the Krypteia were similar in some respects: youths spent a period of time in the wild, lacking weapons and exhibiting cunning. Inversion of norms of adult warfare dominates both sets of practices. The young men of tragedy are arguably at the stage of initiation into manhood (e.g. Ion, Philoctetes, Hippolytos). As we will discuss more fully in Chapters 4 and 5, in plays based on the House of Atreus myth, Orestes in particular is often represented as having to resort to trickery to win out over Clytemnestra and Aigisthos.

Like tragedy, coming of age was sometimes also associated with sexual inversion or cross-dressing, for instance in the ritual known as Oschophoria, where two male youths were required to dress as women when they led off the procession from Athens to the shrine of Athena

Skiras. The Oschophoria was said to commemorate the return of Theseus from Crete, a separation which itself might have signified initiatory activities. Every year Theseus was required to take seven young men and seven young women to be sacrificed on Crete in the labyrinth of the minotaur (a mixture of bull and man). One year he took two extra young men, who were dressed as women, and this deceit enabled him to carry out his plot to end the Athenian servitude to Crete (Plutarch, *Theseus*). Here we see elements of the deceitfulness of the Apatouria. There is also a homoerotic potential of cross-dressing, which characterized women's transition to married status in Argos (where the bride wore a fake beard) and in Sparta (where the bride dressed as a man, shaved her hair, and lay alone on a mattress in the dark) (Plutarch, *de Mulieris Virtutes* 4.245; Plutarch, *Lycurgus* 15.5). In these accounts it seems that in order to mature as a man, you had to go through femininity, and there were some parallels for women. This structure of initiation can be related to male playing the female in tragedy.

Ritual Practice in Tragedy

In recent years, considerable attention has been devoted to the ways in which ritual acts, especially sacrifices, are evoked and staged in the plays. Let us look at Aeschylus' *Oresteia* as an example. The opening of the trilogy intertwines omens and sacrifices. The Chorus describes the events leading to the sailing of the Greeks, mentioning the impossibility of softening the anger of the gods with any kind of sacrifices—burnt or poured (69–71). They then see Clytemnestra in the background and ask her why she is sacrificing (87, 91). They continue their narrative of past events with the reading of the signs and with the sacrifice of Iphigeneia (150, 214, 224) that took place at the embarkation of the army. Clytemnestra uses the traditional word for women's ritual cry when she describes the sacrifices she has ordained (*anóloluxa* 587) because she has been informed that the Greeks won at Troy; at the end of the play, she defines her action against Agamemnon as a sacrifice to Zeus (1385–7), to Justice, Atê, and the Furies (1431–3; on the corrupted sacrifice motif, see Zeitlin 1965, 1966). The second play in the trilogy, the *Libation Bearers*, begins with Elektra pouring libations at her father's grave, and the Chorus, Orestes, and Elektra specifically try to raise the spirit of their dead father.

Finally, Orestes performs traditional actions of supplication and purification in the *Eumenides*.

That play explicitly refers to the possibility of a curse of violence on Athens, which is averted by Athena, who allocates a proper place to the Furies, now to be known as the Kindly Ones; they will bless the city instead of harming it and will continue to do so if they are respected. The honoring of the goddesses is enacted on the stage, since in the last moments of the play, a procession is organized in which the Kindly Ones don new attire that mimics the ceremonial garb of metics in the processions of the City Dionysia and Panathenaia. Their activity of marching off is brought virtually into the laps of the audience. While we may debate how optimistic and conclusive this ending is (to be discussed in Chapter 4, *Oresteia*), there can be no doubt about the ritual echoes the original audience would have "heard."

Coming of age and initiation are other ritual patterns that can be seen in tragedy, as I indicated earlier. There are many stories that are congruent with rites of passage. In the *Oresteia* Iphigeneia is the sacrificial object, but as we have seen, human sacrifice may be metaphoric and stand for initiation. Her dress is described in a way that might remind the audience of little girls playing the bear in Brauron, and her virginity is emphasized. Indeed, Iphigeneia had a tomb at the shrine to Artemis and received offerings there on behalf of women who died in childbirth—that is, who failed to make a successful transition to motherhood.

There are three crucial points of transition for women—marriage, childbirth, death—and Iphigeneia is connected with all of them. Marriage ritual is particularly important as a referent in tragedy; the *Iphigeneia at Aulis* is the most obvious example. Agamemnon lures Iphigeneia to Aulis with the promise of marriage to Achilles, but he really intends to sacrifice her so that the army can go to Troy. Again, the perversion of the ritual adds to the emotional experience of the audience. The sacrifices that are fitting to the wedding become, through a series of *double entendres*, the sacrifice of the bride. The irony of killing the pure Iphigeneia to regain the promiscuous Helen is not lost on Agamemnon or Clytemnestra. Antigone, Polyxena, and Kassandra are all young women whose deaths are similarly associated with the language of marriage.

Men's initiation experiences are also central in tragedy. Orestes typically returns from exile when he is of age to assume his rightful inheritance; in the *Oresteia* in particular his action as healer of the city depends on his having reached his majority. Neoptolemus in Sophocles' *Philoctetes* is committing himself to war, being initiated into the military role. Euripides' Hippolytos seems to resist adult male status; the son of Theseus and Hippolyta, an Amazon, he is associated always with Artemis and the hunt and has just returned to the city. He announces that he does not wish to take on heterosexuality when he shows his disdain for Aphrodite; and when he justifies himself to his father (*Hippolytos* 1002–20), he simultaneously declares his chastity and his lack of desire to rule (Rabinowitz). When his stepmother Phaedra falsely accuses him of rape, his father curses him with exile and calls on Poseidon to kill him. Hippolytos does not make the transition to adulthood safely but is only reintegrated into the city on the point of death. His connection to initiation is displaced onto women.

Many of the plays refer to the establishment of cult, often at the play's end; these can contribute to tragic resolution. This occurs, for instance, in the case of three of Euripides' eponymous protagonists: Alcestis will be given honors at the festival of Apollo known as the Karneia; maidens will dedicate their hair to Hippolytos on the celebration of their marriages, and they will sing of Phaedra's love; and Medea establishes a cult in honor of her children having buried them in Hera's shrine. The deaths of heroes or heroines and their tombs were also the centers of worship, becoming sites for the celebration of festivals or rites of passage; these cults would still be active in the lives of members of the audience.

Although Greek religion did not have a sacred text or set of texts, religious practice was partly verbal, in that there were particular prayers for particular occasions and gods—the paian to healer Apollo and the dithyramb sacred to Dionysos. These prayers could be and were imitated in tragedy and might lead the audience to bring their extra-theatrical experiences to bear on their experience as spectators, adding to the religious dimension of the overall effect. The *ololugmos*, or ritual cry, given at the successful completion of sacrifice would have had a chilling effect when used inappropriately in tragedy.

It is even possible that tragedy began as a response to a change in one ritual song, mourning, or lamentation. In the early periods of Greek history, aristocratic funerals (and weddings) were lavish affairs; there is a history of Athenian attempts (from Solon to Perikles and beyond) to limit lamentation and funeral practices. The state increasingly took control over from the families who had been in charge of mourning, replacing individual funerals with a funeral oration for all the war dead. The public speech forbade or discouraged crying and particularly silenced women. Tragedy may have taken over that ritual function of public grieving, in the process ironically forcing the men who were playing women to do what was relegated to real women historically. We have already seen in Chapter 2 that Euripides' *Suppliants* begins with the grieving of mothers, but when the conflict over the bodies has been resolved, the hero Adrastus offers a funeral address which becomes a praise of the dead heroes, not a lamentation. The women's excessive mourning is problematic and threatens trouble for Theseus, because it makes him afraid for his own mother (cf. Eteokles in *Seven Against Thebes*). The praise of democracy in that play is then related to the funeral speech and to the suppression of women's tears.

Summing up this section, we can see that not only was tragedy performed as part of a ritual event honoring the god Dionysos, but it also referred to various rituals familiar to the audience. The divergences from common practice, as in the case with the sacrificial imagery, are telling; in the world of tragedy, reintegration from the wild is accomplished only with difficulty.

Greek Gods and Mortals

In this section, we will look at the ways in which the Greeks organized their pantheon of gods. Crucially, the Greeks were polytheistic; the history of their gods is based on strife and interfamily competition. The earliest generation, Ouranos (Sky) and Gaia (Earth), had children known as the Titans. The eldest and most important of these was Kronos; Ouranos kept his children prisoner within Gaia by having endless intercourse with his wife so that they could not be born. Kronos, with the help of Gaia, castrated his father, who then flew up into the sky. Aphrodite was born from the foam where the genitals of the god fell into the sea. The other Titans, including Prometheus, the god of fire and the god who devised the first sacrifice, were defeated in turn by the younger generation of gods, the Olympians who dwelt on Mount Olympos.

We have already had occasion to mention some of the Olympians: Zeus, Dionysos, Apollo, Artemis, Athena. Each of the major gods and goddesses had responsibilities for various aspects of human existence.

Zeus, for instance, was associated with the thunderbolt and storms, as well as hospitality, as we have seen. His wife, Hera, was the goddess of marriage, while Aphrodite was and still is synonymous with sexual love (*eros*). There is really no accurate way to divide up the powers and areas of the gods, especially since they had overlapping functions: for instance, Athena and Hephaistos were often paired because of their connection to technology. In simple terms, however, the following general assignments may be useful as a shorthand: Hestia, hearth; Ares, war; Hephaistos, crafts; Artemis, hunt, maidens, childbirth; her twin, Apollo, light and purification; Hermes, travel and the underworld; Dionysos, wine and moist nature, ecstasy; Demeter, grain; Poseidon, sea; Hades, death. Each of the gods not only had specific areas of interest, but also had symbols that could be used by poets—Apollo, the bow and the lyre, for instance. The paian in his honor is a song that addresses him as a healer, but his attributes mark his association with fighting and music, respectively.

There were in addition many divine elements in the human world: sites like streams and trees could be sacred, and inhabited by spirits—naiads in the woods, oceanids in the sea. And as we saw earlier, heroes and heroines were honored with cults as well. In *Oedipus at Kolonos* Oedipus had to be buried in a grove that was sacred because of its relationship to the Furies, goddesses of vengeance. His burial there confirms the holy status of person and place. Thus walking through the world could be a religious experience for the ancient Greeks.

The Olympian gods also interested themselves in human affairs, even causing the Trojan War. Eris (the goddess of discord) was not invited to the wedding of Peleus and Thetis, so she threw down a Golden Apple with the instructions that it was "for the most beautiful." That action led to a divine beauty contest between Hera, Athena, and Aphrodite in which the Trojan prince Paris was the judge. Each goddess offered him a bribe; when he selected Aphrodite, he was granted Menelaus' wife, Helen, as his reward. The gods also took sides in the progress of the war. Paris remained Aphrodite's favorite, and in one scene in the *Iliad* she whisks him away from danger, insisting that Helen come to his chamber. In addition, the gods mingled with mortals sexually; the male divinities often engendered demigods, like Herakles. Achilles was the son of Thetis, a goddess, and Peleus, to whom Zeus gave her since it was prophesied that any child born from his union with Thetis would be stronger than he. Importantly for us, Dionysos was the result of Zeus' coupling with Semele.

Because there were many gods and because they intervened in mortals' lives, they could conflict with one another and place mortals in a double bind. In the *Oresteia*, for example, Agamemnon is acting for Zeus in going to Troy to punish Paris, but he angers Artemis, who then demands the sacrifice of his daughter, Iphigeneia, if he wants to continue to Troy. Apollo enjoins matricide on his son, Orestes, but the Furies of his mother, Clytemnestra, persecute him for it. Thus acting as one god demands is no guarantee that you will not be punished painfully by another one. The many gods exemplify the fact there are many and competing demands on humans; they do not, however, constitute a simple fate. Moreover, while the gods live forever, and have limitless choices for themselves, they are for the most part constrained by natural law when it comes to human beings. Mortality is constitutive of human life: we live within time limits with very few exceptions—the goddess Dawn gives eternal life to her lover, but she neglects to give him youth, so even her boon is ineffectual.

Information about the gods' wishes came not only from omens but also from oracles, especially associated with Apollo at Delphi; he spoke through his priestess, the Pythia. Prophets were typically full of the power of the god they serve. While the seers were never "wrong," there were, however, many ways in which an omen or prophecy could come true. In *Oedipus Tyrannos*, when Oedipus tells Jokasta about the prophecy that he would kill his father and sleep with his mother, she replies that many men dream of marrying their mothers (981–2). Then, too, prophecies could turn out to be metaphorical as well as literal: Aigeus in *Medea* has been to the oracle to find out how he could have children; he is told that he must not uncork the wineskin until he reaches home. Medea tells him what the oracle means. Finally, it was possible that the prophet was deceitful or bribed, as is suggested by Oedipus in Sophocles' *Oedipus Tyrannos* and Kreon in his *Antigone*.

As a result of the multiplicity of divinities and the ambiguity of prophecy, human beings are constrained, yet they also have choice, especially in tragedy. While the Greeks believed in goddesses called the fates, the Moirai, who spun mortals' lives on their day of birth, the concept of fate in tragedy is more often a combination of the divine will and human behavior; the gods don't ordain despite character but through it. Though tragedy is fascinated with myths of families subject to fate and curses, human beings in the plays are shown exercising free will. The gods don't typically force people but make demands within which mortals exercise freedom and reveal character. To take one well-known case, though Oedipus was destined to kill his father and marry his mother, the play takes place after he has fulfilled his fate and emphasizes his agency in bringing those events to light. Similarly, Athena makes Ajax mad in Sophocles' play of that name, but it is his own wrath at not winning Achilles' armor that leads him to act as he does. To make matters more complicated, in addition to gods, nameless *daimones*, or spirits, were also said to accompany an individual and shape the character. Aeschylus' *Persians* repeatedly intermingles human and divine causes for the destruction of the Persian troops. Xerxes' character *and* some unknown god, as well as the skill of the Athenians, are responsible for the catastrophe.

The organization of Greek religion with its many layers of divinities from Olympians to nameless spirits was crucial for tragedy. On the ethical level, the divinities present the human characters with dilemmas and limits; on the aesthetic level, they presented the playwright with situations redolent with difficult human choices and with a set of symbols and associations that would speak to the audience. And of course the gods were characters in some of the tragedies as well as myth, to which we will turn now.

Tragedy and Myth

Athenian tragedy was in general based on stories from the past; as Aristotle said, the same families recur and seem to make for the best tragedies. History and complete fiction were very infrequent sources of tragic plots, unlike comedy, which was from the realm of the imagination and frequently made contemporary political references as well. Mythic subjects elevate the plays from the realm of the everyday and make it, in Aristotle's terms, more philosophical: tragedy is about what might happen, he says, not about what has happened. The preference for mythic stories may be explained by the fact that the mythic material was both distant from the audience's own experiences (so that the suffering was displaced) but also relevant, since many elements from that heroic past were still operative in the fifth century. In particular, there were continuities of hero cult. The contradiction and tension that characterizes tragedy comes from the clash of two time periods— the heroic past of Argos comes into contact with fifth-century demagogues and political practices.

The use of myth does not completely control the author, however, because it does not entail using the same version of the story. Although Aeschylus is said to have called his plays slices from the "banquet of Homer" (*Athenaeus* 347e), indicating that many of the plays' plots come from the Trojan War cycle, they take place before and after the war. The causes and effects seem to be more suited to tragedy than the acts of war themselves. In Homer, Agamemnon remains the "lord of men," but tragedy fully scrutinizes his actions. Euripides shows his indecision, and makes him the victim of fifth-century dema-goguery in *Iphigeneia at Aulis*. Differences of detail show the leeway the playwrights had. For instance, Helen is sometimes raped by Paris, sometimes seduced by him (this ambiguity is endemic to tragedy); and in some versions, she does not even go to Troy (Euripides' *Helen*). *Iphigeneia at Aulis* tells the story of the sacrifice of Agamemnon's daughter Iphigeneia in detail; but the *Oresteia* simply refers to that event. Then, too, in myth Iphigeneia does not always die but may be rescued by Artemis and become her priestess (*Iphigeneia among the Taurians*).

Aeschylus enacts the murder of King Agamemnon by his wife, the revenge by Orestes, and its consequences, including setting a trial in Athens. All three dramatists took Elektra and Orestes as the subjects of drama, but neither of the others enacts the conclusion. Elektra is married in Euripides, but living as a slave in the house of Aegisthus and Clytemnestra in Aeschylus and Sophocles; only in Sophocles is she represented with a sister (though they are mentioned in Homer). In Sophocles she hears a report that Orestes is dead, but not in any of the others. In short, to say that a large number of tragedies are based on the stories of the House of Atreus does not mean that the poets did not have flexibility in arranging their plots.

While mythic heroes like Herakles play a role in several tragedies, and Ajax and Philoctetes are also appropriate tragic subjects, Thebes' ruling family offers an important cluster of plays that centers on that city: Sophocles' *Oedipus Tyrannos*, *Antigone*, *Oedipus at Kolonos*, Aeschylus' *Seven against Thebes*, Euripides' *Suppliants* and *Phoenician Women*. Given the performance of tragedy in Athens, this focus on Thebes has seemed a distancing device, like the use of myth in general. What is set away from Athens suggests that it is somebody else's problem, that Athens, for instance, does not practice incest. At the same time, the advantage of using myth is arguably to broaden the specific and make a play seem applicable to many, if not all, of its viewers. Indeed, one reason that tragedy can still seem relevant today is that it is not set in a particular historical time and place. When we read ourselves into the past, we are only doing what the original audience was already doing.

Euripides' Bacchai

I will close this chapter with a consideration of the ways in which Euripides' *Bacchai* (another name for the maenads or *lênai*), one of his last plays and produced posthumously by his son, sheds light on the questions we have been addressing of the role of ritual and myth in tragedy. Dionysos, as we have seen above, has civic festivals that are stately and calm, as well as orgiastic mysteries, associated with him. The sacrifices and festivals of Athens are said by Perikles to bring "release from toils" (*anapaulai ton ponôn*, Thucydides 2.38), a phrase that is consistent with both mystery terminology and something more modest and upbeat; Dionysos is the god of freedom (*eleuthereus* and *lusios*), which might be threatening to a city dependent on the maintenance of good order, but in the end his rituals also brought the city together. Both these aspects are evident in the play. *Bacchai* gives an outline of the myth of Dionysos as well as some of the practices of the maenads. He is preeminently the god who comes from outside and who is received badly at first, while the experiences of Pentheus, King of Thebes, mirror elements of the god's myth and ritual, particularly the sacrifice and the inversion of mystic initiation; the initiand is a double of the god, and his enemy.

The play opens with a prologue delivered by Dionysos, who has returned to his birthplace of Thebes from the east with a following of converted maenads from Lydia; he is masquerading as his own priest. Thebes is the first Greek city to which he has given his rituals. His aunts have denied his divinity, saying that his mother Semele had actually been impregnated by a mortal and that Zeus had punished her lie with the thunderbolt; as a result, Dionysos has driven them all mad (literally, stung them with mania). When the play opens, they are off in the mountains, having abandoned their women's work; they are wearing Bacchic garb. Despite themselves, they are now indistinguishable from the Lydian maenads. The god predicts that city will learn the cost of being uninitiated in his ritual (1–40). Thus, this is an example of a story of resistance to Dionysos' worship.

The Lydian women enter singing a traditional cult song in which they list the attributes of followers of Dionysos, and they include both the beneficent—blessedness, ritual silence, purity, the magic wand (*thyrsos*), ivy wreaths, snakes, the dance, music, spontaneously flowing milk and honey—but also the violent signs of animal possession—they wear fawn skins, hunt goats, and consume raw flesh (64–166). Both peaceful and violent aspects of their song are reflected in the later descriptions of what happens on the mountainside with the "false," Theban maenads. When they are undisturbed, their behavior is idyllic and peaceful; the land literally spouts with milk. When they are interrupted, they turn violent, rending cattle limb from limb in a realization of the *sparagmos* described by the Lydian maenads. The audience, familiar with such songs, having perhaps participated in choruses themselves, would be brought close through this use of ritual forms, even though the time and place were remote.

Pentheus, son of Agave, grandson of Cadmus and cousin of Dionysos, most especially resists the god. In Pentheus' case, the resistance may be psychological. He is hostile to the god's feminine looks, assumes that his rites include lechery, and insists on imprisoning the god and his followers—perhaps a sign of repression of the same desires and elements in himself. But his resistance has a collective side: the women's defection from their work upsets the order of the city. As the leader, Pentheus feels he must return the women to their places inside their homes. The threat of disorder is also part of the cult and myth: Dionysos arguably makes his worshippers strangers to themselves. As we have seen in his myths, Dionysos was a threatening god: the wine that he brought could change people, leading to madness and kin murder. Divine madness, then, might signify the confusion of opposites, or a more general loss of control, which is at odds with a desired order and might thus be resisted out of fear.

Dionysos reveals himself to Pentheus through miracles (he escapes from his chains, burns the palace down), but Pentheus is unconvinced by these displays and declares his intention to fight the maenads in the mountains. At that point, the god changes his tactics. He plays on Pentheus' desire to see the women, convincing him to dress in women's clothes and hide his masculinity; in a rare scene of tragic transvestism, the god helps Pentheus to fix his costume so that he looks like his mother. Pentheus is then led through the city to the mountain dressed as a bacchant. In the end, his mother, Agave, mistakes him for a lion and tears him limb from limb. She returns to consciousness, sees that the "lion" head she holds is her son's, and recognizes what she has done with horror; she is sent into exile with the other members of the royal family.

The *Bacchai* is the only explicitly Dionysian play that we have; it is consistent with other stories about the god in several ways and may reveal his appropriateness as the god whose celebration included a theater in which men disguised themselves (often as women) and participated in violent actions as well as lament. He is traditionally accompanied by women; the predominance of women in tragic choruses may result from this association. He instigates violence in his worshippers if they meet opposition and uses violence against those who oppose him: for instance, in the case of the daughters of Minyas. In that case, too, the women who don't resist the god have an essentially peaceful form of trance, while the women who do resist are turned murderous, violent against their own children. The departure of the maenads to the wilderness in the play reflects the outsider aspect of the deity, also seen in his liminal identity as Dionysos of the Marsh.

The *Bacchai*, too, refers to initiation. First, there are important similarities between rites of passage (withdrawal from the city, reintegration after a period of separation) and the maenads' retreat to the mountainside and the return to domestic activity, or marriage in the case of the unmarried women. Second, what happens to Pentheus in the play is a failed initiation: he undergoes ritual transvestism when he dresses as a woman and leaves his old identity, but he does not successfully gain a new one. The *sparagmos*, or tearing to pieces, of Pentheus is also typical of Dionysos' cult and myth, but he will not experience the rebirth that is held out by the mythic example of the god and by the promise of initiation into mystery cults.

The *Bacchai*, then, informs us about Dionysos, at the same time that it can be seen to relate to other plays because it utilizes and refers to general cult structures such as sacrifice and initiation. There is considerable debate about the meaning of the play. Richard Seaford sees the successful institution of Dionysos' cult at Thebes as a significant resolution; others point out that since our attention has been relentlessly focused on the individuals, the city is of little concern to us. To be sure, the ending is one of the most pessimistic of any Greek tragedy: the royal family, even Kadmos who accepted the god, is driven into exile. The play offers no easy answers, and that has led some to see only irresoluble contradiction in the ending. Nonetheless, in watching the play in a setting dedicated to the worship of Dionysos, the fact that Thebes suffered for not accepting the god could not have gone unnoticed; the audience has an experience that offers integration to it even if those within the play experience only the tearing apart. In short, the ritual setting of tragedy in ancient Athens cannot be ignored in terms of what the members of the audience actually felt and thought as they watched.

Suggestions for further reading

In addition to the works cited, on Greek religion in general, see Louise Bruit Zaidman and Pauline Schmitt Pantel, *Religion in the Ancient Greek City* (Cambridge: Cambridge University Press, 1992); and on Athenian religion, see Robert Parker, *Athenian Religion: A History* (Oxford: Clarendon Press, 1996).

On female initiation, see Matthew Dillon, *Girls and Women in Classical Greek Religion* (London and New York: Routledge, 2002); Ken Dowden, *Death and the Maiden: Girls' Initiation Rites in Greek Mythology* (New York: Routledge, 1989); and Deborah Lyons, *Gender and Immortality: Heroines in Ancient Greek Myth and Cult* (Princeton: Princeton University Press, 1997).

On lament and funeral oration, see Nicole Loraux, *The Invention of Athens* (Cambridge, MA: Harvard University Press, 1986) and *Mothers in Mourning* (Ithaca: Cornell University Press, 1998).

On the play and Dionysos, see E. R. Dodds, ed., *Bacchae*, 2nd ed. (Oxford: Clarendon Press, 1960) and Richard Seaford, ed., *Bacchae* (Warminster: Aris and Phillips, 1996).

Part II

Thematic Approaches

In Part I, we looked at the conditions in ancient Athens as they affected the production of tragedy, focusing on performance in the civic and ritual contexts. In relating tragedy to the city, I pointed out that while the democracy was radical for citizen men, it was also inextricably connected to rule over others, both in the empire and at home—where it excluded both women and resident aliens and was based on slavery. In this section of the book, I will offer more sustained readings of selected plays from the perspective of certain themes (war, family, and the relationship of mortals to gods), by working through the binary oppositions referred to earlier: male/female, Greek/barbarian, free/slave, king/subject, and mortal/immortal. I have chosen plays that are frequently studied, and that lend themselves particularly well to analysis through these groupings; choices of text and approach are subjective, of course, but had to be made because it was impractical to present all the plays in detail. Euripides' *Hippolytos*, for instance, has been left out, even though it does build on some of these elements. In the background are the questions raised earlier: How do these plays relate to ideology? Do they reinscribe it or question it? How do they draw on the religious or festival setting?

This section of readings is indebted to structuralist, as well as feminist and multicultural, modes of analysis. Structuralist criticism in Classics (see the Introduction) emphasizes such binary oppositions, which also seem to arise organically from Greek thought. A famous statement attributed to Thales, a pre-socratic philosopher, or sometimes even to Socrates, says that "he gives thanks to fortune for three things, 'first, that I was born a human and not a beast, next that I was born a man and not a woman, third, that I was born a Greek and not a barbarian'" (Diogenes Laertius 1.33). Classicists have long recognized the dominance of a kind of polarity in Greek thought. We may take as an example the Pythagorean table of opposites, which they thought organized the universe. In that system limited/unlimited, odd/even, unity/plurality, rest/motion, square/oblong, light/dark, right/left, good/evil, and male/female were lined up against one another; in the plays, concepts like custom and nature, word and deed, friend and enemy are frequently set off against one another and may establish a matrix for interpretation.

We have already seen some of these concepts at work in the structuralist analysis of ritual sacrifice, which takes it to organize relationships between animal, human, and god on the vertical axis and relationships within the community on the horizontal axis. Sacrifice connects the human being performing the ritual killing and the animal killed, the one who eats cooked food, and the other who eats raw meat; at the other end of the spectrum are the gods who received the sacrifice in the form of smoke. Man/woman and Greek/barbarian are ideological oppositions that are similarly useful for the analysis of ancient society. Moreover, the way the Greeks conceptualized them has echoed down the ages. Therefore, these oppositions have meaning not only in antiquity but in the present as well; throughout Part II, we will be considering what the tragedies mean to current readers. Finally, though as ideological constructs these oppositions are primarily political and intellectual, they are elements of plays not essays. As plays performed in the theater, they sought an emotional reaction from the fifth-century audience; as we discuss the plays, I will also suggest that we pay particular attention to the emotional and ethical level of response. To what extent do they have such an impact on readers in the twenty-first century?

The elements in these oppositions are not easily separated but are rather mutually constitutive. As we can see from Thales, Greek men defined themselves as not women, not barbarian, but the borders between are somewhat porous; maintaining order involves policing the boundaries, which shows up as contestation in the plays. Other significant arenas are drawn into this tension, since in ancient Greek culture male/female was mapped onto public and private (which often appear in the plays as war and family). Though the framing as an opposition suggests distinction, the elements are frequently intertwined. For example, the city and the household are not separate since the city depends on households and is made up of them; moreover, the household (*oikos*) is itself made up of family members as well as outsiders (slaves). Since the wife moved to her husband's house and left that of her natal family, she was to some extent viewed as an outsider, though she stood at the core of the new family, producing its lineage. Plays sometimes depend on these ambiguities. In Euripides' *Alcestis,* King Admetos is able to persuade his friend Herakles to stay with him even though he is in mourning for "a woman" who has just died. He does this by convincing Herakles that the deceased woman was an outsider when she was actually his wife. He can do so without lying because the wife is also "a woman" and an outsider. The ways in which the plays confront these tensions and ambiguities are relevant to us today because the ideological association of the female with the inside and the private realm, the male with the outside and the public, is not limited to ancient Greece.

In Chapter 2 on tragedy and the *polis,* I pointed out that the categories of slavery and barbarian were overlapping especially in Aristotle. We can also see that class and gender are interrelated in a different way: in wartime, it was typical to enslave women and kill the men. An interesting story from Herodotus (6.13) shows the connection: in a time before there were slaves, Athenian girls used to fetch water themselves, but after they were raped by the Pelasgians, slaves were used to do that work. Thus Athenian women's safety from rape was dependent on slavery, but nowhere are we given the gender of the slaves. We seem to have women, on the one hand, and slaves, on the other, as if there were not significant areas of identity between the two categories. Slavery remains one of the understudied elements of tragedy and antiquity in general, but the ways in which barbarians and slaves are treated in the plays may also help readers understand the ways in which ideas of otherness can function in modernity. As Classicists are fond of saying, the Greeks (and I would emphasize tragedies) are good to think with. These plays raise questions that are still perplexing audiences today.

The following chapters are organized by theme—war and empire, the family, violence and its consequences, relationships to rule—but the themes cannot be separated out neatly in part because of the binary oppositions. So, the relationships of war connect to family and to kingship, and the family ties conflict with demands of war and power. In each chapter we will approach specific plays via the polarities that seem to predominate there—as a result, not every binary will be useful for understanding each play.

4

War and Empire

Our earliest extant play (472) relates to race, gender, and war, and not only employs but also helps to establish many of the binaries under consideration: Greek/barbarian, free/slave, king/subject, male/female, mortal/immortal. Its ideological position and usefulness to Athens have been much debated. The plot is a simple one: the Persian King Xerxes and his army are away in Athens; a Chorus of older men has anxiously come to the tomb of the former king of Persia, Darius. Queen Atossa approaches them with her fears for the army; she has had unsettling dreams. The Chorus suggests that she make an offering to her deceased husband. At that point, a herald enters and announces that the army has been destroyed and that only Xerxes will return. The Chorus and Queen then conjure up the ghost of Darius; he instructs the queen to take new robes to Xerxes, who has torn his clothes in grief. She exits; Xerxes enters and intones a long lament with the Chorus. The play ends without his ever receiving the clothes that have been such a central part of the play.

For years, Aeschylus' *Persians* was taken as evidence about the Persian kings, the Achmaeonids; external sources corroborate some of what we see in the play (for instance, prostration before the great monarch is attested to in sculptural reliefs from the period). Aeschylus knew Persia; he had been in the war, and he was probably present when the booty from Persia was displayed in Athens. Moreover, it is likely that some Persians were taken prisoner in Greece and that some Greeks had worked in Persia, so that there could have been an exchange of information between the two cultures.

More recently, the play has been taken as the first example of "orientalism" (Said 21), defined as a way of presenting the orient and making its "mysteries plain for and to the west." Asia is enabled to speak by the European writer. Edith Hall has written extensively about the play as a production of the Athenian imagination, "an absolutely truthful record of the ways in which the Athenians liked to think about their great enemy, and a monument to Aeschylus' poetic inventiveness, however 'racist' it may now seem, in his evocation of Persia" (Hall 1996: 5). In this view the representation of the other is used for the purposes of the definition of the self, not as a way of understanding the other. Thus we should not take as accurate the image of the Persians produced in this play. As we will see, the Persians are for the most part defined as not-Athenian. The polarization of East and West, feminine and masculine, slave and free, stupid and clever, hubristic and law-abiding, cowardly and brave, is perhaps similar to media representations of the early twenty-first century's polarity between Islamic fundamentalism and the democratic west. Do we see our enemies through our own cultural productions, be they cartoons or the press?

The *barbaros*/Greek dualism is intertwined with female/male. The Persians are made to speak of themselves as *barbaroi*, using the Greek word for non-Greeks (337, 391, 635). Thus, they objectify themselves, a sign that they are an imaginary creation of a Greek speaker. Furthermore, they are effeminized, while the Athenians are associated with much-prized manliness. The young Persian men are all gone, and we will later discover that they are dead; on stage are powerless old men and a woman who rules in place of her husband and son. The emptiness of Persia is alluded to repeatedly (115–19, 289, 548–9, 730), and the strong, young men are marked as absent. In contrast, the men of Athens remain (349). Moreover, the longing (61–2) for the absent Persian men has erotic overtones that are emphasized because we are told the city misses them (511–12) as the women, as brides, miss their husbands. The Chorus of old men is fearful, anxious about the fate of the army, like a woman in Greek ideology.

The Queen stands for the city, and has the largest speaking part in the play, another feature that feminizes the Persians; moreover, her character can be seen as reflecting the stereotype of the Persians as callous (she cares only about her son not the other dead), though she may also be seen as thoroughly dignified and maternal. She replies to the Chorus, but not reassuringly; instead, she recounts a particularly upsetting dream she has had (176–99). In this dream, there were two women, one dressed like a Persian and one like a Dorian (a Greek from the Peloponnese), one taking Greece as homeland, one "the barbarian land" (187). When the women seemed to be in conflict, Xerxes tried to yoke them together; one took the bit (the Persian), the other struggled and threw him. In Queen Atossa's dream, both Persia and Greece are imagined as women to be yoked, but the Greek woman breaks free and fights, while the Persian woman is subdued. Moreover, Xerxes not only fails to yoke the woman, he also tears his clothing in despair, a traditionally female gesture of mourning for the Greeks. Lament was the role of women and had been controlled by the state since the time of Solon; thus Xerxes' mourning is paradigmatic of the characterization of the Persians as feminine.

In the dream, Xerxes tries to tame Greece with the yoke of slavery (cf. 50), as a husband would a wife or as a master would a slave, but he fails. This brings us to a second major difference: the Persians are slavish, while the Greeks value freedom (403) and are "the slaves of no man" (242). The old men prostrate themselves before the queen, and the Athenian victory will not only end the empire, it will also encourage the people to speak freely (591–2) because the yoke has been removed.

Though following their leaders, the Persians are also characterized as lacking order in their retreat (422, 470, 481), while the Athenians are self-directed but orderly (374, 400). The Persians are lamenting while the Greeks give a battle cry and dedicate themselves to the fatherland. The Persians turn tail and run; the Hellenes hold their positions, each master of his own weapons (380). The Persians outnumber the Greeks greatly, but the overabundance of Persian people is of negative significance; the Athenian land is an aid because it starves off excess population (794). The Persian overpopulation is related also to the incredible wealth of the empire: from the very beginning of the play, Persia is associated with gold and the opulence of the court, while Athens depends on silver from the mines (238).

Why does the play end without Xerxes replacing his tattered rags with new raiment? The ripping of clothing has been mentioned by the Queen and the Herald, and enacted and pointed to when he returned; the new robes were given significance by the ghost of Darius and the Queen. The lack of closure, then, must be important. Critics have hypothesized that the same actor played both Atossa and Xerxes and therefore they could not appear on stage together, but that is not sufficient reason; moreover, the actor playing the Herald could have played Xerxes. Whatever the division of roles, we have here an example of the use of ritual by tragedy. New clothing was a sign of new status, as we have seen in the discussion of initiation; the repeated references to Xerxes as young and a child, as well as his youthful impatience that led him to attack Greece, might make him in need of such a rite of passage. He is contrasted with his father, who, though he was also defeated at Marathon, did not cause the same hardships to the empire. Xerxes' maturation is not complete at the play's end. While finery and robes are associated with the East and with women, his lack of that apparel marks him as a failed man, not as masculine. He goes into the house, the realm of the female, having suffered greatly in the warrior's world. The shame that pricked him on to act as the aggressor against Greece has rebounded back on him; he comes home alone, having shamefully fled the battle scene. He is shown by this inconclusive conclusion to lack manliness (McClure).

It is clear that Aeschylus wants us to focus on the Athenians; he introduces them once so awkwardly that it seems calculated to draw the audience's attention to what he is doing. After the dream speech and before the Herald enters, Atossa asks the Chorus about Athens: where it is, whether they are sufficient men in its army, whether it has sufficient wealth, and how the Athenians fight. The answers are interesting: Athens is where Lord Helios (sun) sets, and Xerxes was desirous of capturing it because by doing so all Greece would become subject to him (234). The power of Athens is exaggerated, as it was in the passage cited above. It has sufficient men to have harmed the Medes before (236, see also 338–47), and its wealth comes from the vein of silver in the earth (238). The Athenian way of fighting is stressed and contrasted with that of the Persians: spears not arrows, and close ranks of shields; they do not follow any one leader; they are not slaves or subjects of any one man (241–2). Twice the words "remember Athens" (285, 824) are heard, each time in the context of Persian suffering. When Darius says it, he explicitly takes it as a warning against intemperate behavior.

But the Athenians also remembered Salamis and the Medes in their prayers at the opening of the Assembly and at the Eleutheria festival; there may even have been a regular presentation of a tragedy on the subject at the City Dionysia (Hall 1996: 4). Did they remember it only as cause for celebration or also as a cautionary tale? While for years critics saw the play as a victory song to Athens, more recently writers have emphasized the sympathy of the representation of the Athenian enemy. The empire of Persia could be taken to stand for the empire of Athens, and its fall might presage the fall of the latter. If this reading is accurate, then *Persians* is a truly amazing play; written early in the fifth century, only a few years after the end of the Persian Wars (the second ended in 480–79, and the play was presented in 472), it puts the enemy on stage, with no Greeks in sight. Given that Athens had been occupied by Persians very recently, and that the audience might be sitting among the wreckage in full view of the destroyed sanctuary of Athena on the Akropolis, this would be quite a startling device; it is analogous to putting the Nazis on stage in London while the city was not even rebuilt, say in 1950, and having their grief dominate the stage. As a result of this potential, the play has been reproduced with explicit reference to the Gulf War and the Iraq War (Auletta/Sellars, see Chapter 8, on Modern Peformances), as well as to other modern wars. The power of the play comes from the fact that it asks its audience to do two things at once: not just to see the enemy as its opposite, but also to see the potential for identification with them. One could argue that it is the quintessential example of the power and demands of theater.

The Athenians might have taken this message away with them because the extreme wealth of Persia is related to the more general meaning of the tragedy. Queen Atossa articulates anxiety about the significance of wealth. "Great wealth may kick blessed happiness into the dust" (163–4); thus the text makes a contrast between material possessions and happiness. Darius is said to have acquired a reasonable amount of wealth. Xerxes has gone too far and squandered what his father accumulated. Aeschylus also attributes Xerxes' disaster to the gods when he has Darius say that Zeus has fulfilled his unspecified prophecy—though he thought it would take longer, he is not surprised. He makes this aphoristic statement: "but whenever someone rushes on himself, a god joins in" (742–3). The god and Xerxes' own youthful impetuosity conspire in causing these events (on *daimôn*, or gods and character, see Chapter 3). "For *hubris* flowered and fertilized the grain of destruction (*atê*) and from it reaped a harvest of lamentation" (821–3). Here Aeschylus uses natural imagery from flowering to reaping for the ways in which insolence against the gods leads inexorably to tears. Xerxes exemplifies the point that for the Greeks *hubris* was not just an attitude but an action, in this case violence against the gods' shrines and holy places. He foolishly thought he could yoke the sea and overcome the gods, including Poseidon. When Darius asks why the war took place, the Queen tells him that Xerxes was taunted by bad men who found his manliness wanting in comparison with Darius' own; in order to live up to his father's reputation as a soldier who acquired great wealth for Persia, Xerxes invaded Hellas. Thus, empire, impiety against the natural order, and gender are all correlated as causes of the Persian defeat.

Xerxes will have to learn to be moderate with Zeus as his teacher; the lesson is characteristic of Greek morality: don't think thoughts beyond your human station. This generalization applies to all, not just Xerxes. The problem of excess wealth leading to the flowering of *hubris* is similarly typical of tragedy. The difference that is stressed between Xerxes and his ancestors suggests that his extreme shame should not then be taken as typical of Asia, or exclusively so. It is possible for Persian or Greek to avoid the trap of Destruction (*Atê*) by avoiding his behavior.

The ancient audience could have responded in a number of different ways. It seems plausible that the play allowed the audience to fulfill a desire for lament vicariously; the audience experiences the characters' grief by watching its representation, as the actor experiences grief by enacting it. It is also possible that an Athenian citizen would have distanced himself by displacing the events securely onto the Persian other, thinking "That man was an arrogant Asian; he was effeminate, luxurious and soft, given to shrieking and tearing his clothing. I am a manly Athenian, moderate in all things." Nonetheless, though the barbarians may seem to mourn excessively, there is a similarity between what they suffer and what the Athenians suffered in battle for the purpose of gaining an empire.

Similarly, the audience today might take the play as securely distant—this is about the Persians and the crafty, well-organized Athenians. Hurray for god-fearing citizens of the democracy. If the viewer is open, however, to seeing the Persians' irreligious desire for conquest as like that of the U.S. and U.K. in Iraq, for instance, the play might be disquietingly close. The relative costs of the two Persian expeditions are analogous to the Gulf War and the invasion of Iraq, George Bush, Sr. and George Bush, Jr. Reading the play this way means identifying with your enemy and seeing that "there but for the grace of God go I." In Robert Auletta's version of the play, the suffering of the Iraqis is made palpable, and references to the application of sanctions imply that the Americans/Athenians were the aggressors, though, of course, it was the Persians who attacked in antiquity. But you can dislike that which reminds you of things you would rather not know about yourself, and the audience can always walk out if it finds a performance unpalatable—there are many ways to move a crowd!

Aeschylus' *Oresteia*

The binary oppositions we have seen in *Persians* continue prominently in the plays about the children of Atreus (Menelaus and Agamemnon) and their offspring; in legends about the house of Atreus, the gendered division correlates closely with that of the public (male) and private (female) realms, and it is therefore a powerful way to look at those issues. In the *Oresteia*, all of our binaries are once again represented and interrelated through an emphasis on war and the family. The trilogy provides a crux where two strands come together; in the following chapters we will look at the family and violence as they appear as themes in other plays—the later stagings of the myth by Sophocles and Euripides (Chapter 5), and the Trojan War plays (Chapter 6).

The similarity of *Agamemnon* and *Persians* is noticeable. The Greek Agamemnon is explicitly guilty of the same kind of excesses as Xerxes was: he went to Troy and destroyed the temples of the gods. He was responsible for the deaths of many soldiers, leading to the exchange of bodies for ashes (the equivalent of modern body bags), which caused dissatisfaction at home (437–55). In addition, he angered Artemis by sacrificing his daughter, the treasure of the house. While, as we will see, eastern *hubris* is a cliché that can be assumed here, it is also clear that the Greek hero is not immune to the problem. The aphorism from *Persians* about *hubris* and destruction is rephrased: "*Hubris* loves to give birth to *hubris* amongst evil men . . . along with the unconquerable, indestructible, unholy boldness of black destruction in the halls" (763–71). In the responding antistrophe, the Chorus draws the connection between justice and poverty, the dissociation of justice and gold. Reading *Agamemnon* along with *Persians*, then, can lead the audience to see that Xerxes is not the only leader with a tendency to excess. If the Athenians were also open to that interpretation, they would have been led not to boast about their power but to fear it.

Aeschylus was reworking a legend that had been told often in the epic tradition. In the *Odyssey*, the story of Agamemnon's death at the hands of Aigisthos, who has usurped the throne, is frequently told as a cautionary tale to motivate Telemachos to defend his absent father, Odysseus (1.34–43, 293–302; 3.193–200, 249–316; 4.90–2, 514–37; 11.409–34). Aigisthos is the primary villain, and Orestes kills him; we hear that Clytemnestra is buried, too, but the description of her death is vague (3.234–5, 309–10, 4.91–2). She is repeatedly set off against the faithful Penelope, who waits for Odysseus; in contrast, Clytemnestra is seduced by Aigisthos and is held responsible for the plot (3.235, 266–72). There is no mention of Elektra, though Khrysothemis is named in the *Iliad*. Aeschylus makes Clytemnestra the architect of Agamemnon's murder; therefore, Orestes must commit matricide in order to avenge his death. What is a simple political matter in Homer becomes a complicated ethical issue in tragedy.

As in *Persians* the gender and ethnic dimensions in *Agamemnon* are interwoven into a war story, this time that of the Trojan War. Again, its overall political "message" is ambiguous, though it clearly makes extensive use of ritual references. In the *Oresteia* women are central from the outset. The theft of Helen is alleged as the cause of the war (60–2, 681–90), and Iphigeneia is sacrificed to make the war possible. Because Helen was taken from under her husband's roof, while Paris was being entertained as a guest, Zeus Xenios is involved in the mission. Helen is compared to the child (50) taken from the nests of birds of prey; yet, she is promiscuous (*poluanoros*, literally "with many men"), so perhaps not worth the sacrifice (62). There is more than a hint that Iphigeneia is at the stage of initiation marked by participation in rituals at Brauron (see Chapter 3); in addition to playing the bear, girls were said to shed a saffron colored robe which might account for the description of Iphigeneia pouring her saffron robe to the ground (239). The virginity and purity of Iphigeneia are set off against Helen's sexuality, highlighting the costs of a war that might appear to be senseless.

From the opening of *Agamemnon*, male and female oppose one another, yet blend. Clytemnestra has set a Watchman on the roof to wait for the first sign of a beacon that will bring news of the fall of Troy: "Thus ordains the hopeful man-counseling heart of a woman" (10–11). This woman is a ruler in the absence of her husband, and (unlike Atossa, the Persian Queen) she thinks like a man. The male/female issue is highlighted throughout the rest of the play—the elders who make up the Chorus do not believe her because they think it is

"like a woman to trust too easily" (483–7, 1401). An astute inter-
preter, this Queen knows what they have been thinking and taunts
them with it (590–2). Clytemnestra is able to use this stereotype of
female foolishness later as she plays on Agamemnon.

Clytemnestra emphasizes her gender when she says that she celebrated the sacrifices and that, as was normal for women (or in women's
song), women across the city echoed the ritual cry (594). Then she
refuses to listen to the Herald's description of what has transpired, for,
first of all, she has seen the beacon and, second, she will hear the details
from her "lord" and "respected husband," whom she hurries to
welcome. Her speech is duplicitous: the word *aidoion* (translated as
"respected"), and typically used of a chaste woman, is here applied to
Agamemnon, for whom she has no respect. The remainder of this
portion of her speech defines the woman's role, as if it applied to
her:

> What else
> is light more sweet for woman to behold than this,
> to spread the gates before her husband home from war
> and saved by God's hand?—take this message to the king:
> Come, and with speed, back to the city that longs for him,
> and may he find a wife within his house as true
> as on the day he left her, watchdog of the house
> gentle to him alone, fierce to his enemies,
> and such a woman in all her ways as this, who has
> not broken the seal upon her in the length of days.
> With no man else have I known delight, nor any shame
> of evil speech, more than I know how to temper bronze.
> (600–12, trans. Lattimore in Grene and Lattimore)

Her claims of ignorance are powerful because they call up the ideal
woman, pure and ignorant of weapons, at the same time that they, by
denying this knowledge, remind the audience of what is really going
on. The next two lines are given to Clytemnestra by some editors, but
to the Herald in the manuscript (and in Lattimore's translation): "A
vaunt like this, so loaded as it is with truth, it well becomes a highborn
lady to proclaim." A literal translation makes it more pointed: "the
speech is not shameful for a noble woman to shriek aloud." Here the
use of the word "shame," which is opposed to modesty (*aidôs*) for a
woman, again hints about the existence of her lover, to those who

know. Moreover, at the same time that Clytemnestra is claiming the role of the quiet and faithful housewife, she is playing the head of state, speaking in public and taking over.

The battle of wits between Clytemnestra and the Chorus is only a hint of what will come, a battle of wills between Clytemnestra and Agamemnon, itself a non-violent version of the internal physical scene in which she murders him. Agamemnon enters on a chariot, with Kassandra, a Trojan princess who possesses the gift of prophecy; she is silent but by his side throughout. It is important that we imagine the staging here. Seated or standing on his chariot, Agamemnon makes a long speech to the gods of Argos, whom he credits with his homecoming. He also addresses the Chorus; he completely ignores Clytemnestra. She then makes a similarly long speech (which he implies is too long—like his absence) in which she again performs the role of the faithful wife, though pointing out that as such she should not speak in front of the citizen men. The speech is full of *double entendres* that the audience will catch, but not Agamemnon. For instance, she begins by saying, "I am not ashamed of my husband-loving ways," but the word for husband can just mean "man" and thus refer to her lover or to more general promiscuity. (The whirring of the gnat's wings that kept her awake [892] may also be a reference to sexual desire, since it raises the issue of how lightly she slept.) Clytemnestra points out how hard it is for a woman when her man is away for ten years at war; though her suffering might have been real at one point, she has not been idly standing by in his absence. She claims to have used up her tears, and that again may well be true, but what has been left in their wake is not sadness but rage. She has had dreams of his wounds, another ambiguous reference: were these anxiety dreams, as she implies, or wish-fulfillment dreams? Throughout, Clytemnestra can count on the fact that a Greek man would assume a woman to be tamed in marriage and not a threat. She effusively praises Agamemnon and his masculinity: he is the watchdog, the post or pillar—both phallic symbols—of the house, a position she claimed for herself in the speech cited above (607).

When Agamemnon is about to descend from the chariot, Clytemnestra stops him and insists that he walk into the house on garments spread for him. These cloths, often translated as carpets, are valuable fabrics; crucially, they were not meant to be walked on. The richness of meaning in this symbolic scene cannot be overestimated. As Iphigeneia was a "treasure of the house," so are they; Clytemnestra urges the king to be bold in walking on these signs of the abundance of the house. By convincing him to step on the symbolic representation of the wealth of the household, Clytemnestra makes him appear to be its destroyer. Clytemnestra thus makes the opening move in her planned vengeance for the death of Iphigeneia and in her self-justification for that revenge.

This scene is explicitly cast in terms of gender. In conversation, Peter Meineck said that he sees the purplish red color of the tapestries as blood, even menstrual blood, and the house as womblike. It is also related to ethnicity; the family's great wealth orientalizes them. After she first bids him walk on the materials spread before him, Agamemnon refuses. He knows his place: he is a man not a woman; he is a man not a god; he is a Greek not a barbarian. He fears the vengeance of the gods and recognizes that what Clytemnestra proposes would make him vulnerable to their jealousy:

> And all this—do not try in woman's ways to make
> me delicate (or to make me a woman), nor, as if I were some Asiatic
> bow down to earth and with wide mouth cry out to me,
> nor cross my path with jealousy by strewing the ground
> with robes. Such state becomes the gods, and none beside.
> I am a mortal, a man; I cannot trample down upon
> these tinted splendors without fear thrown in my path.
> I tell you, as a man, not god, to reverence me.
> Discordant is the murmur at such treading down
> of lovely things; while God's most lordly gift to man
> is decency of mind. Call that man only blest
> who has in sweet tranquility brought his life to close.
> (920–30, trans. Lattimore in Grene and Lattimore)

Clytemnestra protests; Agamemnon again says that he won't be made soft (like an easterner or a woman). She continues to push him to yield, using Priam as a model (935) and saying that the Trojan king would have done what she asks. But the point is, of course, that Agamemnon is not Priam, and should not appear to be. There is an implicit association here of the east and tyranny; if he behaves like an oriental despot, in a Greek city, he will win displeasure from the people. She counters that no one can be admired without exciting envy as well (939). At this point, Agamemnon retorts that her combativeness is not womanly; she replies "Oh yield! The power is yours. Give way of your free will" (940, 943). In this way, she reassures him that he has not lost his masculine authority by giving in to her. But he has put himself completely in her power and revealed himself to be arrogant, irreligious, and soft like a woman. She, in contrast, is in control. Her last speech in this episode shows the danger of her tyrannous rule when she speaks of the endless wealth in the sea and the fact that she would willingly have promised to "trample many splendors down" in order to bring him home. She terrifyingly calls on Zeus to bring her prayers to pass (963–74).

All this time the defeated Trojan has been a silent reality on stage; Kassandra's barbarian status would have been marked by her costume; it is further underlined by the interchange between the Chorus and the Queen. When she does not respond to Clytemnestra's order that she come inside to the altar (supposedly to celebrate a sacrifice, really to be a sacrifice), the Queen explicitly speculates that Kassandra might use barbaric speech. Her other thought is that she is like the swallow (1050), a reference that makes her an animal, but also might allude to the Prokne story: Prokne was the wife of a barbarian king, Tereus; he raped her sister, Philomela, and tore out her tongue. The two women killed Prokne's son Itys in revenge. Prokne became a nightingale, and her cry was thought to sound like her son's name (Itys), Philomela a swallow; later on Kassandra is explicitly compared to Prokne crying Itys (1144).

The male/female conflict ends with the murder of Agamemnon, effeminized by his location in a bath; the fact that a woman is the murderer adds to the horror for Kassandra and the Chorus. Kassandra stresses that the woman is killing the man (1231), compares them to cow and bull, and highlights what she takes to be the unnaturalness of the act by giving Clytemnestra the names of well-known monsters ("Skylla," "amphisbaena," 1233). The Queen has a great deal of masculinity in her; she hid her manly nature, pretending to be a weak woman and fawning on Agamemnon (like a dog, as Kassandra says, 1228) in order to win her victory over him. While dominance and masculinity were contested between the two of them in the tapestry scene, in the last episode, we see another feminine man on stage— Aigisthos, the strengthless lion (1224), the wolf who goes to bed with the lioness (1228–9). In the *Odyssey*, Aigisthos is the primary figure; he has his own motives: revenge for what Atreus did to his father Thyestes—serving him a stew made up of his own children (Aigisthos' siblings). This story is recounted by Kassandra, so it will have been fresh in the audience's mind, and will heighten the contrast with this version of Aigisthos who hid behind Clytemnestra. The Chorus mocks his lack of manliness, waiting at home while real men fought at Troy (1625, 1635, 1671).

The gender confusion is pronounced: Clytemnestra is a woman who acts like a stereotypical man in her assumption of rule and lust for power; Aigisthos is a man who acts like a woman. Each gender also causes disaster when it adheres to its "proper" role, whether in public or private, the city or the family. For instance, Agamemnon must choose between war and family: whether to desert the navy or to sacrifice his daughter. His manliness requires that he not abandon his men, but performing that action changes him drastically for the worse: "changed, and from the heart the breath came bitter and sacrilegious, utterly infidel" (219–20, trans. Lattimore in Grene and Lattimore). The changes in Agamemnon may be taken as symptomatic of what happens to soldiers in wartime. Moreover, the deaths of the young men have caused political grumblings at home. In particular, the irrationality of waging a war, killing his daughter and many other young people, to regain a "woman of many men" (62) is emphasized.

Though the city's elders, along with the other Argive citizens, were angry at the deaths of the Argive soldiers, they welcome their king home and hope he will restore order. Clytemnestra, on the other hand, ruins the city to exact payment for a loss on the level of the family. In its exchanges with the Queen, the Chorus judges her according to traditional women's roles, but she defies those expectations. The Chorus is especially appalled at the murder because Agamemnon was both her husband and the Argive king. Her action has brought down the legitimate authority and left a tyranny in its place (1355). The Chorus then threatens her with exile; such a woman has no place in the city at all.

The human level is thus divided along lines of gender and nation, but the borders are continually being crossed. Kassandra is a barbarian, a wild seer who seems not to understand Greek, yet she speaks the language and knows better than the Chorus what is going on in the house. On the mortal/immortal axis, things are hardly any clearer. The Chorus in this play plays the dual role we discussed in Chapter 1: it has a clearly defined character *and* speaks philosophical and ethical truths. So, it is composed of weak old men who are dominated by Clytemnestra and Aigisthos. Yet, they have a power to see, and in that vatic capacity they give voice to fundamental Greek beliefs about the role of the gods in human existence. Some of the most often cited passages from tragedy come from the Chorus in this play, for example: "justice so moves that those only learn who suffer" (250–1). Especially in the early parts of the play, they sing about justice and moderation in wealth, and relate them to the fall of Troy and specific incidents there. They see Zeus Xenios' authority in what transpired: "He acted as he had decreed. A man thought the gods deigned not to punish mortals who trampled down the delicacy of things inviolable; that man was wicked" (369–72, trans. Lattimore in Grene and Lattimore).

The maxim also applies to Agamemnon, who sacrificed his daughter in order to gain favorable winds from Artemis and who sacked the altars of the gods at Troy. In mythic thinking, Agamemnon was guilty of violence at Troy before he even went because at its embarkation the gathered forces received an omen of eagles eating a very pregnant hare. The omen causes Artemis to send ill winds that stall the fleet, but she does not tell Agamemnon that he *must* sacrifice his daughter. If he wants to go, however, he must comply. Agamemnon actively puts the "yoke of necessity" on himself (218).

Nonetheless, he does have some pressure as well as right on his side: he acts for Zeus Xenios. He is a vengeance spirit, a Fury, launched by Zeus. It is when he acts excessively, exacting double payment from Troy (a whole city destroyed for one man's misdeed), that he becomes a justifiable target of the gods. Therefore, Clytemnestra's desires and justice seemingly come together. Agamemnon and Clytemnestra both claim justice and the support of the gods. The first play reveals the complexity of vengeance—it shows the people's anger against Agamemnon, the paradox of this war to win back a "promiscuous woman," and Agamemnon's arrogance, but also the people's trust in him. Clytemnestra, too, has more than one motive—vengeance for her daughter, jealousy over Kassandra, and perhaps the desire for continuing rule with Aigisthos as her consort. Therefore, there is no clear right and wrong here.

In *Libation Bearers* (*Choephoroi*), named after the opening action of pouring libations at the tomb of Agamemnon, Orestes returns from exile having been directed by Apollo to avenge his father's death by killing his mother and her lover, Aigisthos. He reports his own death in order to catch the rulers unawares. Much of the play consists of a lament sung jointly by Chorus and actors in order to obtain Agamemnon's help in the vengeance. After Orestes has killed Aigisthos and Clytemnestra, he is driven off the stage by the Furies (vengeance deities also known as Erinyes) of his mother.

Gender and the gods are clearly still very much at issue. There are two parallel male/female pairs: Orestes and Elektra, Aigisthos and Clytemnestra. Orestes is anxiously awaited because it is he who must act; the woman's part is to wait and encourage him. The Queen, who was so very much in charge in the first play, here (disingenuously perhaps) disavows masculine power, offering to give the newcomers warm baths and clean beds, but telling them that, for "affairs of state," they will have to talk to the man of the house (673). Clytemnestra tries to keep Orestes from killing her by showing him her breast and reminding him that she is the mother who nursed him; her status as mother is challenged, however, by the presence of a Nurse, who tells the audience that she was the one who took care of Orestes as a baby. In fact, a large part of what is typically held against Clytemnestra by her children is her flawed performance as a mother: she claimed to care for one daughter, but the remaining children are evidence to the contrary. Elektra is dishonored in the house (445–6); Orestes has been sent away (913).

In Orestes' confrontation with his mother, he specifically argues that the sexual double standard is based on the work that the man does in war: fidelity in marriage is a woman's duty, while her safety is guaranteed by the man's courage in battle (919–21). Agamemnon's death was particularly shameful in that it unmanned him (345–71, see above on the *Agamemnon* Chorus' similar response). The humiliating way in which he was killed is emphasized through the display of the net and the devices that hobbled him (981–2); it was not a warrior's death—they all would much rather he had died at Troy (345–7).

The image of the evil woman as a viper or snake is woven through this play, too (994–6, 1048–50)—but as important, in a significant ode, the Chorus generalizes about the terrifying nature of women and contrasts it with the male. Men are characterized by will, women by passion that destroys marriage (594–601). The ode goes from individual women in various family situations, to the general example of the Lemnian women, who killed all their husbands (631). While the female subverts culture with desire, Orestes is depicted as a culture hero bringing political liberty. Two snakes, Aigisthos and Clytemnestra, have ruled the city as tyrants, and Orestes is a hero for ending their despotism. Thus, once again, animal/human, male/female, city/household are linked, creating a system on the basis of which the ancient Greek audience member would be moved to judge the characters.

The sweep, imagery, and moral complexity of the first play are missing; it is more simply a revenge action. The play restores Agamemnon to his status as noble father and king; Clytemnestra is deprived of any right, though she makes an appeal based on her physical maternal body. While in *Agamemnon*, the king had an imperfect claim to justice—he was responsible for the death of his daughter, exceeded justice at Troy, and walked on the tapestries that were a sign of his arrogance—in this play, he is exonerated. Iphigeneia's death is mentioned briefly, but Agamemnon is not held responsible for it (242). In *Agamemnon*, Clytemnestra had her own claim to justice—she was avenging her daughter; in this play she seems to have no acceptable motive; it is as if she started the killing.

Orestes recognizes the conflict between his obligation to father and mother; the Chorus advises him (828–9) to "Cry father when she cries child," that way he will bring "innocent murder." Orestes recognizes that he only has a partial right, but he is obedient to the god Apollo, and he is encouraged in his murder by his male friend, Pylades, who seemingly exists only to utter the lines telling him to proceed and be faithful to the god. Though Orestes has the blessings of Apollo, he must nonetheless face the "winged hounds" of his mother, who literally drive him off the stage. The goddesses who pursue him continue the evil female imagery since they are likened to Gorgons (women with snakes for hair; Medusa is the most famous one) and bloodhounds (1048–50, 1054). As was the case for his father, there is no absolute concept of fate insisting that he act; caught between two opposing forces, he must choose who he will become.

The staging reveals the difficulty that Orestes faces: he stands over the two dead bodies of a man and a woman who have been rolled out from the palace (see Chapter 1 on *ekkyklema*), and the audience must compare him to his mother. He needs to be more pure for the play to work. But is he? Even Orestes admits that he (like Clytemnestra) had multiple motives: his father's suffering, the god's oracle, his loss of his estate, and the fate of the citizens who are ruled by a pair of women (299–304). Gender and civic politics are intertwined in his motives because he can't stand to see the men who defeated Troy ruled by these two women. We must also take seriously his claim that in part he is here to better his material state. The *moira* (910, 911) that is invoked in this play may be translated as destiny, but it is also related to the word for lot or portion (*moros*). The question of lot suggests that Orestes is in transition to manhood; he has returned to take up his rightful position as leader of the family and to gain his inheritance, thus becoming a man (6–7). Orestes seems to be an ephebe; he must be Perseus, the Chorus says; his strongly marked use of deceit (*dolos*) is related to this initiatory stage. Of course, the reintegration is not completed in this play, for although he has been away and returned, the ritual action is not ended by the death of Clytemnestra; it will take purification and trial to make him a man.

The trilogy is not only about large themes like gender and justice and humans' relations to the gods. It is also importantly about a family, and modern interests in psychology, as well as the mother/daughter tie, have led to an emphasis on that dimension of the myth in performance. Both children have to come of age; Elektra mourns her unmarried state (her name can mean "unmarried," without the marriage bed), and she is willing to give up marriage and instead dedicate her dowry to her father's tomb (486–8). On the psychological level, we can say that the daughter is overly attached to her father, while the son must separate himself from his mother, with the most extreme form of action (murder). Both children feel abandoned by her, betrayed for her lover. Sophocles and Euripides treat the family dynamics and the effect on the children of the violence of the parents (see below); as we will see, there are differences in each version. How attached is Elektra to her father? Is her attachment out of control?

The *Eumenides* takes the mortal/immortal references and literally embodies them. The gods and goddesses are on stage, even making up the chorus. The scene shifts to Delphi, where Orestes has gone to be purified for the murder of his mother; the Furies are pursuing him, spurred on by the ghost of Clytemnestra. After Apollo takes full responsibility for having persuaded Orestes to commit murder (84), the action shifts again to Athens, where Athena announces that she will create a court of citizens (the Areopagus, see Chapter 2) to hear the murder case.

The female principle is made disgusting, while the male is represented by the golden Apollo. In the opening scene, the priestess of Apollo (Pythia) traces the history of the oracle back to a past female, Phoebe, who has no independent existence and who seems to have been invented for the purpose of giving Apollo a feminine shrine that he traditionally had to win with a dragon combat. The Pythia is horrified at the monstrous Furies she sees inside her temple; they are utterly repulsive:

> In front of this man slept a startling company
> of women lying all upon the chairs. Or not
> women, I think I call them rather gorgons, only
> not gorgons either, since their shape is not the same.
> (46–9, trans. Lattimore in Grene and Lattimore)

The Pythia cannot figure out what to name them; they are hideous, snaky, but anomalous, beyond comparison (cf. 411–12). They are foul creatures, as Apollo agrees (67–73). They are monstrous and not fit for his sanctuary:

> This house is no right place for such as you to cling
> upon; but where, by judgment given, heads are lopped
> and eyes gouged out, throats cut, and by the spoil of sex
> the glory of young boys is defeated, where mutilation
> lives, and stoning, and the long moan of tortured men
> spiked underneath the spine and stuck on pales.
> (185–90, trans. Lattimore in Grene and Lattimore)

Thus, an unsightly, slobbering gang of old women, out for blood and defending ties of blood by castrating young men, is set against the youthful Olympian Apollo (150), god of light, his young suppliant Orestes, and the god Hermes, who is present but silent. The Furies live in the dark (396), while Apollo is bright. This scene is reported (probably apocryphally) to have caused women to miscarry because it was so terrifying.

This level of divine male/female hostility and vituperation is transmuted into oratory at Athens, where the Furies and Apollo compete. The Furies argue that it is simply wrong for a son to kill his mother. Apollo defends Orestes by saying that he had to avenge his father, and that Clytemnestra was not really his mother: he who mounts is the true parent; the mother's body is only the nurse of the seed (657–61). Since this was the position of the Pythagoreans and was a common medical opinion of the day, we cannot simply dismiss it as laughable, or as a sign that Apollo is not meant to be taken seriously. On the other hand, it should not be taken as evidence of Greek naïvety about the role of the mother in reproduction, as this statement by Telemachos makes clear: "My mother says I am his. . . . Nobody really knows his own father" (*Odyssey* 1.216–17). The trial is a clear articulation of ideology, more than the state of biological knowledge.

The positions taken by the Furies and Apollo fit in with the play's larger oppositions of male/female, young/old, light/dark, Olympos/ underworld in the play, bolstering the impression that Apollo expresses an ideological view that is endemic to the larger culture. The court ultimately divides evenly; Athena has already said that if the matter comes to her, she will vote for the acquittal of Orestes because, born from the head of her father, Zeus, she sides with the male in all things (735–41). Therefore, Orestes wins his acquittal. Vendetta and endless familial bloodletting are brought to an end; in its place are the state and democracy. The Furies are furious at the outcome of the trial; as a result, there is another stage in which they must be persuaded by Athena to bless the city instead of cursing it as they had threatened to do. She is successful in her persuasion, and the play ends with the integration of the Furies into the city of Athens; they have changed their names and become "Kindly Ones" (*eumenides*).

There have been debates over the ending of the *Oresteia*: to some it is clear that it does not settle anything permanently, to others it is a triumph of justice. It seems that we can argue either way, since, on the one hand, the cycle of bloodshed is ended, but, on the other, the remaining threats to peace are very real. Fear must be in its place for the violence to end. Given the ethnic conflicts after the fall of communism or the dictatorship of Saddam Hussein, it is folly to be condescending about the good that is created by establishing the fear of the Furies as a safeguard. As we saw in Chapter 2, the founding of the court and the promise of a permanent treaty between Argos and Athens situates it very much in the play's own period. Is Aeschylus questioning the democracy or supporting it? Again, given the complexity of the trilogy, it is hard to see it taking a particular stand on the contemporary changes in the court, though Aeschylus refers to them.

In terms of gender and the status of women, there are also multiple interpretations. In one view, the resolution is accomplished through the control of women and the subordination of ties of blood to ties of marriage; in other words, the powerful Clytemnestra of the first play is the loser, and the claims of the father are triumphant. George Thomson long ago claimed that Aeschylus "regarded the subordination of woman, quite correctly, as an indispensable condition of democracy.... Aeschylus perceived that the subjection of woman was a necessary consequence of the development of private property" (288). The goddesses have been defined as disgusting and then made

more presentable before being stuffed back underground as a necessary evil. Orestes has achieved his independence of the mother, not
only by killing her, but also by separating from anything that might
be remotely feminine and siding with the male gods. In another
reading, however, the Furies are really given stature. As Kindly Ones
they are granted enormous power to restrain intra-city violence. Fear
of them will produce order.

The spectacle, however, would lead the audience to leave the theater
not questioning but convinced that they had witnessed a great victory.
At the play's conclusion, Athena welcomes citizens bearing robes
which the Furies don as a sign of their new goodwill to Athens. The
Athenian audience would have seen this as reassuring and reminiscent
of their own pageantry in the Panathenaia. Their costumes echo the
robes that the metics of the city processed in earlier and overturn the
deadly use of fabric in *Agamemnon*. Through the spectacular incorporation of the Kindly Ones, the trilogy gives a ritual solution to a
political, psychological, and sexual problem.

What does the modern reader or audience member make of it?
Ariane Mnouchkine's lavish productions seek to reclaim the ritual
effect through recourse to costume and dance drawn from eastern
traditions, and that strategy is very effective. For those of us reading
the plays without such visual stimuli, however, interpretation requires
an active imagination. Many readers resist the interpretation based on
ritual because they cannot intellectually accept the positive evaluation
of a location under the city. Can we transform the negative associations
with the basement or underground? Was that indeed Aeschylus' point?
The ritual interpretation may seem to the modern reader to celebrate
the control of femininity that has been made to look monstrous
through myth (see Froma Zeitlin's classic article [1978]).

Euripides' *Iphigeneia at Aulis*

Aeschylus used the trilogy form to trace a transition from vengeance
to trial by jury, based on control of the female. His treatment formed
the backdrop for later plays based on the House of Atreus. The sacrifice of Iphigeneia became the subject of a play by Euripides (*Iphigeneia
at Aulis*), having been an embedded narrative in one choral ode in
Aeschylus; her subsequent life as a priestess was made into another
play by Euripides (*Iphigeneia among the Taurians*). In this section we

will be looking at *Iphigeneia at Aulis*, which takes place before the Trojan War, and continues the trend of integrating questions of war and family.

The play was produced posthumously in 406–5 with *Bacchai*, almost at the very end of the Peloponnesian War; the Sicilian Expedition had ended in ignominious defeat ten years earlier, and Sparta's overall victory was around the corner. There are echoes of Aeschylus' treatment of the myth, and the *Oresteia* might well have been reproduced recently, making familiarity with the trilogy plausible. There are large textual questions about this play, including the order of the opening and whether Euripides ended the play with the sacrifice or with a messenger's speech recounting Iphigeneia's rescue by Artemis and replacement by a deer. In this presentation of the myth, Agamemnon has brought his daughter to Aulis on the pretext of a marriage to Achilles, and her presence and that falsehood are major elements in the plot. *Iphigeneia at Aulis* relates women to the cause of pan-Hellenism, or union of the Greeks, by generalizing the rape of Helen to that of all women and therefore setting Greeks against barbarians.

The play most likely opens with Agamemnon writing to Clytemnestra retracting his original letter, in which he instructed her to bring Iphigeneia to Aulis to be married. When this note is intercepted by his brother Menelaus, a struggle ensues. Though Agamemnon persuades his brother to his way of thinking, it is too late to prevent Iphigeneia's arrival. Once she hears what is to happen to her, she pleads with her father not to kill her, but by the end of the play she is transformed into a young woman willingly embracing death.

Even more than Aeschylus, Euripides questions men's motives for war by juxtaposing family and military obligations. We first hear Agamemnon's straightforward narrative of what he considers the facts—he objected to murdering his daughter until Menelaus convinced him (96–8). Immediately, however, a dialogue between Agamemnon and Menelaus seems to undermine his account. Menelaus argues that Agamemnon eagerly desired the leadership of the army (337) and this opportunity to win fame and honor (*kleos*, 357; *philotimon*, 342, 385).

The text's opening and the debate about Agamemnon's motives bring into play many of the larger issues of Greek culture, especially gender and class. The male value system is set against a female code, the public/military vs. the private/family. The Chorus makes it explicit that each sex has its own mode of seeking excellence: "To hunt after excellence is a great thing. For women, excellence means chastity; for men, a kind of personal harmony which, multiplied, makes a great city greater" (569–72, trans. Gamel in Blondell et al.). Agamemnon's masculinity is debated throughout the play; even his slave finds him somewhat lacking as a "noble man" (28), and his brother thinks he is a glad-handing politician who is "*kakos*," meaning cowardly, ignoble, or bad, not loyal to his friends (340, 349). The entire code of Athenian masculinity is here held up to scrutiny in the person of Agamemnon. In terms of the play, the heroic aristocratic man is contrasted with the slave and found wanting; Menelaus alludes to that code when he says that the barbarians are laughing at the Greeks (371–2). A Greek aristocratic man typically wanted to help his friends and harm his enemies; he could not tolerate being mocked (see below on *Elektra, Medea, Antigone*). The Greek free male set himself against non-Greek and slave, but Agamemnon fails to uphold the standard. He'd rather be a slave (446–53) because then he could cry more easily and say what he liked; he furthermore admits that he is a slave to the crowd (450). It is almost as if Agamemnon is a politician in a democracy, dependent on pleasing the crowd, rather than a man born to royalty; the use of loaded terms (*kleos, timê, kakos*) reveals the shift from the heroic past in which the play is set to the present in which it was staged.

The war was supposedly waged for a woman's love, or love of a woman, but there is ambiguity about the role of Helen, as there is in the *Oresteia*. Characters blame her over and over again (e.g., 76, 467, 573–89 [Paris and Helen], 683). If she left of her own free will, then she has failed to fulfill the role of virtuous wife. Agamemnon asks why he should sacrifice his daughter so that Menelaus can regain his bad bed-mate (389). In this line of thought family is pitted against family, daughter against wife.

Euripides' attention to the female victims of war allows the play to articulate a female/family value system even though it takes place in a military camp. The ideology of the normal separation of male and female spheres is made explicit by Agamemnon's plea with his wife to go home, by Achilles' embarrassment in facing her, and by Iphigeneia's modesty in facing him. As a maiden, Iphigeneia should remain inside if at all possible (993–4, 998–9, 1340). Because of Agamemnon's deception, however, the public/private and male/female binaries have been destabilized. While the *Oresteia* talks about the sacrifice of a maiden, *Iphigeneia at Aulis* represents it and juxtaposes it consistently with marriage (at 461, Agamemnon says she is not a maiden but bride to Hades; at 1397 she is to be married to Greece). When a messenger enters with the news that Iphigeneia has been sighted, he adds that the whole army is gossiping about whether a wedding is planned, and the rituals for a wedding are described—the consecration to Artemis, crowning, the feast, song and dance (435–49, also 1110–14).

From the beginning, Agamemnon is especially upset that Clytemnestra has come. She enters on a chariot, introducing the luxury of the home into what must be a very tense situation—the army has been encamped waiting for favorable winds for quite a while and is desperate to get moving. Her concern for the wedding highlights the gender differences underlying the action, and her insistence on performing her appropriate role in the marriage ritual (610) will bring on the crisis with Agamemnon. Euripides emphasizes women's role by having her refer to her first marriage, mentioned nowhere else in the literature: "You married me against my will and took me by force, having killed my husband; my infant you hurled to the ground having torn it from my breast" (1149–52). She became a model woman/wife, however: modest in matters of Aphrodite (*es t'Aphroditên sôphronousa*, 1159) and causing the house to grow and flourish. The inside/outside opposition is central to her claim: "so that you were happy when you came home, and seemed a fortunate man when you went out" (1160–1, trans. Gamel in Blondell et al.). She pleads with Agamemnon not to turn her into the wicked woman that she typically is in legend. By giving this history to her notorious vengeance, Euripides humanizes Clytemnestra and to some extent justifies her.

But the public and private are tied together. Helen was courted by many men, and her father Tyndareos exacted an oath from her suitors that they would help her husband if anyone, Greek or barbarian, took her from him (62–5). The single woman stolen away comes to stand for all Greek women who must be protected from barbarian rapists (1266, 1275, 1380–2). The very grounds for the war are debatable: is it for the glory of Greece, or is it for Menelaus' private pleasure in the wife he could not even control (382–4, 389)? In neither case does it seem to be rationally motivated. Menelaus suggests that the war is Greece's chance to do something really noble and worthwhile that would prevent barbarians from laughing at them (370–2); in reply Agamemnon calls his own country ill (411), says he doesn't want to be ill like his brother (406), and later says that Aphrodite has maddened the army (1264). He thinks the suitors were insane when they swore the oath to Tyndareos. One person's nobility is another's idea of madness.

The public/private, male/female dichotomies are worked out through Iphigeneia's decision to die; we see her transformation. At first, she resists her fate vigorously, which allows Euripides to underline the costs of war. In response to her plea for her life, Agamemnon takes on Menelaus' position, which he had opposed earlier: "It is Hellas for which I must sacrifice you whether I want to or not; we are less than it. Greece must be free, as much as it is possible for you and me, and Greeks must not have our wives taken from us by force, by barbarians" (1271–5). Nationalism is a male sentiment in this framing (and often implicitly in modern times as well); all the Greeks are men in this sentence—Iphigeneia will not, after all, have a wife—and she is asked to give up her life for their manliness. Iphigeneia does not accede immediately; she still does not want to die and indeed she laments her death and blames Helen and Paris in the song immediately following (1279–335).

At a crucial moment, however, Iphigeneia changes her mind and supports her father. Aristotle draws attention to the unlikelihood of this transformation (*Poetics* 15.5), which should give us pause as well. She sacrifices herself for the greater good, to protect other Greek women from rape by barbarians (1380–1), but also for her own glory. Iphigeneia becomes the ideal Greek woman: she specifically says that her death means less than that of Achilles or his soldiers (1394, 1419). Her words may be hard to stomach in the present because of her self-abnegation. On the other hand, Iphigeneia also adopts a heroic stance: her marriage was private, but now she is marrying all of Greece, and the sack of Troy will replace her children (1398–9).

How are we to interpret her moment of glory? Would it have supported women's subordination in ancient Athens? Iphigeneia takes Agamemnon's self-servingly specious speech and makes it real; we see the effect of her self-sacrifice on Achilles—he falls in love with her. If we put the play in its fifth-century context, with Euripides' other plays on the Trojan War theme and his self-induced exile, it is hard to believe that he simply cheers Agamemnon on. On the other hand, given the glory of this Iphigeneia and the effect she has on the Chorus, the internal audience that Euripides carefully deploys, it is also hard to dismiss her as a dupe.

It seems that Iphigeneia faces necessity; fate in the form of the forward movement of a military that has gained its own momentum.

Earlier in the play, Agamemnon sounded paranoid or even duplicitous when he argued that he had to go ahead with the sacrifice because Odysseus knew and the army would come to Argos to attack his family. But that fear has been symbolically realized: Achilles has just told Iphigeneia that his own men have turned against him (1344–67). There is indeed no way out. In Chapter 3, we saw the effect of sacrifice in uniting the group. In keeping with the ideology of willing sacrifice, Iphigeneia must accept her own death. Instead of allowing herself to be dragged off, she assumes subjectivity by committing herself to the war effort. Her decision underlines the cost of war in terms of the lives of a nation's young; it also illuminates the kind of delusion that makes war happen again and again.

It is possible that Euripides mocks the transformation, as translator Don Taylor would have it: "Clytemnestra being transformed into an avenging fury, and Iphigeneia becoming that most tragic of spectacles, an innocent allowing herself to be used as an icon of vulgar patriotism and destruction" (xxvi–xxvii). It is also just possible that Iphigeneia would be taken as heroic in a time of war. Much will depend on the point of view of the individual audience member or reader. We might have here an example of the way in which the heart and the mind can be in conflict. The audience has evidence that Agamemnon is self-serving, that Achilles is not half the man that Iphigeneia is, yet her speech is moving. Does Iphigeneia's choice lead the audience to forget her father's base motives? Perhaps. Achilles praises her (1421–3), and the female Chorus immediately begins the process of glorifying Iphigeneia for her sacrifice: "Your glory will never leave you" (1504). It is not surprising that these young women do so, for they entered the stage singing the praises of the Greek army (164–302). The Chorus reaffirms the heroic masculine project, while Iphigeneia is co-opted into supporting nationalism and pan-Hellenism. Her quest for fame through sacrifice apparently succeeds. Iphigeneia can make one ask, "What are the benefits given to women and others who oppose war in order to win them over?" Is it a threat (of violence) or a promise (of reputation)? Iphigeneia shows how those two modes of persuasion work.

In this play, the immortal/mortal dynamic interacts with the gender and Greek/barbarian dynamics, but not to clarify what is at stake. Unlike Aeschylus, Euripides alludes to the story of the divine beauty contest that Paris judged—in which Aphrodite offered him the most beautiful woman in the world as his bride if he chose her as the winner

(178–84, 580–9). Helen in this version is merely used by the goddess and cannot be blamed as she routinely is. The power of love is personified in Aphrodite and Eros, however, and in the choral ode to Aphrodite internal desire as much as the goddess as external force seems to act (543–57, vs. 584–5).

Artemis is typically significant in the myth because she demands the sacrifice of Iphigeneia, but the debate between the brothers in this play undermines any sense that there was a requirement by the goddess. Agamemnon states that Kalkhas ordained that he sacrifice his daughter Iphigeneia to Artemis (90); Menelaus also says that the prophet said that they could sail to Troy if they sacrificed Iphigeneia. The goddess is never consulted (though it is discussed), and she never speaks; there is no reference to her anger or cause for this "demand." In *Agamemnon* the King puts on the yoke of necessity, and a yoke is mentioned here as well (443, 511), but in this case it is said to be crafted by the army, not the gods (514). Indeed, only the infatuated or patriotic Iphigeneia gives the goddess as a motive (1395–6), and even then, she simply says, "if Artemis wishes to take my body," a weak version of divine command. Zeus is not involved, as he was in *Agamemnon*. Without the admittedly ambiguous authority provided by the gods, this death seems even more politically motivated. The word for murder is often used, so that the very language reveals the thin line between murder and sacrifice (see Chapter 3). Mortals seem to be left to their own devices.

The ending of the play throws all this up for grabs yet again. As I said earlier, there are textual difficulties: the opening and closing have been challenged on the grounds of metrics, language, etc. The play is sometimes presented with the entry of a second messenger, who reports that the goddess saved her at the end (e.g., Gamel). If we accept that ending, then we have one interpretation: Iphigeneia is a young girl on the verge of marriage; as we saw, initiation can mean the death of the maiden and her rebirth in the new stage of maturity. Here, the death will be that of the ordinary girl, to be reborn as a priestess of Artemis. This is consistent with her myth and cult, in which both girls and animals are involved (see Chapter 3 on the cult). Even in this optimistic ending, however, Clytemnestra is left questioning the truth of the messenger (1617). In a play that depends so little on the gods, the divine intervention seems inconsistent or ironic.

If we don't accept the ending with the messenger, we are left with the death of the young woman to make possible a war of aggression masquerading as a war to save women, a war that intensifies East/West oppositions by labeling the East as source of rapists and works by getting the young to accept patriotic ideology. As I have pointed out, Euripides was writing in the context of a war with other Greek cities that left many young dead; would the audience have seen themselves in Iphigeneia, Achilles, Agamemnon, and Menelaus? Given the complexity of the play, it is reasonable to assume that a modern reader could take it to question our own investment in wars around the globe, as war is questioned by this play. It reveals the causes alleged for war to be lies, as well as the way in which ideology can become reality by deceiving the innocent.

5

Family Romance and Revenge in the House of Atreus

Both Euripides and Sophocles addressed individual episodes in the House of Atreus story without adopting the trilogy format; as a result, they narrowed the focus to the family. Sophocles and Euripides present the children's revenge by writing *Elektra* plays, while Euripides also wrote an *Orestes*, which covered the time period after the matricide and before the trial in *Eumenides*. Writing in the wake of Aeschylus' *Libation Bearers*, each made significant changes of detail while keeping to the basic revenge plot. Though the chronological relationship between the two is not secure, both probably date from the last ten years of the Peloponnesian War, a time during which Athens was subject to factional infighting. In connection with internal strife at Corcyra, Thucydides draws attention to an important factor, the changed meanings of words:

> So revolution broke out in city after city, and in places where the revolutions occurred late the knowledge of what had happened previously in other places caused still new extravagances of revolutionary zeal, expressed by an elaboration in the methods of seizing power and by unheard-of atrocities in revenge. To fit in with the change of events, words, too, had to change their usual meanings. What used to be described as a thoughtless act of aggression was now regarded as the courage one would expect to find in a party member; to think of the future and wait was merely another way of saying one was a coward; any idea of moderation was just an attempt to disguise one's unmanly character; ability to understand a question from all sides meant that one was totally unfitted for action. (3.82, trans. Warner)

The internal conflicts and ethical crises caused by the Peloponnesian War may be reflected in the action of these plays. The traditional obligation to do good to one's friends (*philoi*) and harm to one's enemies (*ekhthroi*) runs into difficulties when definitions shift, when family members become enemies (see also *Antigone* and *Medea*), or when duty to father and mother conflict.

As we have seen already, the House of Atreus myth was suitable for tragedy because of the ethical problems it presented. The fact that all three tragedians wrote plays dealing with the murder of Clytemnestra and Aigisthos provides a fascinating basis for comparison between them. In these plays, we find a more intimate psychological focus. They ask what happens to the children of violence. The barbarian/Greek axis is deemphasized, and the role of Apollo in the revenge is more limited than it is in Aeschylus.

Euripides' *Elektra*

In Euripides' *Elektra* the eponymous heroine is married to a farmer; unlike Aeschylus' Elektra, she does not immediately recognize her brother. Orestes murders Aigisthos while he is away from the palace sacrificing to the nymphs. They both plan the murder of Clytemnestra, which takes place when the Queen comes to Elektra's home for the celebration of rituals on the birth of Elektra's supposed child. In the end, Elektra and Orestes are separated, as Castor and Polydeuces, the immortal brothers of Clytemnestra, send them each to meet their fate.

A fundamental question for those of us reading revenge plays in the twenty-first century must be "how are we supposed to judge the avengers?" Homer minimized the matricide and made the murder a political solution; Aeschylus vilified Clytemnestra and devised an elaborate purification ritual in order to take the blame off Orestes. In a single play, Euripides cannot enact the aftermath to revenge, which makes judgment more difficult. The changes that he makes, in particular his decision to have his Elektra married to a farmer and to delay the siblings' recognition, will affect audience response.

Because this Elektra is living with her farmer husband in his house, the play is set outside the palace. The setting encourages an everyday tone and lengthy discussions of Elektra's clothing, as well as what she and her husband can afford to feed Orestes and Pylades. The marriage itself leads to a philosophical conversation about wealth and virtue. Though Elektra is married, she is still a virgin because her husband has not touched her. Euripides uses this element to raise the question of what makes true nobility; the farmer is one of nature's nobles though he is not wealthy (he is naturally pious [253] and temperate, *sôphrôn* [261]). Orestes makes a long speech on this point: wealth does not predict virtue. Later on, Elektra also depreciates wealth, saying that Aigisthos made the mistake of thinking that money made him someone; she asserts that nature is more trustworthy and lasts longer (939–44). This nobility of the humble farmer may lead in turn to the audience's questioning of the supposedly heroic characters and their values.

Elektra's role as an unmarried wife is anomalous; she is in social limbo. The marriage is like death (247, 911), twice even the death of Iphigeneia (1092–3). Her flowering into young womanhood (20–1) and courtship by nobles (including her now immortal cousins, Castor and Polydeuces, 312–13) was effectively cut off by Aigisthos' strategy of marrying her to a commoner, which was a replacement for cutting off her life altogether. Though the Greeks sometimes imagined marriage as the death of a maiden, or compared the premature death of a maiden to marriage to Hades (e.g., *Iphigeneia at Aulis* and *Antigone*), for Elektra marriage beneath her station is a form of death. This marriage has taken from her the status that she was entitled to as a member of the royal family; she is, like her brother, an exile from the house (209).

Gendered norms of behavior are explicitly used to judge the characters. For instance, Elektra thinks that manliness is at issue for Orestes; the farmer says that it is shameful for a girl to talk with men outside (344). These codes tell us what the Greek audience will have had in mind as it watched, what clichés and stereotypes about gender (as well as class) were active. Elektra repeatedly criticizes her mother for her behavior as a woman, although she herself is certainly not a typical demure Greek maiden. In exulting over the dead body of Aigisthos, Elektra issues several sexual insults: she blames him for shamefully marrying her mother, imagining that she would be faithful to him, then accuses him of being a woman's possession instead of the other way around, and derides him for his girlish looks (931, 949).

These values also play a role in the rhetorical contest between Elektra and her mother. Clytemnestra justifies her murder of Agamemnon by pointing to his failures as father and husband, the death of Iphigeneia, and the presence of Kassandra—not only a lover, but a second wife in the bed (1033–4). She explicitly brings up the double standard. She calls Helen a lewd woman and traitor, not worth the war to regain her; Elektra counters by pointing out that she is like her sister. The Chorus evaluates Clytemnestra as a wife: her justice is shameful; like a good wife she should have acceded to her husband's wishes (1051–3). Elektra attempts to distinguish herself from Clytemnestra; however, despite her sexual purity, her hatred has made her like her mother (on Clytemnestra's rage, 1110).

How, then, are we to respond? Elektra presents herself as a victim; she enters singing of her lineage. She is in mourning for her wretched life (118–21) and her father's fate, slain by his wife and Aigisthos (123–4); lest we misunderstand, she uses a traditional word for women's ritual lament to refer to her song (*goos*), which she seems to intone nightly (141, 125). She mourns not only the dead but also her absent brother, who should come to free her and avenge his father. At the same time, she is impatient and angry at his delay (245, 263, 275). Her pain is increased by the contrast with her mother. Clytemnestra's children are in exile, while the mother lies in a bloody bed with her new husband (212). When Elektra speaks to Orestes, she sharpens her claim to pity by comparing her situation with Clytemnestra's luxurious life, which is after all based on Agamemnon's victory at Troy ("she sits on a throne with Phrygian spoils, with Asian servants that he took," 314–16); finally she returns to the original theme of the shame to her father; his killer rides in his chariot and holds his scepter (321–2).

The audience may not sympathize with her, however, because Elektra might seem to wallow in her mourning. For instance, Euripides introduces her carrying a water pitcher on her head. The Farmer explicitly tells her she doesn't have to fetch water from the spring, but she insists in order to make a point about Aigisthos and Clytemnestra: they have acted with "*hubris*" toward her (58). When the Chorus invites her to participate in a celebration that unmarried girls will hold for Hera, goddess of marriage, she declines this as well as their offer of robes. She then emphasizes her ragged apparel throughout, especially when she tells Orestes how she suffers. She underlines her physical suffering, her house, her labor at the loom (300–10), and her isolation because she doesn't have the right clothes. It is not clear that Elektra has to wear rags any more than she has to collect water; her life is not threatened, and it is not in fact so dreadful. It seems that anything less than regal would strike her as lacking for the daughter of Agamemnon (175–89), the sacker of Troy. The Chorus, like the Farmer, underlines the excess of her actions by suggesting that prayers might have better results than groans (195–7).

By marrying Elektra off, the play (and Aigisthos) offers her the possibility of a change, a new life: she is not dead or beaten, and while she may have adopted the look of a slave (shaven head, rags), she is not actually a slave in the palace. Why can't she be happy in her marriage? Ancient and modern emotions might well diverge here. For someone steeped in myth, as the members of the Greek audience were, it would be understandable that the daughter of Agamemnon would consider her marriage tantamount to social death. To the modern reader, this might seem self-indulgent, particularly because we are told that she has a very fine man for a husband. Is this an example of a heroic character going too far (a question we ask again in the case of Sophocles' Elektra and Antigone)?

We can perhaps respect her, however, as someone who will not cease seeking justice. She cannot "get on with her life" because she resists the idea of disloyalty to her father. On the psychological level, the play reveals that we can sink ourselves in our own mourning, condemning ourselves to a living death by attachment to the past. Her over-identification with Agamemnon and the possibility that her desires are incestuous, introduced as a question earlier, are possible interpretations here. Taken in this way the play can provide a way of thinking about the normal. How long should we grieve before living the remainder of our lives? The everyday setting makes this royal action more apparently relevant to a modern audience.

Critics are divided about how we are meant to feel about Orestes, as well. He enters with no plan, and is prepared to leave if that seems necessary. He is cautious if not downright cowardly. He delays in telling Elektra who he is, though he supposedly returned to make her his ally. Moreover, he has less divine assistance than his Aeschylean forebear. He has come from some nameless god's mysteries (87); Apollo is identified late (971) and then only to have his role actively criticized. Orestes says that it was stupidity "to order him to kill his mother, whom he should not kill" (971). He wonders if the god even spoke, or whether it was not rather some vengeance deity (979); he finally says that he does not believe that the god prophesied these things well (981). How can you believe in a god who ordains murder? Was it even the god who spoke? Castor and Polydeuces challenge

Apollo's wisdom as well, though they have no doubt that it was he (1302). This play questions the proposition accepted by the *Oresteia*.

The morality of the matricide is also discussed at length: instead of a few lines between Orestes, Pylades, and Clytemnestra, we have a scene in which Orestes debates with Elektra as they watch Clytemnestra approach; the sister presents the father's vengeance as a counter to the mother's right, but Orestes explicitly challenges the truth of the oracle (978–81). When Elektra rails against Aigisthos, Orestes agrees with her, but he says that it is a dreadful thing for him to kill his mother (985–7). The murders are potentially made more problematic because Aigisthos and Clytemnestra are portrayed somewhat sympathetically. Aigisthos, though he has been cruel to both children, is hospitable to strangers and is performing appropriate ritual actions at the time of his death. Clytemnestra saved Elektra from the worst of Aigisthos' violence (attempted murder) and presumably cares enough about her to come when she is called to perform the ritual at her supposed child's "birth." It is noteworthy that Elektra is sure that their plot will work and has no doubt that her mother will appear.

Even if it was necessary for Aigisthos and Clytemnestra to die in the end, the children feel themselves to be polluted for being the agents of vengeance. According to Castor, it was a just act, but their doing it was not just (1244; cf. Clytemnestra's murder of Agamemnon, 1051). Euripides chooses to show the children suffering mentally for what they have done—the Furies are yet to come, but they feel terrible guilt. Elektra in particular takes responsibility for her attack on the mother who bore her (1182–4); she urged Orestes on and even held the knife (1224–6). The Chorus criticizes her for pushing her brother, who was unwilling (1205). Elektra can only look forward to a life like the one she has led up until then—what dance can she participate in, what marriage can she anticipate (1198–2000)? Orestes blames Apollo for making him a murderer and city-less (1190–7). The pressure brought to bear by family, fate, necessity, and the god Apollo (1301–7) seems unbearable in the present. But the very end suggests that the children are shortsighted in their criticism of the gods: Orestes will have his trial in Athens, and Apollo will take the pollution from him; he will be released from his suffering, as will Elektra, who is promised to Pylades in marriage. The release from toils echoes the phrases of mystery cult, which also promise blessedness to initiates (1291).

The conclusion may, then, reinstitute the traditional order. Are we meant to see it as ironic? I believe so. The pair's final punishment is that they can no longer be together. The family has in fact collapsed under the weight of the required revenge. The play may also challenge the traditional ideal of harming one's enemies and helping one's friends by showing the suffering that it causes. The view that Euripides was a radical supporter of democracy as well as a writer who made changes in the art form can predispose us to see this play as critical both of the myth and of Aeschylus' version (which is directly held up to ridicule in the recognition scene). On a political level, can we see these two young people as analogous to modern-day victims of exile? The complexities of Euripides' *Elektra* can help us to think about comparable situations in our own day. What pressures shape today's youth into martyrs?

Sophocles' *Elektra*

While we don't know its date, and so can't tell its specific relationship to Euripides, Sophocles' *Elektra* is similar in general outline to the other two accounts of the myth: Orestes has returned from exile, though he is accompanied by his aged Tutor (*paidagôgos*) as well as the trusty Pylades; as in Aeschylus, Elektra lives at home with Clytemnestra and Aigisthos; Clytemnestra has had a different fearful dream but once again sends offerings to the tomb; Orestes' death is reported as an important part of the revenge plot. It is significantly different from Aeschylus' and Euripides' treatments in crucial ways, however: the murder of Clytemnestra precedes that of Aigisthos; there is no questioning of the matricide, no regret afterward, and no explicit mention of any punishment to follow the revenge. Sophocles includes Elektra's sister, Khrysothemis, who was mentioned in Homer. It is also different from each in other, more subtle ways, namely in the manner of the way and timing of the scene in which the two siblings recognize one another. While the *Libation Bearers* and Euripides' *Elektra* show Orestes and Elektra plotting together, this play postpones the recognition until very late in the play; in the interim, Elektra along with Clytemnestra is deceived by the tale of Orestes' death so that she comes to the point where she is willing to act.

The main debate about Sophocles' *Elektra* regards its judgment of the vengeance. The play ends with Elektra expressing confidence that Aigisthos' death and ejection outside the city will bring purification from past ills (1489–90); the Chorus' last line promises the accomplishment of freedom (1509–10, cf. 1256). Is this, then, the view of the play as a whole? One group of scholars, following the edition of R. C. Jebb, sees the vengeance as simply laudable (xxiii). Those offering this interpretation tend to argue that Sophocles is not referring to Aeschylus so much as to Homer, and that he accepts the Homeric version in which the revenge is glorified as a son's duty to his father and is held out as a model to Telemachos (see above), and in which Aigisthos assumes priority over Clytemnestra as the villain, thus minimizing the problem of matricide. It is significant, then, that Sophocles includes Khrysothemis, who is mentioned in Homer but not in Aeschylus or Euripides.

There is definitely an epic tone to the play, not only in the plot but especially in the prologue, which stresses Orestes' patrilineage: "oh son of Agamemnon, once great general at Troy" (1–2). The notion of the *kairos* is emphasized in this play (the word appears more often here than in any other single tragic text) and is associated with Orestes' coming of age: the Tutor says that he took him from his sister and saved him and brought him to this stage of flowering youth, to be the avenger of his father (12–14). Because Orestes has reached the appropriate age, it is the time (*kairos*) for revenge: "It is no longer the right time for hesitation, but high time for action" (22). In addition, the god determined that this is the time to put the plan into practice (1264).

As a youth in the epic mold, Orestes is concerned with his honor (64–6, 71), as he should be, but there are complications from the beginning. He also has a profit motive (72). Moreover, unlike the reputation-hungry epic hero, he doesn't care what is said about him and he is not afraid to be reported dead when he is in fact alive (59–60) since his glory will come later:

> For what harm does this do me, when in fiction (*logos*) I die, but in fact (*ergon*) I am saved and win renown? Really, I think that no word is ill-omened if accompanied by *profit*. Yes, often before now I have seen clever men also falsely reported dead; then, when they come home again, they are held in greater honour. Just so, I trust, shall I emerge alive with the help of this report, and shall yet blaze like a star on my enemies. (59–66, trans. March; emphasis added)

This speech is the opening statement of two additional themes of the play: the contrast of words and deeds; and the paradox of living in death, or dying in life.

The Homeric echoes die away quickly, however, or are drowned out by women's voices and lament. Having dedicated himself to action, albeit via deceit and false words, Orestes is primed for the vengeance when he hears a woman's voice crying out. The Tutor thinks it is a servant, but Orestes wonders if it is Elektra and asks whether he should stay and listen to her cries (80–1). The Tutor says no, they must do nothing before attending to Apollo's commands; they must pour libations to his father (51–3, 82–4). The prologue concludes the Homeric portion of the play: the men agree not to stay to hear a woman's discourse of suffering; their aggressive turning away from her sets male against female, god's requirements against human motives.

With the shift to Elektra, we also shift to lyric and enter the women's world of mourning. The role of the children in the family is strongly distinguished by gender. Orestes has been brought up as the avenger, while Elektra has been treated as a servant; dressed in rags, fed crumbs from the family table, unmarried and childless, she must wait for Orestes to begin her life. We see the significance of Sophocles' choices: like Aeschylus he sets his play before the palace; Elektra therefore appears mired in the situation, condemned to live with her father's murderers. Her brother's exit emphasizes her isolation (reemphasized by other characters entering and exiting, while she remains transfixed); the recognition of the two could easily have taken place at the outset. Since it does not, but since we know it is about to happen, we are made pointedly aware of the effects of revenge deferred. Orestes' delay in coming home has already extended Elektra's suffering; putting off the recognition causes more suffering and enables the audience to see for itself the costs to Elektra. I would say that this is a very painful play: the revenge may not be punished on stage, but that does not negate the suffering it has already caused.

Some theorists have stressed the importance of lamentation to the development of tragedy *per se*—a form that focuses on death and indulges in the mourning prohibited in the city (Chapter 3); we can see these traces of that past in the opening to the *Libation Bearers*, where Orestes, Elektra, and the Chorus engage in a *kommos* to activate Agamemnon's support for them, and to a lesser extent in Euripides' *Elektra*. In Sophocles, Elektra laments continuously (103–6, 132–3,

231–2), mourning her father's death and his marriage bed defiled. She longs for her brother (118), who promises to come but does not (171–2, 319), because she has lost the strength to go on (119–20). And she bewails her own suffering—she is childless and unmarried, treated like a foreign servant in the home of her father, dressed in shameful clothes and sitting at an empty table (164–6, 185–92). Elektra elaborates on her tribulations, repeating some elements. Her situation is intolerable: she hates her mother, she lives with the murderers and is under their control; she watches the usurper in Agamemnon's clothes and on his throne, sleeping with her mother (if that is what she should call her, 273), who has even established a festival to celebrate her murder of Agamemnon.

Half of her speech is the report of the kind of insults that she receives from her mother. But she ends by repeating what she has said before, that she endlessly waits for Orestes, who doesn't come. Time has no meaning for her because of this continuous mourning—day and night are the same (105–6, 259). The Chorus assures her that Orestes has a noble nature and will arrive (322), but Elektra is clearly doubtful: she didn't hesitate when it came to saving his life (321). Like Euripides' Elektra, she questions her brother's commitment. Elektra will mourn still more bitterly when she thinks that she has lost her brother, too.

Elektra is in a time warp, condemned to repeat herself endlessly and pointlessly. It is possible that she, like Euripides' Elektra, wallows in her suffering, taking pleasure in it. For instance, the Chorus of local women commiserates with her, but they also urge her to stop, implying that she is excessive and adds to her own suffering (213–20). They add, however, that they say this in love, like a trusty mother (233–5). Thus they do not blame her. In reply, Elektra claims the integrity of her position, the nobility of it—she is well-born, and she is doing the right thing; by mourning, she supports *aidôs* and *eusebeia* (respect or modesty and reverence, 237, 249–50, 257). Her sister Khrysothemis begins by criticizing Elektra for indulging in her vain and empty anger (330–1), and for having come outside. She hastens to add that she is really upset too, but she doesn't have the strength to do anything. Later on she explicitly makes the argument on the basis of gender: as women they cannot fight the stronger (997–8).

With which sister are we meant to sympathize? Khrysothemis accepts the fact that the right is with Elektra (338, vs. 1042), but if she is going to be "free," she says, she must obey those in power (339–40).

In truth, as women neither of them is free: Elektra, though outspoken, can't mourn as she wants (285–6) and wouldn't have come out of the house if Aigisthos were home (310–13, 517). Elektra's public mourning gets her in trouble, but she has no desire for the kind of comfortable life that her sister enjoys (359–62): that is, she might complain about her "empty table," but she does not want a full one at the expense of giving up her mourning. The contrast between Elektra and Khrysothemis is presented as a debate between the idealistic and the realistic; in her accommodation to power, Khrysothemis also occupies the position of "words" in the words/deeds polarity—she claims to mourn, but does nothing (347–50, 357). Clearly Khrysothemis has no principled reason for not helping her sister since she acknowledges that "justice demands immediate action" (466–7).

The moral evaluation of Elektra is, however, not as straightforward as it might seem from what I have just said. She often apologizes for her behavior and acknowledges that she might seem shameless because she is not a proper woman like Khrysothemis is—she is always outside the house lamenting loudly. Sophocles here draws on the ideological association of modest women with the inner regions of the house. Thus, though Elektra is feminine and passive in comparison to the vengeance hero Orestes, she is masculine and daring in comparison to her sister, who is the "good" girl.

A modern debate about identity focuses on the relative power of nature and nurture, or nature and culture; in ancient Athens there was a similar debate between *nomos* (custom) and *physis* (nature), which is relevant to this play. By birth Elektra is in a complicated situation: though she accuses Khrysothemis of siding with her mother (341, 366–7) and would like to and does identify herself with her father (in one staging, she was shown wearing an army greatcoat throughout to demonstrate this allegiance), she was born from her mother, which would determine her biologically (*physis*). At one point, she says that she is good at shamelessness because she is like her mother (605–9). She has been living with her, so that the similarity might be based on environment (*nomos*) as well. Although Elektra claims the moral high ground, she also acknowledges that the suffering of such evils has made her who she is (308–9) and that she is ashamed because she knows that her behavior is not consistent with her real self (618–21, cf. 221, 254). The shamelessness with which she is treated has made her shameless; Clytemnestra's actions lead to her words (624–5). It is possible, then, that she is overly violent in her mourning, and that she has become like her mother, who stands for shamelessness itself. Elektra cannot be properly reverent and restrained, *sôphrôn*, a key concept for women. Learning is thematic in the play, and one way in which we learn is in the family or through our experiences. The modern audience might not see Elektra as so different from her mother, then, and not free of guilt.

The confrontation between mother and daughter, like that in Euripides, is set as a debate; the two women resemble fifth-century orators in the way they argue. The contest might either confirm or disconfirm the legitimacy of matricide. Clytemnestra claims that she acted with justice, giving Iphigeneia's sacrifice as her only motive (528–33). Elektra counters by arguing that Artemis demanded the sacrifice of Iphigeneia, and then attacking Clytemnestra's relationship to Aigisthos and her treatment of her other children. She minimizes the problem with their matricide by pointing out that Clytemnestra was no mother to her (596–8, cf. 273). This Clytemnestra is fully evil (compared to the Euripidean mother): not only has she profited from the murder sexually and politically, but she also feasts and laughs on Agamemnon's death day (277–81); moreover, she further emasculated him by her actions afterward, cutting off his limbs and wiping her sword on his head (444–6).

It seems, then, that Sophocles has given Elektra the better case, and it is smooth sailing until she mentions the problem with revenge: "if we are to take a life for a life, then you would be the first to die, if you were to meet with justice" (582–3). The claim that Elektra makes may come back to haunt her—if Clytemnestra did not have the right to kill Agamemnon, what can she and Orestes reply? On the other hand, if Agamemnon did no wrong, then Clytemnestra's murder of Agamemnon was the first act of violence, not payment for a prior killing; thus it might still be acceptable for the children to kill her in proper revenge. As we know from the *Oresteia* and Euripides' *Elektra*, there are competing "rights" and thus the vendetta could go on forever. There is no next generation held out as a threat, no Furies of the mother enacted, yet Sophocles here has given his audience at least one reason to hold their breath at the end of the play.

This nasty dialogue ends in a standoff, but as if in answer to Clytemnestra's prayers, the Tutor comes and gives what is the longest set speech in the extant corpus of Sophocles; in front of Elektra, he narrates an elaborate story about the death of Orestes at the Pythian games—he won in the foot race, but when it came to the chariot race, he was tangled in the reins of his horses and dragged to his death. The Tutor goes far beyond merely repeating Orestes' words from the prologue, embellishing creatively with details about the races. Its very length must draw our attention to its function in the play. The description is an artistic *tour de force*; it puts the absent hero in front of us as an athlete and fits into the Athenian competitive performance culture in that way. Its effect is ambiguous. One might feel that the real Orestes does not live up to this golden hero, or that the aura of the contest glorifies the somewhat more mundane character of the drama. The description is ambiguous in another way: it describes Orestes' victory but also his death, so that although it is in the Homeric mode of the prologue, it is a reminder of the possibility of failure.

The internal audience for this speech includes Elektra as well as Clytemnestra. Clytemnestra mourns briefly, drawing attention to the contradictory feelings that arise when family members become enemies, but she recovers quickly. Now she will be able to sleep (780). Elektra is devastated; she feels that Orestes has killed her with himself, for now all her hopes are dashed. She will have no avenger and must return to her life of slavery (808–14). At the end of that speech, she seems at her nadir, her only recourse to lie outside the palace door, friendless, and wither away; she'd rather be dead (817–22). The audience alone knows that she is mourning a deception of a deception. Will we be distanced from the action as a result? Less engaged on an emotional level, more engaged on an intellectual one?

Khrysothemis returns at the summit of happiness: Orestes must be alive, for someone has made offerings at Agamemnon's grave. Elektra ridicules her and tells her what she has heard; and in a new version of their earlier scene, she tries to convince her sister to join her in killing Aigisthos. She fails and decides to act alone (1045). In psychological terms, then, Elektra is enabled to grow up by the "death" of Orestes. Now it is time for Elektra to turn from lament and words to deeds. She becomes a woman of action; she stresses traditional aristocratic values in her speech to her sister: they will be glorified for their reverence to the dead; she will be known as a free woman and will make a noble marriage suitable to her free birth. They will win "glorious reputation" from citizen and foreigner alike (973, 975) and will be honored for their courage (983). Unlike the Athenian woman of citizen class who was typically not spoken of in public, they will receive the praise appropriate for epic warriors.

Elektra does not go too far into masculinity, however, since the desired fame is defined within the realm of appropriately female expectations: the sisters will attract noble husbands. If they do not avenge their father's death, they will be locked forever in spinsterhood because Aigisthos will never let them marry lest they breed trouble for him. Khrysothemis again counsels caution—keep it quiet and yield (1011, 1014); they are women, and they cannot stand up to the stronger Aigisthos (997). Elektra, however, has the spirit of Ares in her and intends to do just that (1243). This is her shining hour. Though at first the Chorus simply counsels the sisters to listen to one another (990–1) and Elektra to profit from Khrysothemis' good sense (1015–16), it later applauds Elektra's path explicitly for its nobility: she will win fine reputation (1081–9) and is the best of daughters.

There is still more suffering in store for Elektra, however. The play has once again come to the point of action (where it was before Orestes left the stage after the Prologue), but there is another long delay in which Orestes, not recognizing Elektra or pretending not to, presents her with the urn holding "Orestes' ashes." We must ask why there is another postponement. On one level, we might suspect that this Orestes is cruel, playing cat and mouse with his sister. My students felt that he was torturing her. The delayed recognition scene must remind us of the beginning of the play where Orestes asks if he should wait to hear his sister, and the Tutor says no. The boy and girl have sharply differentiated roles to play. In contrast to his Euripidean version, Orestes has never claimed to come back for his sister; he is simply the avenger; therefore, he keeps himself distant from her suffering. If this scene were played with Orestes in good clothing and Elektra in rags, the contrast would be crystal clear. He has been educated for one purpose and can't be distracted from it.

What does Sophocles gain from this strategy? What is his profit? First, by having Elektra experience real pain through a fiction, he creates an analogy for the audience: if we emotionally engage with a play, we are doing what Elektra does. Even though the audience knows it is a deception, the scene is real in its feeling (there is a famous story about an actor who played this scene by thinking of his own son who had died). The audience is always looking on at imitations of actions. Second, it ratchets up Elektra's suffering one more notch: though earlier she had not minded dying, and had thought she would simply wither away, now she believes that she is dead and wishes to be buried with her beloved brother. Finally, the speech before the urn allows the author to show us a different Elektra, the one who loved Orestes. She reveals the meaning of family and family affection; she has lost everyone that she claims as dear (herself included, 1150–2). Having said before that she wished she were dead and would pine away in front of the house, she now wishes to climb into Orestes' little room with him. His grave will be her true home.

The play at this point takes the active Elektra, armed for revenge and ready to take on the male role, and puts her back in her feminine place. When the Chorus finally names Elektra, Orestes is moved to pity, but he is afraid of that emotion, asking how he can control his tongue (1175). Though there are plot reasons for silence, the effect is to make Elektra fit the Greek conception of a woman as too emotional and too noisy. From the beginning Orestes has been kept away from her suffering; it is too intense for him. The theme of words and deeds is brought back again at this point; it is time for deeds, not words (1288–92), that is, Orestes, not Elektra: the urn contains Orestes only in words (1217, cf. 1359–60); silence is called for (1236, 1238, 1322). Elektra wants to speak freely (1254–6, 1261), but the Tutor is very annoyed at their loud rejoicing.

So, having spent most of the play watching Elektra's suffering and listening to her mourning, we come to the revenge. Elektra is given nothing physical to do with the murders, but she participates extensively in words. When Orestes is inside killing his mother, it is Elektra who speaks and answers her. The only sign of her excessive emotion might be the fact that she urges Orestes to hit Clytemnestra a second time. A prayer to Apollo and references to Ares and Hermes indicate that the Chorus believes this is part of a divine plan. Blood for blood is the dominant tone: the murder matches the original act (deceit for deceit, in the same place), but unlike Clytemnestra's act, it is not compromised by adulterous desire or inappropriate desire for gain.

These two bloody children who feel no guilt may, however, speak horrors to us. Orestes says that all is well if Apollo prophesied well (1425). It is perfectly plausible to read that "if" as intensificatory and implying "of course he did; he always does." It is also possible to read it as a genuine question, given Euripides' treatment in *Elektra* and *Orestes*. There are further doubts raised by the murder of Aigisthos. He asks, "Why do you lead me into the house? How is it that you need the shadows if this deed is noble (*kalos*)? Why not kill me handily here?" (1493–4); Orestes gives this reason—he's going to kill him where Agamemnon was killed, which is plausible but not definitively so. Aigisthos replies, "Is it really necessary for this house to look on both the present and future evils of the family of Pelops?" (1497–8). Readers cannot simply dismiss these questions, even though Orestes and the Chorus seem to do so.

Orestes goes inside, herding Aigisthos ahead of him. What happens to Elektra? Is she still outside or does she go into the house? The ending of the play is open, even though the words seem clear enough. Elektra has prayed for release from toils (1490), a phrase that might once again evoke initiations into mystery cult, and seems to have received it: the dead brother has come back to life. And the Chorus claims freedom for the children of Atreus; earlier the only freedom had been Khrysothemis', gained by giving in to those in authority (339–40). There is no hint in this play that any outside force will exact punishment from Orestes and Elektra.

A great deal will depend on the director's interpretation. The suffering must be internal, if at all. The ending with Orestes going into the house may mean either that he is restored to his throne, or that he is condemned to be drawn back into the familial mud. If the house is accursed, equivalent to a wound or a womb, his independence is over. Elektra, on the other hand, may be either inside or outside. And she may be played as triumphant or as still huddled as she was in the beginning. Either way, it is unlikely that a lifetime of hatred and suffering will quickly turn into its opposite. In Strauss' *Elektra*, she dances herself to death. It is critics' assumption that Sophocles was more pious than Euripides that allows them to eliminate these possibilities easily.

In modern times, the vengeance may seem to have political overtones, and that element in the text can be played up (the tyranny of Aigisthos and Clytemnestra, the power of Elektra's mourning to rile up the citizens). Even if a viewer takes the perspective that the play is unambiguous about the children's justice, the endless suffering of Elektra can seem problematic to the audience, and even the characters' self-justification can be frightening. It was, for instance, when the play was produced in Northern Ireland—some members of the audience identified with Elektra, but some criticized her, saying to actress Fiona Shaw, "It's hanging onto your grief like that, that has our country destroyed!" (Shaw 133). What would the play mean in situations of

ethnic cleansing? It is possible to see Elektra as the heroine of a revolution, or as an *agent provocateur*. She has not found a viable way to
mourn yet still live (perhaps by taking on aspects of her father and
embodying them herself), because the norms of fifth-century Athens
within which she lived rendered it impossible. What might we do
differently?

6

Victims and Victimizers

As we saw earlier, *Iphigeneia at Aulis* reveals the way women were used to justify war; gender differences are especially noticeable in the aftermath to ancient war: the men were typically killed, while the consequences for the women of Troy were rape and slavery (as rape, or fear of rape, is the reality for women in the chaos of present-day wars). In tragedies on the war, we see the costs of war as they are borne by the enemy women, and we also see the ways in which the dichotomy of East and West (Barbarian/Greek) intersects with gender and class. Women are not simply victims, however. Like Clytemnestra in the *Oresteia*, Hekabe and Medea exact revenge on those who have wronged them.

Euripides' *Trojan Women*

Troy was the model of a war against an eastern outsider (like the Persian Wars), yet when Euripides was staging many of his plays on the subject, Athens was at war with Sparta, in defense of an empire won after decisive encounters with the East in the Persian Wars. How does Euripides mean us to understand his own society? The relevant events in the Peloponnesian War might be the taking of Melos or the Sicilian invasion, actions at Plataea, Mitylene, or Scione, but the quest for specific political referents is often very limiting (see Chapter 2). What we will be doing here, as indeed throughout Part II, is looking not for the opinion of the historical Euripides, but for what the ancient interpretation might most likely have been, and then trying to see what the plays can mean to us.

Trojan Women seems to be the anti-war play *par excellence*; the Greek victors are made despicable, and their victims are noble. It takes place after the war is over, on the shores just beneath Troy; it focuses on the Trojan women, who wait to see which Greek man will be their master; the Trojan men are all dead (except for Astyanax, the youngest prince) and the Greek victors appear only briefly. Hekabe is the fixed point in the (limited) action; her daughter Kassandra and daughter-in-law Andromache enter and are taken away. At the play's climax, Hekabe has to bury her grandson, Astyanax, and watch as the city of Troy is put to the torch.

Poseidon, the god of the sea, presents the prologue, telling the audience that Polyxena has been sacrificed on Achilles' tomb, and that Agamemnon has forcefully bedded Kassandra, the mad prophet of Apollo (44), thus dishonoring the gods. Athena wants to punish the Greeks for the rape of Kassandra at her altar; therefore, these former enemies come together in a compact to hinder the Greeks' return home. The prologue shows the dangers attendant on victory. At the time of its production in Athens (415), the Athenians were in a brief respite from war, but about to embark on a campaign in Sicily; men in the audience might have identified as the Greeks versus the Trojans, the men versus the women, and hoped to be the victors.

Like *Agamemnon* and *Iphigeneia at Aulis*, this play debates the causes of the war and reveals its costs. The consideration of the causes of the war leads to a discussion of the role of the gods, thematic to the play, as is obvious from their presence at the opening. They are invoked variously through the play, but Hekabe in particular runs the gamut of responses. First she calls on the gods but asks why she bothers with such bad allies (469–70); she basically ends up saying that she does so because it is customary. She then holds them responsible for building towers out of nothing and tearing down those seeming to be something (612–13)—the towers of Troy are in the background, and it is from the walls that her grandson will be thrown to his death. Later she wonders what to call the gods, though she expresses belief in the divine justice that directs the affairs of mortals (888); finally, she regrets the sacrifices she has wasted since she never got anything for them. The gods have meant nothing but suffering for her (1240–2), and it makes no sense to call on the gods (1280) since they don't listen. The prologue and choral song (1060–80) reveal a central feature of ancient Greek religion: the gods receive worship from and should protect mortals, but they leave when the city falls. The Chorus wonders if Zeus cares at all about his temples in Troy. These questions, like Job's complaints in the Bible, do not necessarily mean that there are no gods, just that they don't give much comfort to suffering mortals.

Euripides makes a very strange move in terms of plot. He has Hekabe gratuitously call for a trial of Helen—Hekabe, who fears Helen's seductive powers and is trying to convince Menelaus to kill her in Troy and not take her back to Greece. This unlikely turn of events allows Euripides to bring out certain elements of the situation, in particular, Helen's discursive seductiveness. While she is on trial for her life, Helen addresses the power of the gods but she blames Hekabe and Priam first of all, for having given life to Paris (who was fated to do what he did). She next blames the Divine Beauty Contest, claiming that Paris came to her with Aphrodite at his side, and that the goddess was irresistible. In a very rationalizing rebuttal, Hekabe questions the myth; she doubts that goddesses would participate in a beauty contest; she asserts that mortals use Aphrodite as an excuse for their own lechery, and in Helen's case, her greed. Hekabe's skepticism is consistent with a rationalizing strand of fifth-century culture; while modern secularists might agree, it is not clear that she would have been perceived as the victor by an ancient audience. We know that the gods will cause harm to the fleet on the way home; therefore it is not a foregone conclusion that Aphrodite did not empower Paris, as Helen claims. Modern stagings may assume that Hekabe is correct; they may ignore the prologue and the role of the gods, in an effort to update this and make it into a more obviously anti-war play; in doing so, they undermine the play's expansive perspective.

Hekabe's argument, however, makes us ask to what extent we mortals are responsible for our own fates. Indeed, the position of women, who historically have not made war but do suffer its effects, is a particularly poignant way of raising that general question. Hekabe's interpretation brings us to the issues of gender and the fate of women in war. She blames Helen for betraying her husband and argues that killing her will make other women chaste (1031–2); Menelaus echoes her sentiments (1055–9). While Helen claims that she was raped, taken away by force (962), Kassandra and Hekabe, as well as Menelaus, believe that she went willingly (1037). Yet, Hekabe has a sense of the ambiguity of will; she acknowledges the power of desire when she tells Menelaus not to take Helen on board ship with him, because she is irresistible (as was Paris).

But the force of desire is quite different from the force of rape. The Trojan women will experience the latter. They are sexual slaves. The language of force is deployed from the beginning of *Trojan Women*. Scamander is echoing with the cries of the "spear-won" women who are waiting to be allotted their masters (28–39); Poseidon further says that Agamemnon impiously and forcefully (*biaiôs*) married Kassandra in a "shadowy bedding" (43–4). And as we saw, Athena's ire was inspired by the *hubris* against her when Ajax forced Kassandra from her temple (69–70). So the key terms are force and *hubris*, used interchangeably here against Apollo's priestess and against the goddess Athena. Because of the different fates of men and women in war, the opposition of free/slave is brought to the fore, as well. The slavery that awaits these women is thematic, from first to last (158, 165, 192, 277, 422, 492, 507, 600, 678, 1271, 1280).

The fate of the defeated women is also made similar to the more typical fate of women, for the discourse of rape is countered by the frequent appearance of words for marriage and bride. Kassandra enters brandishing torches and seems to be raving. One of the significant signs of her madness would appear to be her "mistaking" her sexual slavery for a marriage. This is a royal wedding, blessed (311–13); she ends her speech calling her captor "husband" with the unambiguous term *posis* (341). But how mad is she? In fact, she is not alone in her view. We are told that Kassandra has been chosen especially by Agamemnon (248) not as slave to his wife (249–50) but as the shadowy bride of his bed (*lektrôn skotia numpheutêria*, 251). From the herald Talthybios' perspective, her selection by Agamemnon is a great thing (259). He leads her off, calling it once again a fine marriage (*numpheuma*, 420), and she echoes his language, hurrying off to her wedding in Hades, claiming her bridegroom (*numphiôi gêmómetha*, 445). Hekabe makes the connection explicit: "I never thought that you would make such a marriage at the point of a spear or a sword" (346–7). It is a marriage, but one made by force. The main inconsistency is that Kassandra was not given by her father in lawful exchange, but was taken by violence.

Kassandra, then, is neither mad nor suffering from false consciousness. In her confused speech, she reveals the resistance that lies beneath her joyful embrace of her fate by indicating that this marriage will not be happy for the famous prince Agamemnon (357–8). Her marriage union will be deadly for her enemies (405), as she explains at length. Euripides uses the ambiguity, uses the language of marriage, to underline the pathos but also the danger: not only does Kassandra threaten the house of Atreus, but Talthybios fears that her "marriage torches" are meant to set fire to the inner chambers of the house they stand before (298–9).

Euripides correlates the fall of the city with the rape of the women, the Greek victory with appropriation of the reproductive labor of Trojan women (566). The women of the Chorus have been taken by violence (signified by the spear) and will make children for the Greeks, leaving pain for the Trojan fatherland. Moreover, their song leads into the entrance of Andromache; she is placed on a cart piled high with the other spoils of war, holding her son. She and he are both objects of value, but in different ways. The play culminates in the painful death of Astyanax, making explicit that in war death is the fate for men and boys, while slavery and rape are the fate of women. Andromache's future children will be owned by the enemy.

Andromache's situation points out the ways in which sexual slavery can become marriage. First, Andromache was especially desirable to the Greek soldiers because she was virtuous and a good woman/wife to Hektor (658–60). Neoptolemos, the son of Achilles, wants her; ironically, her loyalty to Hektor will make her a slave in the house of his murderer. Second, she knows that "they say" it only takes one night in bed for a woman to get over her anger. She understands that she must choose between getting used to her new husband, thereby becoming a traitor to Hektor, and living in enmity with her new husband; her mother advises her to make Neoptolemos love her (700). But Andromache has already said that she loathes women who are disloyal (667–8); so, like women slaves in other periods, she will live in division against herself.

Trojan Women, like *Iphigeneia at Aulis*, undercuts a traditional polarity in tragedy and Greek thought. While the Persian Wars and Trojan War pit East against West, and presumably barbarians against Greece, here the Hellenes are called barbarians (764) and fearful (1159) when they take the life of a small child lest his noble blood lead to a Trojan uprising. The horror is underlined by having even the Greek herald commiserate with the boy's mother and grandmother (e.g., 710). The barbarian theme is complicated again when Hekabe asserts that Helen was won over by barbarian gold, not by Aphrodite, raising the possibility that the Greeks were motivated by the prospect of ruling Troy and its wealth (991–7). The imperialistic element is mentioned explicitly in Helen's version of the Beauty Contest. Helen argues that Paris was offered rule over Greece or rule over Asia, but chose her instead; as a result, the Greeks should thank her for their freedom (933–4). And Andromache mourns for her son Astyanax in part because he was to have ruled Asia (748). The barbarian/Greek polarity is further undercut by the privileging of the Trojan women, especially Andromache and Hekabe, over the Greek Helen. Andromache is virtuous and loyal, in contrast to Helen, and Hekabe has the force of reason on her side, traits that Greeks (like Jason in *Medea*, for instance) liked to reserve for themselves.

Athenians in the audience, male or female, could also have identified with the victims—they might have thought of their own women and children who had been taken as slaves at Plataea, for instance; if so, the nobility of the Trojans would be consoling. If they identified with the victors, however, either as men or as Greeks, that nobility and strength of character could of course be intimidating. In the version that I saw in New York City, the point was being made explicitly that the women of Troy were like the women of Afghanistan, left widowed, without housing, and without food, and, like many war widows, the victims of sexual assault. In that production, the women's strength came through loud and clear. It is significant that Kassandra will be responsible for Agamemnon's death.

This analysis is embedded in larger questions about the universal versus the specific meanings of tragedy. In its ancient Athenian production, allusions might have been seen to the Peloponnesian War and to perverted rituals of marriage, as well as to the specifics of warfare between barbarian and Greek. Cautiously, I would say that these plays can also elucidate structures in the relationship between gender, war, and power; there are similarities between the Athenian imperial democracy and modern imperial democracies. In particular, the contemporary reader may find instructive the false excuses given to justify war and the ways in which war's effects may fall differentially on men and women. What do our rulers claim as motives? What happens to women in war today?

Euripides' Hekabe

Hekabe similarly makes it clear that the result of war is death to men, slavery and rape for women. The Trojan Queen is once again the main point of interest, yet her plight is not just her own since she is part of a defeated nation; again the fall of the city is identified with the rape and enslavement of its women. Hekabe in this play, however, is like Clytemnestra (and Medea, as we shall see), a strong, powerful, and deceptive woman who uses rhetoric and social assumptions about femininity to gain revenge; her passive suffering turns to active aggression. We have no date for the play, though, on the basis of metrical evidence, scholars tend to date it to between 428 and 415, and thus during the Peloponnesian War, a time of much cruelty. It is tempting, then, to read its violence as a comment on that wartime situation. That said, the play also makes important contributions to political debates and general themes common to tragedy as a whole.

The action takes place in Thrace during the Greeks' voyage home (see Figure 7). It opens at dawn with a prologue spoken by the ghost of Hekabe's son, Polydoros, who has been killed by the Thracian Polymestor, the family friend (*xenos*) to whom he, along with great quantities of gold, had been entrusted for safe keeping during the war. The first half of the play shifts almost immediately to the sacrifice of Polyxena at the grave of Achilles; at mid-point, the body of Polydoros is found, and the rest of the play is devoted to Hekabe's revenge against Polymestor. Critics have often objected because the structure seems to fall apart, or at least to break in the middle, but the rationale for the structure is made clear in the prologue: Hekabe will suffer the loss of both her children in one day. The body of Polyxena is foregrounded at first, but she yields her place to the body of Polydoros. The two are merely gendered aspects of the same struggle: that of the mother in wartime, doomed to bury her children instead of being buried by them, as was (and is) considered proper.

The play emphasizes marginality in several ways. First the setting would have been marginal for the Greeks, since Thrace was not quite Greece, yet not Troy. The audience is asked to look back on the fallen Troy that has disappeared as well as toward the Greece that lies ahead. The theatrical use of space would have emphasized this duality since the aisles through the theater lead in two different directions, one to the camp and the other to the sea (see Figure 5). Second, the prologue emphasizes the location of the play betwixt and between two other realms, for Polydoros is separated from his body and sends dreams from Hades. He also appears as a ghost. He seems to flit about over his mother's head. The ebb and flow of the waves that wash him ashore emphasize the border quality, as well. Third, as we have seen in other plays, values are fluid and are contested in wartime. Polydoros' speech emphasizes the instability of alliances, and the undermining of codes of human behavior. As we saw in Part I, codes of behavior formed a context for the experience of the audience at tragedy. Guest-friendship (*xenia*) was a system of gift exchange that organized relationships between cities; it, along with suppliancy and the duty to return favor for favor (*kharis*), are put into question in this play.

Polydoros predicts the imminent demise of his sister Polyxena, who will be offered at the grave of Achilles so that the army can return home; thus, beginning and end of the Trojan War were marked by calm winds and the death of virgins. The specter of a beautiful young woman sacrificed to glorify a soldier who was already dead underlines the horror and pointlessness of war. It raises ethical questions that must be asked of any war: Is it honoring the dead to get out of an ill-conceived war, or is it honoring the dead to send more soldiers to replace them? Euripides uses these myths of human sacrifice to question the ideology of war.

What does the first part of the play suggest about masculinity and femininity? The public realm of the male victors and the private realm of female victims are set off against one another there. At first, we seem to be in a play of relentless suffering, like *Trojan Women*. The murder of Polyxena takes place (though offstage) instead of being recounted as a past event (*Trojan Women* 270, 621–30). Hekabe enters from the tent of Agamemnon, and her entrance establishes her exhaustion: she depends on slave women to hold her upright (59–60). Her change in status is emphasized: she is old and, though formerly their queen, she is now a slave like them. The passive tone continues as she recounts her fearful dreams: "I saw the dappled deer killed in the bloody claw [or jaw] of a wolf, having been seized pitilessly from my lap." Then she saw the ghost of Achilles at the crest of his tomb, and he demanded a prize from the much-suffering Trojan women (90–5). Hekabe's speech and her dream reveal her (correct) fears about both her children rolled into one: Polyxena will be seized from her lap; Polydoros has been killed by Polymestor, who is turned into an animal in the imagery at the end of the play. With the emphasis on her lap and breasts, the reader is shown the intimacy of the mother/ child dyad, though Polyxena hardly sits on her mother's lap any more, nor is she a nursing infant.

In contrast, we have the men of the army and their deliberations. As the Chorus narrates it, Achilles only demands that his tomb not go without prize (*ageraston*, 115); he does not specify what the prize should be. A debate ensues about whether (118–19) and what (120–40) to sacrifice. Agamemnon defends Polyxena, but the sons of Theseus retort that they are not going to cheat Achilles for the sake of Agamemnon's relationship with Kassandra (122–9). In the conflict, Odysseus' voice is decisive. While the Athenians put it in terms of sex, he puts it in terms of class: the army ought "not to reject the best of all the Danaans [Greeks] to avoid sacrificing a mere slave" (134–5). The favor that Achilles did for the Greeks must be repaid with a favor in kind.

Hekabe's passivity soon yields to action. She moves quickly from lamentations to speech, noting that she might not be in a position to speak at all, as a slave woman, to a free man (234); her arguments are extremely logical and work against the overwhelming sense of the women's passivity. Throughout her speech she refers to the codes of noble behavior that Odysseus deviates from. She rouses herself (as she does in *Trojan Women*) and attempts also to rouse Odysseus' sense of shame (arguing that "this is bad of him," 251) and of obligation, using the concept of "favor" (276). She reminds him that he was once in her power, and she protected him. He returns her good deeds with bad, as is typical of his ungrateful (*akhariston*) "breed"—those who seek honor by making speeches to the people (254). Hekabe thus attacks the honor of politicians, who attempt to woo the masses and betray the code of helping friends and harming enemies (255–7).

She makes a claim to justice, criticizing the decision to sacrifice her daughter: an animal would have been more appropriate, or if Odysseus wanted to harm those who harmed him, why not kill Helen instead (as Clytemnestra elsewhere looks for a replacement for Iphigeneia)? She is even familiar with Greek law, arguing that it is their *nomos* (law, custom) to treat free and slave the same. At this point in her speech, she has recourse to the generalizations that so often lie behind tragedy: power should not be abused, and everything can change in a day (282–5). Thus, a woman and a slave, by definition lacking power, Hekabe is a consummate rhetorician, even though she criticizes faulty rhetoric as demagoguery. In the speech, as opposed to her duets with daughter or Chorus, there is nothing specifically feminine or barbarian about her; she and Odysseus appear to share a common set of values that she can call upon to enlist his support with the army.

Odysseus' reply to Hekabe's request is not totally without reason. He will save Hekabe, he says, but only her; he will not comply with her request to convince the army to change its decision (302). The military must honor Achilles because if they don't, how will they ever

get soldiers to enlist? The glorious death trumps life, or so he says
(317–20); *kharis* in death is imperishable. In the end, he lumps all the
barbarians together, saying that he hopes that they follow a different
code than his, for if they don't honor the dead, then the Greeks will
win. He takes "doing good to friends" to refer to doing good to the
dead Achilles, not repaying Hekabe for her favor to him.

The women in the play (and perhaps the play itself) critique this
masculinity, pointing out its weaknesses. So, for instance, the Chorus
calls Odysseus a glib man, sweet talker, and one who tries to curry
favor with the people (*dêmokharistês*, 132). They immediately make
the connection to their own powerlessness as slaves (332–3); they have
to bear anything. In this contest, Hekabe appears to be bested, yet
she shows her graciousness as a barbarian queen, and her rhetorical
skill. In the stage action at this point, we must imagine Odysseus trying
to sneak away or in some way avoid Polyxena, for she points out that
he is afraid to meet her gaze and be supplicated by her, lest he have
to do what she asks:

> I see you, Odysseus, hiding your right hand under your cloak, and
> turning your face away, so that I cannot touch your chin. Be brave . . . I
> will follow you, not thanks to necessity, but because it is good to die;
> if I did not think so, I would appear a low woman and a woman too
> much in love with life. (342–8)

The sight of a young woman telling a veteran of the Trojan War
not to be afraid, that she won't touch him, is powerful. Polyxena
enunciates aristocratic virtues here, honorable death over ignoble life,
and she will expand on this theme as the scene continues. She claims
her freedom and says again that she can't bear to be a slave (550–2).
Though she makes much of her freedom of choice, Polyxena nonetheless occupies an object position: as a girl she was bred to be the bride
to a king, and she was looked at beyond other girls and women (355).
She was and will be a prize to be given. On Achilles' grave, she will
again be the object of the gaze.

Her death scene is described very strangely: first she rips her clothing
away from her breasts and chest, then she asks Achilles' son if he would
like to strike her in the chest or cut her throat. Translators debate
whether this action is more sexual or pitiable, but there is no reason
it cannot be both. After she is struck, she falls, taking care "to hide
what should be hidden from men's eyes" (570), probably a reference

to her genitals, since her chest is already bare. As a result of her nobility, Polyxena gains gifts—leaves that might signify masculine athletic victory and the clothing and items of adornment that signify feminine excellence. Despite this evidence of the army's respect, Hekabe is worried about what might happen to her child's body because "in a vast army the undisciplined mob and anarchic sailors can be stronger than fire" (606–8). This line refers to the low status of the sailors in fifth-century Athens, but it also indicates that there is an erotic charge to the sacrifice. Polyxena is after all to be a "bride who was no bride, the maiden who is no maiden"; this, along with the other emphasis on her as a young animal and as a maiden, underlines her sexuality. She is, like other sacrificial heroines, a bride of Hades.

The modern reader has to decide, as we did with Iphigeneia, what to make of Polyxena's apparent freedom. Polyxena's choice, unlike Iphigeneia's similar decision, does not include ratifying a pan-Hellenic, masculinist vision, but it does make her look better than Odysseus, as Iphigeneia upstaged Agamemnon and Menelaus. Her willingness to die also makes it easier for the Greek army, who we remember needed that consent for an efficacious sacrifice. Does she simply reaffirm and give life to aristocratic masculine values that the men no longer sustain? Or does she undercut those who claim to hold those values by virtue of being a virginal female and yet braver than the men?

Hekabe praises her daughter's fine words, but reflects that such nobility brings her pain (382–3). She goes back to the question of virtue later; here she refers to the culture/nature debate and allows for a kind of mixed causality. Nobility is constant, but there is also a role for education: "the worthless are always bad, while the noble is always noble, and their nature is not corrupted by what they experience but are always good. Do the parents or the upbringing make the difference?" (596–9). Hekabe does not take much joy in these reflections, however, as her closing words indicate: "Such things [household wealth and honor among the citizens] are nothing, nothing but resolutions of the will and boasts of the tongue. That one is most blessed to whom nothing bad happens through the day" (627–8).

In the second half of the play, when Polydoros' body is discovered, Hekabe's initial response is a shared song of lament with the Chorus, but once she has identified the murderer and his motive (greed for gold), she turns to speech (as opposed to lyric) and action as opposed to suffering. Mourning is no longer adequate; the situation calls for revenge. Her retaliation provides one of the ethical cruxes of the play:

Does Hekabe become a monster? Does she lose the audience's sympathy? Not necessarily, from the Greek set of cultural assumptions; as Anne Burnett has carefully argued, it was possible to be the instrument of a just revenge, but women were not supposed to be the architects of such actions. As we have seen in the Elektra plays, a woman revenge hero presents fit material for tragedy because of the very problems that it proposes. In *Hekabe* Euripides re-presents the earlier contest of words with Odysseus, staging a scene of persuasion in which Hekabe again faces a Greek hero; this time she asks Agamemnon for his assistance in taking revenge. She specifically invokes his relationship to Kassandra. Hekabe acts as a suppliant; thus ritual gestures link the two scenes in the audience's mind. In each scene the personal claim is tied to a more general norm or law, and in each case the barbarian woman seems more honorable than the Greek man. Hekabe calls not only on the law of hospitality, but also on the universal laws of the gods (798–800). "We believe in the gods because of the laws, which distinguish unjust from just," she says (800–1). Later she adds that it is justice to treat bad men badly (845).

Agamemnon offers Hekabe her freedom (as Odysseus had done earlier), but she turns it down (754–8). What is long life for her? She wants his aid. He rejects her plea because he can't seem to be favoring Hekabe, which would reveal him to be besotted with Kassandra. As we have seen, the "law" of doing good to one's friends and harm to one's enemies depends on the definition of friend; the army thinks that Polymestor is their friend and ally, so Agamemnon can't help her. At this point, Hekabe, like her daughter, takes the high ground and says, "I will free you from fear" (869). Again the woman with nothing to lose is braver than the man with a reputation to uphold: "no mortal is free; one is the slave of possessions or fortune or to the many in the city or written laws that prevent one from acting according to his own judgment" (864–7). Ironically under the circumstances, Hekabe encourages Agamemnon to be brave (875, cf. 345).

Up to this point, it would seem that Hekabe is a pitiable old woman who has the courage of her convictions, though her emphasis on persuasion and sexuality may be of questionable morality (816, 828–30). Then she says that she will "make it all come out well" (875), and we don't know what to think. She will be successful, but is she good? Now the play's evaluation of her perhaps begins to shift. Agamemnon raises gender as a factor, asking her how she, a mere woman, can pay Polymestor back. When she replies that she is not alone but has a community of women in the tents, he is still incredulous—these are slaves, prisoners after all, and still only women. Then Hekabe reminds him of the power of women—to do evil. She mentions the Lemnian women, who were legendary as murderers of their husbands (see *Libation Bearers*, for instance).

Polymestor will later emphasize the fact that women have done this to him (1061–4, 1120–1) and draw a typically misogynistic conclusion: women are evil (1178–81). Moreover, the horror at the vengeance is exacerbated by the way in which the women succeed, which is markedly feminine. Looking at the cloth of Polymestor's robes and delighting in his children, they play on and reverse those gendered assumptions. They pass his sons from hand to hand, until they are out of his reach. In addition, they blind him with clasps that hold their women's robes together, and they kill the children with knives they have hidden in their robes. Thus, women's attire enables them to be successfully deceitful and violent.

The internal scene as described by Polymestor is indeed terrifying and might seem excessive. Even if we accept revenge as a primitive form of justice, Polydoros asked only to be buried; Hekabe blinds Polymestor and kills his two children in retaliation for what he has done. In her defense, however, we must note that Agamemnon has no problem with Hekabe's plan except for his own lack of courage in the face of the army, and he supports her in the contest against Polymestor. Moreover, when Polymestor first enters, he confirms what we have heard about him. He is greedy, a stereotype of the Thracian, and disloyal to his friends; he lies to Hekabe and tries to make his crime seem a virtue by claiming that he acted out of friendship (that word *kharis* again) for the Greeks (1175) and killed Polydoros because he was a Trojan and their enemy.

It is not clear how we are meant to feel—do we blame Hekabe when we see Polymestor's suffering, or do we not pity him? Looking at the element of performance might help: Polymestor enters on all fours, crawling like an animal (1057–9); when he hears that Hekabe is nearby, he wants to tear her to pieces and bloody her flesh (1125–6, 1128). Polymestor is thus bestial when he returns to the stage and does not emphasize the children as he (and Euripides) might have done to increase pity for him. He has to be calmed down by Agamemnon, who tells him to throw savagery (*to barbaron*) from his heart and speak so he can judge. While Hekabe is also a barbarian, that is, a non-Greek, to this point, she has not been represented as a barbarian in the pejorative sense; although both Odysseus and Agamemnon make distinctions between Greek and barbarian in ways that would seem to equate the two foreigners, the stereotype does not hold up since they are so clearly differentiated (as women in the play are differentiated, yet women continue to be lumped together). Has Hekabe in her violence become not only the stereotype of the harmful woman but also the stereotype of the savage barbarian?

Let us not forget, however, that Euripides has also shown the flaws in the Greek men, and Hekabe's initial experience of violence was at their hands. Euripides discourages us from falling into clichés. As we might recognize in the present, terrorism is a technique, not an ideology, and both Greeks and barbarians can use it. If this scene is played coldly, it might seem that this is just a fact: if you push people around, some of them will push back, and they may push a little harder because of the extent of their suffering. How you as an actual reader or viewer will feel will depend in part on the performance, if you see it, and admittedly also on your personal predilections and tolerance for violence.

The play ends with Polymestor delivering a very enigmatic prophecy in which he predicts that Hekabe will become a dog with blazing eyes, and, on her death, the monument on her grave will be a sign (*tekmar*) for sailors (1271, 1273). Readings of the metamorphosis will depend on the moral view you take. It might seem to make her a beneficent signpost keeping sailors from a dangerous passage in the sea, a headland that did exist. Given the political reflections of the play, critics have also taken her as a sign to the audience about the costs of violence, which have been alluded to throughout the play, as well as a reminder that nothing lasts forever. In this context, she could also have been a sign to the Athenians about the ways in which their violence to Sparta might rebound—if you take slaves, you can also be enslaved. Or putting the value differently, we can say that she has now become an animal like Polymestor. It is this kind of ambiguity that makes Greek tragedy so important outside of its own time period.

Euripides' Medea

Medea was produced as the Peloponnesian War was about to begin (431), and it may be that we can see in this play the shadow of the decline of Athens that is to come (page x). Like *Hekabe*, *Medea* depicts a female victim who wreaks vengeance by using deceitful rhetoric. With this play, we leave the huge Trojan War and House of Atreus cycles and enter the wake of the Argonauts, but as will be clear, since Medea is a woman, a foreigner, and semi-divine, the male/female, Greek/barbarian, mortal/immortal oppositions are prominent here as well.

The legend is a complicated one. Like the myth of the House of Atreus, it begins in a dispute over a throne. Pelias killed his brother, Jason's father, and denied Jason his heritage; when Jason returned to claim the throne, Pelias required that he bring him the Golden Fleece, hoping of course that he would fail. Indeed, he might have, for Aietes, the owner of the Fleece, set him the seemingly impossible task of yoking fire-breathing oxen to plow a field, then sow that field with dragon's teeth, and then kill the "sown men" who would grow up from those teeth. Aietes' daughter Medea fell in love with Jason, however, and gave him the tools he needed to accomplish the tasks. The couple had to flee as a result, and in order to facilitate the escape, Medea killed her brother and chopped up his body, strewing the pieces in the sea to slow her father's pursuit of them. When the pair reached Iolkhos again, Medea convinced Pelias' daughters that she could give Pelias youth if they cut him up and boiled him, but he died instead. Jason and Medea then fled to Korinth, where the play opens. By now Jason has taken a new wife, the daughter of the king, Kreon; Medea is about to be sent into exile for the threats she has made against the royal family. She executes a complicated revenge plot, killing the princess, her father, and her own children with Jason; she then escapes in a dragon-drawn chariot.

Medea has been largely defined by that infanticide. A central question in the literature has been why she chooses that method of revenge. Medea's identity is mixed: she is a woman and mother, but she is a foreigner, too, and Denys Page states in his edition of the play that she kills her children as a barbarian and escapes as a witch: "She embodies the qualities which the fifth-century Athenians believed to be characteristic of Orientals" (xxi). That is not strictly true, for she exits in a dragon-drawn chariot sent by her grandfather, the Sun. She is the divine (in the mortal/immortal pairing) as well as the woman (who is masculine) and the foreigner (who lives within the Greek city). Thus, though Jason thinks that Medea acted as a barbarian, stating famously that "there is no Greek woman who would have dared to do these things" (1339–40), we must also consider her as a woman "wronged" and as a demi-mortal.

The dominant narrative in the beginning of the play is that of the abandoned wife, and as such Medea has full sympathy from those around her. The prologue is spoken by an old Nurse, who identifies strongly with Medea, even generalizing about servants sharing their masters' pain (54–5, as do other servants, like the tutor in Euripides' *Hippolytos*). She thinks that Medea is a woman who has been betrayed by Jason, who is now "bedding down in royal marriage" (17–18). The Nurse and Medea are both depicted crying; Medea is wasting away, not eating; she is repeatedly called a "poor wretch." Later Aigeus, King of Athens, enters. He has been to Delphi seeking a cure to his childlessness. He concurs with the Nurse, calling Jason shameless, and is particularly shocked about the way his children are being treated, with their father's tacit approval (695, 707). Medea has right on her side in their eyes, and both Chorus and Aigeus promise to help her: the Chorus with silence (822), Aigeus with the offer of a safe harbor if she accomplishes her goal.

The Nurse ties Medea's suffering to women's lot; she calls it the greatest salvation whenever a woman (or wife) doesn't disagree with (literally, stand apart from) the man (or husband), but in this family, she says ominously, what should be loved is now hated (14–16, cf. 77). When she addresses the Chorus, Medea similarly emphasizes the need for a woman to get along with her husband in marriage. She gives a blistering analysis of the situation of women, the most miserable of creatures (230–1), that applies directly to fifth-century Athenian women (though, as we will see, not to her). She describes the typical marriage, in which a woman is exchanged between men. First, a woman has to buy a husband, a master for her body, and he might be a bad man at that. Then, she has to learn how to get along with him. If it works out, life is "enviable" (243); if not, then a woman might as well die right then, but a man can take a lover (246). The double standard is based on men's role in war; as Clytemnestra was told by Orestes in *Libation Bearers*, women are supposed to be grateful for their life without danger at home. Medea disagrees: she would rather stand behind a shield three times than bear one child (250–1). On the basis of this speech, she gets the Chorus' commitment to help her.

The Chorus sees Medea's situation as part of a general cultural bias against women. The world is topsy-turvy (410–11). Because men sing the songs, they tell malicious stories saying women can't be trusted, but it is actually men who falsify pledges. The Chorus predicts that things are about to change—honor is going to come to women (410–30). In the next strophic pair the women of the Chorus move on to Medea's particular situation. Does that imply that they find hope in Medea's situation? Not in what they say here, but their words suggest that they foresee a time when women's song would tell their side of things. After the plot is well under way, they return again to the unequal access of men and women to the power of song. At this point, they make a generalization: it is better not to have children at all, because that way we suffer less (1081–115). In these songs, the Chorus has referred to the Greek misogynistic literary tradition, assuming that it would be different if women were the poets. The audience must ask what part this text plays in that tradition.

Medea and Jason both give voice to those misogynistic views. Medea says first that women are cowardly in battle, but bloody if wronged in matters of the bed (263–6); then she adds that they are good with poisons (385), least skillful in nobility (*esthlos*, 408), most clever practitioners of evil (408–9). When she claims her status as wife on the basis of her aid to Jason and the oaths that they swore with their right hands (492–5), Jason attacks her as a woman, using a common Greek assumption that women were overly lustful. He gives the goddess Aphrodite credit for everything that Medea did, saying that she had no choice because of her love for him (remember Hekabe's attack on Helen in *Trojan Women*). He asserts that women care only about the "bed" (570), meaning sex. Jason takes the hatred of women to its logical conclusion: a wish that "mortals could engender children from some other place, and there were no race of females; that way there would be no evil to men" (573–5, cf. the misogyny of Hippolytos, which leads to much the same conclusion).

The word for bed, however, stands not only for sexual activity, as Jason thinks (569–73), but also for a woman's position as a wife. Given what Medea has said before, if an ordinary Greek woman does not have a husband, she is without social standing. Medea has given up all for Jason. But, of course, she is not the typical Greek woman whom she analyzes for the Chorus, as she herself acknowledges. She is a foreigner, and even more isolated than they; she does not have a father or a city to go back to, as she later admits, because she destroyed her past to help him (222, 252–8). Her father did not give her away in marriage as was typical in ancient Athens; rather, she was the one who shook hands with Jason, as if they were equal partners. Moreover, the favors that she did for him, such as enabling him to acquire the Golden

Fleece, hardly resemble the dowry a typical woman uses to buy a husband (232). A great part of Medea's success comes from the fact that, like the male actor that she is, she can mimic being a woman, to the Chorus, to Kreon, to Aigeus, and to Jason. When she needs Jason's help to further her plan, she fawns on him as she did on Kreon. She pretends to be the little woman, who should have helped him with his new marriage.

As an imitation woman, Medea is complex and dangerous. She is not simply the sympathetic betrayed woman. From the beginning the Nurse directs us to fear for the children (36, 89–91). Medea presents the murder or sacrifice of the children as inevitable, but it is only inevitable because she has chosen to use them as bearers of the gifts, and even then, if she can get away, why can't she take them with her? It might be awkward but not impossible, as she admits briefly. The more compelling reason has been hinted at from the beginning: she hates the children as a sign of her past relationship to Jason. Moreover, the only way to destroy Jason completely is to kill the children, not because he loves them so dearly (she loves them more) but because it was very important for a Greek man to leave progeny. If she did not already know it, Aigeus' quest for children and Jason's expressed hopes for the children tell her how best to hurt him. She will take her revenge by destroying the future of his house.

The Nurse explicitly worries that Medea will turn her rage against a loved one instead of an enemy (95). Part of what is frightening about Medea appears to be her masculinity, indicated by the code of the warrior applied to her (she is concerned for her honor and justice 20, 21, 26, 33); she won't let someone sing a victory song over her (45), as if she were a contestant in the games. Medea is motivated by aristocratic heroic values: she wants, like the heroes of old, to do good to friends and hurt her enemies, but, of course, as we have seen repeatedly, it is not so simple to define the terms in tragedy. In helping Jason, her beloved, she betrayed her father and killed her brother, also loved ones. The past murders are alluded to once by the Nurse (9, 31–2), then by Medea (502–5), and again by Jason at the end (1332).

Like a typically heroic male, Medea adopts a value system in which what is good (*kalos*) is bravery, and what is bad (*kakos*) is cowardice or softness. The values of noble masculinity conflict with her love for her children: she does not want to provide her enemies with the opportunity to laugh at her (383).

I cry out at such a deed that must be done next; I will kill my children; there is no one else who will rescue them; having torn down the entire house of Jason, I will leave this land, fleeing the murder of my dearest children, having dared the most unholy deed. For to be laughed at by enemies is not to be borne, friends. (791–7)

She is in conflict between two traditional values. Avoiding laughter requires that she harm her loved ones.

Medea also has to go against her feelings as a mother in order to accomplish her heroic goals. There is a very famous monologue in which Medea debates with herself whether she should actually go ahead with her plan. When the children are an abstract tool of her vengeful right hand, which Jason has betrayed, she has no problem contemplating her action, but when she sees them, and, more particularly, touches their soft flesh and feels their sweet breath, she is almost broken. In this reading, at the end of the play she moves toward the heroic male, away from normative female behavior.

In Jason's view, she is also moving toward the barbarian, not the Greek, pole. Indeed, the male/female opposition seems to map onto that of Greek/barbarian. Medea is from Kolkhis, which in myth was settled by Ethiopians; Herodotus called them dark and woolly haired (2.104; also Pindar, *Pythian* 4.212). In the play, her foreignness is marked; she comes from the far side of the Black Sea, past the crashing rocks of the Symplegades (2). Costume could be significant here. If she wore typical Greek dress until her escape, that would indicate that she has changed status in the end; but if she were consistently dressed in foreign garb, she would have been marked as different throughout. In either case, the barbarian theme is explicit. Medea believes that Jason has tired of her barbarian bed (591) and wants a royal bride. Jason, on the other hand, thinks that he doesn't have to be grateful to Medea, doesn't owe her any favors, because he has already given her the benefits of Greek civilization (532–41), justice and law, and fame for her wisdom. If she were in a barbarian land, she would not have these great advantages. Medea laughs at the idea that she has benefited from the rule of law that he boasts about, and she surely does not benefit from her reputation for wisdom (Kreon mistrusts her and exiles her precisely because of this reputation). Jason sees himself as a rational, Greek male—he has made this new alliance out of the best motives for his present family, not out of lust. He has a plan for political and material gain: his sons will have new brothers and an assured position in a foreign land (559–67, 595–7). He makes a final distinction between Medea as a barbarian and any Greek woman (1330–1), saying that he ought to have known what she would be like given what she had done to her father. Medea has many of the stereotyped attributes of the "barbarian" ascribed to her, though of course the Greeks were no strangers to emotionalism, gold, violence, and so forth.

At the same time, as we saw above, she is more an aristocratic Greek man than Jason, holding onto the oath that they swore to one another, and she has a claim to justice. Fifth-century Athenian concerns about clever people (the sophists) are subtly represented in her defense of her behavior to the Chorus and to Kreon, and the Chorus explicitly asks her how Athens will be able to receive a child-killer. As you recall, Athenians excelled at rhetoric but were simultaneously concerned about its power (Chapter 2); Medea explicitly disdains Jason's skill in rhetoric and would punish him even more because of his way with words (580–1). Scholars point out that Jason, like Agamemnon and Odysseus in the other plays, seems like the real-life Athenian man, not the commander of the legendary Argonauts. At this point, when Medea is at her haughtiest, it would seem that, as in *Agamemnon*, *Iphigeneia at Aulis*, and *Hekabe*, the "realistic" contemporary male looks shabby compared to the heroic female. But nothing is simple in this play, and, as I mentioned earlier, Medea is herself a rhetorician with the best of them.

Medea is also not quite human. She is so willful that she is from the beginning described as impassive, like a force of nature, a rock or the sea waves (28–9, cf. 107, a storm cloud). The Nurse calls Medea savage and hateful, self-willed (103–4); she is a bull and a lion, a wild thing (92, 103, 187, 188). In the end Jason accuses Medea of being a lioness (1342). She also participates in the divine plane, with immortal ancestry (her grandfather is Helios, and her aunt is the sorceress Circe), and she may be the "spirit" who is angry and will bring destruction to the house of Jason (129–30). Medea makes the claim that if Jason is not punished, there will be no more reciprocal oaths nor modesty (492–5); in Medea's view, she is the agent of the gods maintaining the sanctity of the oaths that he betrayed (1013–14, 1059). That divine status is corroborated in her final appearance in the place usually reserved for the *deus ex machina*, and her declaration that she will found a cult.

Her behavior is, therefore, quite complex in its motivation. What about the emotional effect on the audience? There is reason to think that she forfeits the audience's sympathy. For instance, the Chorus initially sided with Medea, as we saw. But the infanticide goes too far for the women of Corinth. They try to talk her out of killing her children, and explicitly say that her action will be against human laws (812); they tell her not to do it (813, 853–5) and predict that it will make her the most wretched of women (818). They wonder how Athens can welcome such a person, an unholy child-murderer (849–50). They ultimately come to feel sorry for the princess, though they still feel that Jason suffers justly (1232). Euripides may be making Medea monstrous since she practically salivates over the long and luxurious description of the painful death suffered by the princess and Kreon (1135, where she is somewhat like Clytemnestra rejoicing in the fertilizing blood bath from Agamemnon).

Are there grounds for continuing to side with Medea? What other recourse did Medea have if Jason had to be punished for breaking his oath, as they agree he did? Medea and the Chorus have already talked about the wrongs of women. Of course, an ordinary woman would simply have had to accept the hand she had been dealt (according to Medea's early speech to the Chorus). But Medea is not ordinary. Her escape in the dragon-drawn chariot may help here. There is not even the hint of punishment in store for her except for the suffering that she has brought on herself. This escape does not have to signify divine approval of Medea; it might stand for her transformation into a god, and therefore her subjection to different codes of behavior. Gods are capable of great cruelty (see, for instance, the *Bacchai* or *Hippolytos* of Euripides). In this reading, she is no longer subject to mortal justice or mortal feelings, of either pleasure or pain, and the author would not expect her to arouse pity, only fear.

The problematic revenge and the rescue, however, have many potential interpretations. For the ancient Greek, the play may confirm Greek fear of barbarian excess in showing the victory of a foreign wise woman over a Greek hero. Because that hero does not seem very heroic, the play may also critique the masculine values in the person of Jason. The presentation of Jason's mealy-mouthed rhetoric and his lack of masculinity might also sound like a critique of fifth-century politicians. It may critique those values through Medea as well, since her acceptance of that ideology led her to kill her children. The play shows the price that must be paid if you have that warrior mentality, and shows it up more clearly because the words come from a woman's mouth. It might, then, have made Greek men in the audience fearful about this code when they saw that it would cut off the future by devouring the young. Given the date of the play's first performance, it might have seemed to the audience like a reflection on the coming war.

If ancient women were in the audience, they might have responded differently from either citizen men or foreign men. The infanticide might support a misogynist belief in women's dreadful capability for evil: this is the most fearful thing that a woman could do. Sentimentality about the children might, however, be *our* problem; Euripides certainly spends little time on them, compared to the time spent on Jason and Medea's suffering. In fact, however, Medea doesn't really succeed as a woman or as a human but rather by killing off the maternal/human side of her duality in order to become more fully the divinity that protects oaths (Burnett). She is then free of the constraints on her life as a woman, imposed by childbearing.

Modern readers will bring different emphases to the text. I will sketch in a few of them here, but there are many others. Because of the escape, the play can be taken as a feminist tract. Euripides does not discipline or punish Medea, and some viewers or readers respond "bravo Medea" for her bravery. A modern woman might also interpret *Medea* as an example of the double bind that afflicts women in modern life: the only way to achieve success in the world is by eliminating the feminine and maternity. If we take seriously the fact that Medea is an imitation of a "real" woman, that is, an actor is behind the female mask, we can emphasize the fact that she is not a woman at all. She is a radical "other." Given all that, can the play still arouse terror at women's ascribed capacity for violence? This play with its infanticide and its freeing of Medea in the end seems to insist that the audience question simple dichotomous thinking.

7

The King and I

In this chapter, we turn our attention to another family, that of the Labdacids, the royal family of Thebes; Sophocles' *Antigone* and *Oedipus Tyrannos* address the relationship of king to subject, placing it in the context of gender relations and the relationships of mortal to god. Thus, these plays interrelate two of the ways of looking at tragedy in its Athenian context set out in Part I, the political and the religious. We will start with *Antigone* since it was written first, though it takes place later in the mythic cycle. As you will remember from earlier discussions (Chapter 3), it had been prophesied that Oedipus, son of Laios and Jokasta, would kill his father and marry his mother; although his parents exposed him, he survived and lived to fulfill the prophecy while he thought he was avoiding it. He blinded himself when he discovered what he had done. After the end of the *Oedipus Tyrannos*, he leaves Thebes, wandering with Antigone until he reaches Kolonos, where he dies (in other versions, he remained in Thebes). His sons, Polyneikes and Eteokles, who were to have shared the throne instead fought over it. At the opening of *Antigone*, they are both dead.

Antigone was probably written around 442 or 441, judging from a summary preceding the text (called a *hypothesis*) that tells us that the poet was awarded a generalship in the Samian expedition after his successful production of this play. Unfortunately this possible correlation of political and theatrical success does not indicate in any secure way how we should interpret the play. It does, however, encourage us to take into account the political climate in interpreting *Antigone*. Perikles' program of celebration of Athens was in full swing, and the building of the Parthenon had begun. Officially at peace with Sparta, Athens was nonetheless consolidating its power in the Aegean, expanding in Southern Italy and asserting its power in Samos. The play was composed at a time when the democracy was fully established, yet, as with Aeschylus' *Persians* and the *Oresteia*, the threats of tyranny were not far in the past, and there was tension between the strength of aristocratic families who constituted the ruling elite and the *dêmos*. Remember that the desire to control aristocratic families' rivalry made up part of the motivation for the suppression of lamentation and the establishment of the funeral oration for fallen warriors. These issues came up, for instance, in our discussion of *Elektra*; *Antigone* is like *Elektra* in many ways, and is, as we shall see, intimately tied up with burial and lament.

The central issue in the play is the burial of Polyneikes. Eteokles has been given a lavish public funeral, but Kreon, their uncle and ruler as a result of the war, has forbidden the burial of the brother he deems an enemy to the state. Antigone, acting on the duty she feels as a family member to uphold unwritten laws, defies his order and covers the corpse with dust. Kreon sentences her to death by starvation in a cave that will be her tomb, but changes his mind when the prophet Teiresias informs him that the omens indicate that the gods are unhappy and that he has disrupted the natural order. In a classic case of too late learning, which often marks tragedy, he goes first to bury Polyneikes, and arrives at the cave only to find Antigone dead in the arms of Haimon, her betrothed and Kreon's son. Haimon attacks his father, and when he misses, turns his sword on himself. Eurydice, Kreon's wife, kills herself while cursing him for the deaths of Haimon and their other son who died in the war.

Antigone has been at the center of philosophic interest in tragedy; questions about it relate to the interpretation of some of the statements implicitly made above—i.e., that the play focuses on state vs. family, human law vs. divine law. One of the related debates has been "who is the tragic hero?" Was Antigone the hero and Kreon the villain? Were they both equally "the hero"? As the play has been more contextualized in recent interpretations, that question has become less pressing, and it now seems clear that there is no single protagonist. It is impossible to eliminate one or the other figure: Antigone represents one kind of "hero," the intransigent character who will not yield, but Kreon is an essential participant and dominates the end of the play.

Indeed, he embodies the classic structure of the good man who experiences a fall because of an error.

Though each character seems to stand for a fairly identifiable position that has ethical consequences, there are also no moral absolutes here, and critics can marshal lines of text to support apparently opposite opinions. Hegel treated the play several times and, to risk oversimplifying, held that both Kreon and Antigone were right to some extent, but also both wrong; each is one-sided, and the resolution will be a synthesis (cf. Nussbaum). Hegel's view that the family and the state collide here has been well criticized, and there is no real evidence of progress at the end, yet some account of the divisions (male/female, young/old, *oikos/polis* [household/city], divine law/human law, or individual conscience/city law) must be taken into consideration. The characters share a discourse, but they use it differently because they come from different perspectives—so Kreon might not be irreligious but might simply worship different gods than Antigone does.

Structurally, the play develops through several main confrontations: Antigone-Ismene, Antigone-Kreon, Kreon-Haimon, Kreon-Teiresias. Sophocles chooses to start with a scene between Antigone and her sister Ismene, laying out the assumptions of appropriate behavior for a woman (as he does with Khrysothemis and Elektra in his *Elektra*). Ismene is a passive, fearful woman, while Antigone is brave and fearless (which Ismene interprets as foolhardy). After informing Ismene about Kreon's pronouncement, Antigone asks her to help bury Polyneikes. Ismene explicitly says that they can't go against the edict of the city (44, cf. 7) because they are women (61–2), and therefore they are weaker. Antigone argues that they owe loyalty to the family (45) and to the dead, since death is for eternity (75–6); moreover, it seems noble to her to die in burying Polyneikes (72–5). Antigone is first introduced as a transgressive woman in contrast to her sister, a normative woman, yet like Elektra, Antigone is not completely off the map of femininity; she adheres not only to the laws of the gods, but also to the traditional role of a woman in caring for the dead. She asserts later that her nature is to join in love, not hate (523), which also sounds like part of the definition of appropriate femininity.

But even these seemingly clearly laudable values are questioned. Though loyalty to family is a good thing, this family is incestuous, as Ismene emphasizes (49–57). Later on we will see that Antigone is aberrant in that she does not transfer her fidelity to her husband's family, as the appropriate Athenian woman would. The language implies that her desire to *bury* the dead is a desire *for* the dead: "It is a fine thing for me to die doing this. A loved one, with him a loved one I shall lie, having gone beyond the law in performing holy deeds" (72–4). The task has the chill of death about it, but Ismene says she brings a hot heart to it (88, cf. later when Kreon tells Haimon that he will have a cold embrace if he lies with Antigone [650]). There is an erotic component to her whole project, as is revealed when Ismene accuses Antigone of being in love with the impossible (90). Moreover, at the end of the scene, Antigone reveals that the respect she shows for the dead is not a love for her family in general and in all situations: she is willing to consider Ismene her enemy (93) for disagreeing with her. Thus it is only the relationship to the brother that counts with her (cf. Elektra and Orestes' urn).

Antigone's values deviate from ideological femininity. She, like Elektra, stakes her claim on the nobility and bravery of her position and challenges Ismene to live up to the strength of her forebears (38); she later reiterates her heroic desire to die nobly or well (97). Her version of the good is folly to Ismene and Kreon. She counts early death a profit (*kerdos*, a recurring word in the play) because her life is so unpleasant (461–2); she is the living dead (559–60, cf. Elektra). Like Khrysothemis, Ismene is an ordinary woman, not heroic; the heroine is outside the boundaries of the norm for a woman (and most men)—she will get the glory she wants only in death. Indeed her acceptance of death may enable her to act nobly. Is she sick or a heroine, or is the heroine she who is sick by her society's standards?

Kreon is also a complicated figure. He is not simply a wrongheaded tyrant but has some right on his side. Ismene implies that he has acted democratically, for she uses the word *psêphon*, the pebble used for casting a vote in Athens, for his decree. Though he is called "*tyrannos*," he does not seem to have exceeded his powers at this point (60). As an appropriate constitutional leader, Kreon is coming for a special consultation with the Chorus of elders (156, 160–1). Moreover, Polyneikes posed a real threat, as the first choral song makes clear—the enemy was raging like a maenad (136–7) against the city. Kreon claims to have righted the state; Polyneikes has not been faithful to his fatherland (182), and will not be buried because no enemy of the land can be his friend (187–8).

The desecration of the corpse is described at length, but the Chorus neither criticizes nor endorses Kreon's position. It simply acknowledges his power. The decision might or might not have sounded a false note to an ancient audience—the burial given to Eteokles would have sounded like the public funerals of Athenian war dead and so might have put the present day in the audience's mind. The obligation to bury the (enemy) dead was contested in antiquity, as we can see from other plays (Euripides' *Suppliants* or Sophocles' *Ajax*); however, Athens specifically prided itself on its defense of the Argive dead. Burial of Athenian dead was an issue after the battles of Delium and Arginusae (424 and 406), and the generals at the latter were themselves executed for leaving the dead behind. Finally, even if Athenians denied traitors burial within Attica, they typically allowed relatives to bury them on foreign soil. Kreon is the only surviving male relative of Polyneikes, and as such he actually has an obligation to bury him. The proper woman family member would prepare the body for burial and sing the lament over the corpse. Kreon, however, defines Polyneikes only as the enemy, while for Antigone, Polyneikes is first and foremost a beloved family member.

Kreon's first image as a fair-minded leader begins to erode immediately, however. A guard enters to report that someone has symbolically covered the dead. He beats around the bush, as Kreon notes (237, 241–2), because he is afraid (223–36). When the Chorus raises the possibility that this first burial might be some god's will (278–9), Kreon bristles (280). He starts to sound like the problematic tyrant: the gods can't possibly have supported *his* enemy! It must be a conspiracy of those who were complaining about him before and "won't justly bear the yoke" (289–92). He jumps to the conclusion that there has been bribery and embarks on a strange criticism of the evils of currency. In these scenes, Sophocles delineates a Kreon who is developing away from what at first seemed reasonable in his decision.

When Kreon and Antigone meet after she is caught in the act of burying her brother, the themes of divine law/human law, family/city and female/male are sharply etched. Kreon asks if she has dared to go against the law (449), and she says bitingly: "Surely, since it was not Zeus who proclaimed these laws, nor did that Justice who resides with the gods below ordain them for mankind. And I did not think that your proclamations had such strength to overrun the unwritten and unshakeable laws of the gods" (450–5). She repeats some of what she had said to Ismene, specifically that she has no intention of putting fear of a man ahead of rendering justice to the gods (458–60). Antigone understands that we all die, and it does not matter to her if it is sooner or later; therefore, she is free of Kreon's control. She exults in having performed this action. The state cannot rupture her blood ties; brother remains brother whether he is the city's enemy or not.

Kreon reads this as a gender struggle. He finds her excessive, rebellious in transgressing the laws and reveling in having done so. At lines 484–5, he says, "Now then I am not a man, but she herself is the man, if the power [or rule] rests with her, and she is unpunished." He ends with this statement: "From now on, it is necessary for these to be women, not to be let loose" (578–9). Since brides were conceived of as yoked in marriage, women who run loose would be like his citizens who don't bear the yoke and thus may form part of the political revolt that Kreon fears (291–2). As a man, he believes that he must rule; his place is in the public domain, and women must be kept inside (whether that is in the house or in the tomb that he plans for Antigone). While Kreon started with an almost rational position, his desire for control and his fear of being bested by a woman (not hatred for Polyneikes) later distort his reason.

This ruler who is anxious about his masculinity cannot allow himself to be defeated by a girl. He also cannot be defeated by a younger man, and in particular, must rule his son (726–7). Kreon starts by asking Haimon if he's come raging at the decree against his bride to be, or "are we dear (*philoi*) to you whatever we do?" (634). Haimon says "I am yours," and, unlike Antigone, he commits himself to agreeing with all of Kreon's opinions. He goes further and says that he will not place his marriage above his father (637–8, cf. 639–40). Haimon tries to reason with his father, but Kreon can't tolerate it. He sees two diametrically opposed positions, defense of the woman or loyalty to him as the father. He ends his long speech making it explicit: they, as men, can't be the inferior of women (680, see also 740, 741, 746, 756). Haimon disagrees and says that he is only ruled by a woman if his father is a woman.

There is a general political disagreement at the basis of these arguments. Kreon believes in the absolute power of the city's law and his own authority in it (663–5); Antigone has opposed him with eternal law, while Haimon tries to educate him about the political reality. The son begins by speaking non-confrontationally so that he can get his father to listen to him. He tells Kreon that Antigone has supporters among the people (690–700, cf. 509). His message would have resonated powerfully in fifth-century Athens, as it does today: no city belongs to one man, and if Kreon continues this way, he will be the ruler of an empty desert (737, 739).

In this play (and others, for instance *Elektra* and *Oedipus Tyrannos*), learning is important. There are different kinds of wisdom, as we saw in the opening scene between Ismene and Antigone. Ismene early on says "think" (*phronêson*, 49), and in her parting words she accuses Antigone of being witless, though avowing that she is still dear to her (98–9). Antigone and Kreon each think the other is a fool (562, 469–70). Haimon urges his father to learn (723) and change his mind. As is often the case in tragedy, the Chorus blandly thinks that each should learn from the other (724–5), but Kreon does not believe that youth can teach wisdom to its elders. When he acts like a tyrant, he falls prey to his own warning to Antigone about the danger of "over-rigid minds" (473), as Haimon warns him in turn (710–11). Haimon tells his father that wisdom consists in the ability to learn; there is nothing shameful in not being stretched too taut, and he points out the success of trees that yield (712–14). Although as an adult man Kreon is properly invested with the rule, he has to modify his behavior. As a result of his actions, he loses everything and rules in the desert that Haimon predicted for him.

After the scene with Haimon, the clock is wound and the alarm is set. Kreon embodies an overly rigid masculine principle. He is driven to conquer and enslave all who oppose him, in order to bolster his position as the man in charge, and he has created a fearful populace as a result. Kreon simply does not recognize alternative value systems. Polyneikes is not only an enemy but is also closely related to Kreon. Though the ruler is not completely anti-religious—he refers to Zeus (184, 304)—his confidence that the gods only ratify his city-dominated view of things (288) is a sign of his ignorance. By the end of the scene with his son, Kreon has developed to the point where he is sadistic, threatening Haimon with marriage to a corpse; like Aigisthos in the *Oresteia*, his lack of manliness has made him a bully to those weaker than himself.

What about his opponent, Antigone? Her trajectory is not so clear. Antigone stands for family and the unwritten laws of the gods, and she will not yield to the authority of the king, whose edicts do not come from Zeus. Yet she is from the beginning represented ambiguously—she turns quickly on her sister, for instance, and her devotion to the brother could be a sign of the family's incest. Is she just reenacting the harsh temper she inherited from her father, as is suggested (471–2)? The Chorus asks whether it is not the curse of the family coming out in her, and she admits that she is worried about that possibility (856–62).

The difficulty in making her the principled individualist standing against the state is exacerbated by her *kommos* with the Chorus and her last speech. Here she emphasizes her regret, her status as maiden, about to be married to death (810–16, 867–8), not her glory (cf. Iphigeneia, Polyxena, and the other Trojan women). She bemoans the fact that she will never be a wife or mother, and while the regret humanizes her, it also makes her less heroic. Ironically, the description of Haimon's death suggests sexual relations, with its heavy breathing, embrace, and blood evoking defloration (1236–9). Antigone's earlier longing to lie with the dead Polyneikes comes to fruition in this wedding of corpses: "Corpse lies with corpse, poor wretch, obtaining his marriage rites in the house of Hades" (1240–1).

As she confronts the actuality of death, Antigone (like Medea about to murder the children) is more aware of what she will be missing, and she then articulates her rationale. Feeling abandoned by her family, she wants the respect of the Chorus as she goes to her grave. She goes through a calculation of familial relations and says that she would not have taken her extreme position for just any member of her family, but "Since my parents are hidden in Hades, there can be no other brother born again" (911–12). Critics sometimes go so far as to cut this speech because it seems out of place, but it simply shows that she acknowledges that there are alternative laws (908), that there is no absolute necessity that she give up her life to bury every family member, only the irreplaceable brother (and not a sister). In choosing death over marriage, in choosing her brother over Haimon, she is in effect reproducing the incest that has shadowed her decision all along, as we saw above. Antigone is isolated; she is a marriageable woman surrounded by the male elders of the Chorus who are more judgmental than sympathetic. As a result, she blames the gods (922–3), who have failed her as allies, and complains that she has gained a reputation for impiety though she was pious.

Despite her despondency, she exits once more asserting her piety (lines 924 and 943 use the same word). The judgment of the gods is about to come. Though Kreon believed that he was creating order with his laws, the final conflict, between the blind prophet Teiresias and Kreon, makes it explicit that the king was wrong. He has created the chaos he feared, confusing the living and the dead, keeping above ground what should be buried, and burying what should be allowed to live (1068–71). As a result, the city is polluted, and the birds murder one another (1003–4). In this play, the political and the ritual interrelate; the sacrifices are not successful because of Kreon's law (1006–7, 1019–22). Teiresias' speech refers back to the dialogue between Haimon and Kreon; he, too, urges learning, and says that he speaks for Kreon's "profit" (1031–2). Kreon refuses and accuses the seer of seeking his own profit (1047, 1055). As a tyrant, he sees corruption everywhere, and he refuses even if it is Zeus' will (1040). This is the peak of his arrogance, and he is reviled by Teiresias, who prophesies his doom. In conversation with the Chorus, Kreon decides to yield (1096), even though it is terrible to do so, and he now acknowledges that these are the established laws (1113).

We have spent much of this section on the characters, but the odes in this play address the complex character of the cosmos in which the actors find themselves and relate the specific action to Athenian and contemporary concerns. Right after the Chorus has heard about the miraculous burial of Polyneikes, it sings the so-called "ode on man." The ode starts by calling human beings (the generic term for man, *anthrôpos*, is used here) a "wonder," like the many other "wonders" of the natural world. The word *deinos* has a broad range of connotations, both positive and negative; it can refer to something that is wondrous or frightening (somewhat like the relationship between full of awe and awful). The human tames the natural world in the first two stanzas, and then gains language and airy thought; resourceful in all situations (*pantoporos*), mortals are without resource (*aporos*) only in the face of Death (360–2). But all this can turn to ill if they exceed the laws of the land and the justice of the gods; then from being blessed with a lofty city they turn to being without city (367–71).

This song can be taken to refer to Antigone, who, on the one hand, is represented as part of the nature to be subdued: she has been hunted as a wild thing and is birdlike in her mourning. But, on the other hand, she is also introduced by the Chorus as "a marvel" (376), and, most particularly, she is the one who apparently defies the city's laws. The ode can also plainly refer to Kreon, who seeks to tame the earth and the citizens and use his cunning intelligence to rule. The dual connotation of *deinos* would then also adhere to his actions. In his desire to control, he goes too far. There are larger Athenian resonances as well. The song is a paean to human Promethean ingenuity: fifth-century Athens was the center of culture and progressive thought like that exemplified in the first two stanzas. In that respect the song has been taken as referring to Periklean Athens or even Perikles himself.

After Kreon pronounces the death sentence on both sisters, the Chorus sings another philosophical song. The phrasing situates Antigone's implacable stance in the family curse, implying that she is a Fury (604); but this time the lines also put the troubles of the house of Labdacus in the context of a god-driven destruction that will not leave (584–5). The immortal and timeless gods, specifically Zeus, dominate. And they cause destruction, as the repetition of the word "*Atē*" (meaning disaster, but also infatuation or curse) implies. Though the Chorus specifically refers to Antigone ("the last of the house of Oedipus," 600), Kreon is also one who "mistakes the bad for the good because the gods are bringing him to destruction" (620–5).

When Haimon storms off, mumbling curses that his father does not understand, Kreon announces his full and horrible plan to the Chorus: he will bury Antigone alive with enough food for a few days so that the city will not be polluted. What comes after is a hymn to "Eros the unvanquished in battle." For an ancient Greek audience, the conflict between father and son would have been very disturbing; the Chorus here seems to side with Kreon in attributing the dispute to Haimon's love for Antigone. Eros is damaging, stirring up trouble and strife between these men. The one who feels desire is mad (790). Desire is also described more positively as a "gleaming yearning [either seated in the bride's eyes, or desire for her]" that is "victorious and is enthroned with the great laws" (the text is debated here, 795–800). But there is still the implication of danger, since "Aphrodite the unconquerable strikes." What motivates this song? On one level, the desire would seem to be the sexual love of marriage, given the references to the bride, and thus the ode would seem to be about the relationship of Antigone and Haimon. Or should we say that Kreon was mistaken in fighting against love (family love as well as erotic love), which he did not understand was unconquerable? But it is also perhaps Kreon's *erōs*, his desire for power and control, that led him into this conflict. Finally, the Chorus, and perhaps the audience, looking at Antigone feel the power of desire and are taken off the track of the law (801). Having been reluctant to praise her, they are now smitten as they see her going to her tomb like a bride to her marriage chamber. They acknowledge that she has won praise and fame (817).

The Chorus members continue to place Antigone in the company of the gods. At the end of the next choral song, they summarize a complicated set of mythological parallels with the remark that fate is terribly powerful (951, *Moirai* 987). After the Teiresias scene, when the Chorus is relieved that Kreon has changed his mind, they sing an ode praising Dionysos. While the cheerful surface meaning is an example of irony and acts to heighten the suffering to come, there are also threatening undertones. In the previous song, Dionysos' punitive side was referred to, and earlier references in this play to Capaneus raging like a mad bacchant against Thebes (136), as well as what is known about the god elsewhere, would have perhaps incited fear in the audience. Thus, the male/female struggle for power, the contest between the city and the family, between mortal law and divine law, are all put in the larger cosmos in which the gods have power to bless but also to destroy.

The play ends with the emotional destruction of Kreon, who now replaces Antigone as the living dead (1167). The messenger describes the scene at the cave in which Haimon kills himself after attempting to kill his father and dies embracing his bride-to-be; Eurydice, the wife and mother, kills herself when she hears what has happened and dies cursing Kreon. To return to the question of the play's relationship to Athens: Why would the success of this play, which depicts the failure of a ruler, lead to the political appointment of its author? Is that testimony that this interpretation of his appointment is foolish, or is it testimony to the ability of Athenian citizens to ask challenging questions about power relationships? Or, is it that the chastened Kreon stands for the successful ruler, not that the challenger to his rule is fully embraced? After all, the gods do not rescue Antigone as they do Medea.

Antigone has continued to fascinate writers and readers, especially following the French Revolution up through the present. It has been reproduced and adapted by creative writers more often than almost any other tragedy and has had a place in philosophy, where it is often referred to when questions of conflicting rights are at issue. The character and play have also gained the attention of post-Freudian, post-structuralist psychoanalyst Jacques Lacan. Lacan said of her, "it is Antigone herself who fascinates us, Antigone in her unbearable splendor. She has a quality that both attracts us and startles us, in the sense of intimidates us; this terrible, self-willed victim disturbs us" (247).

But Luce Irigaray interrogates that attraction, reclaiming a political Antigone who "respects the natural and social order by genuinely (not metaphorically) respecting the earth and the sun. . . . Her example is always worth reflecting upon as a historical figure and as an identity or identification for many girls and women living today" (69–70). She has been taken up as an icon by feminists and those seeking justification for civil disobedience. More recently Judith Butler has looked for a way to read Antigone in the context of "publicly ungrievable losses" (24).

In the end, we must ask again how the play affects us, its current readers or audience members. While it is easy for critics to say that we in our time admire those who stand up against authority, it is also easy to see that the definition of resistance is relative. How you feel about Antigone or Kreon in this play will again depend on where you are coming from. My students, for instance, were divided between those who saw Antigone as someone who martyred herself and who wanted attention, and those who admired her for standing up to the powerful ruler. There is an interesting debate about Jean Anouilh's *Antigone*, which is more a version than a translation. It is often taken to be an attack on the Vichy government during the Nazi occupation of France, since it was produced in 1944; the ancient text enabled him to elude the censors. More recently, however, the sympathetic portrayal of Kreon has seemed to challenge that reading, and in fact my students did not see Antigone as a hero. In retrospect, it appears that the censors might not have been fooled but may have understood what Anouilh was doing—issues of morality are rendered complex in the play.

Sophocles' Oedipus Tyrannos

This balance of the responsibility of the gods and the choices of humans is the core of our final text. *Oedipus Tyrannos* (often translated *Oedipus the King*) is one of the most frequently taught and studied of the tragedies, and it is popularly considered an example of the typical tragic plot—the fall of a good person from a high place because of pride. It is difficult but important to try to read the play freshly, unprejudiced by conventional ideas. As with most of Sophocles' plays, we do not know securely the date of the first production, though through stylistic analysis and external evidence (the plague in the play is taken by some to have been suggested by the plague in Athens that killed Perikles and many others in 430), it would seem to be in the middle period; it was written after *Antigone*, but it takes place before.

Like Antigone, Oedipus has a reputation that goes far beyond Sophocles' play. Asked who Oedipus was, most people would probably say something like this, "He was the man who was fated to kill his father and sleep with his mother." Because the history is not narrated directly in the text, readers are forced to piece it together, though most of the original audience would have known the basic outline before coming to the theater (which creates the dramatic irony). As you remember from earlier discussions, Laios and Jokasta had a child, but fearing a prophecy that it would kill its father, they exposed it; the baby was saved and adopted by Merope and Polybos, the Queen and King of Korinth. Hearing accusations that his father was not really his father, Oedipus went to the oracle at Delphi, where he was told that he was fated to kill his father and marry his mother. To avoid that fate, he exiled himself from Korinth. On his way from Apollo's sanctuary, however, he had an altercation with a stranger on the road and killed him and his party. Oedipus, arriving in Thebes after the death of the king (who was thought to have been killed by robbers), solved the riddle of the Sphinx, thus ending the monster's siege on the young men of the city. In gratitude the city gave him the throne and Jokasta as wife.

All that has happened in the past—in the play's present Thebes suffers from a plague. The oracle at Delphi tells the Thebans that they must find Laios' murderer, who is the cause of the city's pollution, and either exile or kill him. In searching for that man, Oedipus finds himself: he discovers that he has killed his father and married his mother, and has sired four children by her. As a result Jokasta kills herself, and he blinds himself. It is often described as a hermeneutic plot, or a detective story, or even as an analogue for psychoanalysis because of its emphasis on self-discovery and knowledge.

Oedipus Tyrannos moves back and forth between the political and ritual dimensions that we looked at in Part I. Oedipus is the king and a ruler, and the play has been taken to reflect on Athens or Perikles. But the text also consistently refers to fate and oracles as conditioning human existence. As we discussed earlier (see Chapter 3), humans are placed between the animals and the immortals, and the myths as well as ritual try to mediate between the spheres; tragedy, and this play in particular, reveals the discomfort of the human position in the middle.

Religion and politics mix as the play opens. We see a crowd of suppliants outside the palace; their priest approaches the king. The people show a tendency to worship the king since they are seated at his palace not a sanctuary and refer to his altars (16); based on his having saved them from the Sphinx, they call on him to save them again (as mortals routinely call on the gods). Moreover, the setting would have been familiar to the audience from the Thargelia (Vernant and Vidal-Naquet 127–35), a ritual observance that purified towns of defilement by driving out selected scapegoats. The god has sent a plague on the whole city, and it, too, is mixed; its effects are both political and natural. The city like a ship founders in bloody foam (an image which draws on the typical metaphor of the ship of state), but it is also withering away: plants, animals, and women can't bring forth fruit (25–7). The Chorus will later develop these themes: the whole city is affected, but the women and children in particular suffer (169–73, 180–5). When Kreon returns from the oracle, he announces that they must "drive away the contamination (*miasma*) which is nurtured in the land and must no longer nourish it until it is past cure" (97–8). The inhabitants are literally breeding death not life; they have to drive out the murderer who killed their former king, Laios (100–4). The attack on the city by the gods is consistent with the notion that the pollution has spread from the ruler, who stands for the city as its head, to the group. Regicide and parricide, city and family, are intertwined. Moreover, the incestuous element of the family is reflected in the emphasis on the failure of crops and women. As we have seen in the house of Atreus myth, the public and private, culture and nature, are not opposites but interrelated elements in a whole system, which is under siege in Thebes.

The Chorus of older men enter singing and wondering which god is responsible for their troubles, but in the following episode, a conflict erupts between the political and religious powers. Confident in his power and knowledge, Oedipus announces a terrible curse on the killer and anyone who does not give evidence against him (236–45). He has already called for Teiresias, thereby placing civic health in the hands of the gods. While the priest and suppliants looked to him as a savior, now he uses the term savior for Teiresias (304). But he doesn't really trust the prophet, and as soon as Teiresias shows reluctance to speak, Oedipus suspects a political plot. His rule, as an outsider, is fragile; he thinks in terms of bribery and conspiracy. It is a short step from suspecting the prophet who won't speak to blaming the one who suggested consulting him—that is, Kreon.

The confrontation of king and prophet is also a confrontation of their respective forms of knowledge. Teiresias presents his knowledge as terrible and his alone; everyone else is ignorant (316, 328–9), but he, though blind, can "see" (324). Oedipus acknowledges that the sightless Teiresias knows something (302–3) and demands that the prophet share this information (330). When Teiresias refuses, Oedipus becomes enraged and denies that the prophet's knowledge has any strength because he is blind in his ears, his mind, and his eyes (370–1, 375). He soon ridicules the prophet and boasts about his own insight. He questions Teiresias' ability to foretell the future, since he did not solve the riddle of the "rhapsode Sphinx." That task was left to "Oedipus, the know-nothing," and his innate intelligence solved the riddle, not something he learned from birds, the source of Teiresias' knowledge. He is challenging nothing less than the power of prophecy as a whole (462).

The theme of knowledge/ignorance is played out through a prominent structure of overturn and reciprocity. Oedipus moves from praising Teiresias to accusing him of being the lowest of the low (334, using the word *kakos*). Teiresias gets angrier and blurts out first that Oedipus has put the curse on himself (350–3), then that he lives together in shame with his closest family and does not see the evil (366–7, *kakos*). And, of course, Oedipus will be blind, though now he has physical sight; he will have knowledge, whereas now he is ignorant. Oedipus is the very pollution that he seeks; he will not drive anyone out but will be driven out himself. After this horrifying interchange, the Chorus thinks not about Oedipus specifically but about the still-unknown murderer. Yet there are subtle ironic allusions to Oedipus—reference to a foot, to tracking, and to the eroticized violence all help tie the song to their king. The misidentification of self as other will ultimately be corrected (Oedipus seeks and is sought, attacks and will be attacked).

The conflict between the prophet and the king, between their forms of knowledge, precipitates a crisis for the members of the Chorus; they are anxious not only about the unspeakable crime (465) but also about what the wise man Teiresias has said. How can they be disloyal to the one who solved the riddle of the Sphinx (511)? They want a touchstone by which to decide (494), and in the end they take Oedipus' solving the riddle for that purpose (510). The ode ends with a vote of confidence in him, in the secular and politics over religion. Knowledge definitely leads to power in this play, where Oedipus is in charge because he answered the riddle, using a kind of intelligence of which he is proud. He assumes that Kreon, as his brother-in-law, wants that power and therefore conspired against him. Kreon has a very rational response to Oedipus' accusation. He shares the rule equally with Jokasta and Oedipus (581) and he sleeps well at night (586), so why would he desire to be *tyrannos*? This lukewarm rationalization does not persuade Oedipus, who moves quickly to invoke the death penalty, rather than the exile the oracle had offered as a possible punishment.

Political contestation leads back to the question of the power of prophetic knowledge because Jokasta tries to reassure Oedipus by telling him about the false oracle she thinks she received. Laios was not killed by his son, as was prophesied, but by robbers at the meeting of three roads. She draws the conclusion that prophecy has no power (709, 723). Her speech leads to further unfolding of the story, for the mention of the murder of Laios jogs Oedipus' memory of his own past. He begins to fear that he is indeed the murderer he has cursed and that the blind prophet might see (747, cf. 768). He tells his story, that he was insulted by a drunkard who said he wasn't the real son of his father, and that he went to Delphi, where he was told, "it would be necessary for him to lie with his mother, to show forth a race unbearable for mortals to see, and he would be the murderer of the father who engendered him" (790–3). He tells Jokasta for the first time that on leaving Delphi he met and killed an old man and his whole party (811–13). He will have to leave Thebes if this man was in any way related to Laios.

Jokasta still holds on to her belief in the importance of human reason and agency. All seems to hinge on a discrepancy in calculation (844). Were there many attackers (842–4)? If so, then Oedipus is not guilty. Reliance on logic and history—the only witness said in front of the whole city that there were many attackers and can't retract that now—is tied to the dismissal of prophecy: Jokasta now explicitly rejects it (857–8). She will continue in this vein in the next scene. When a messenger comes to tell Oedipus that his "father," Polybos, has died a natural death, Oedipus is still concerned about the possibility that he will have sex with his mother. Jokasta once more reassures him: Young men often dream of sleeping with their mothers (981–2).

The choral song in between these two episodes clarifies the problem with this way of thinking (though there are textual difficulties here and the reading is not secure). The men of the Chorus are horrified and pray that they may be "pure and reverent in word and deed, as the lofty [high-footed] laws lay out, laws born from Zeus the father alone . . . nor did any mortal nature of men bring them forth" (863–70). They then turn to a more metaphorical parenting: *hubris* engenders the tyrant. Previously there was no particular moral coloring to the word *tyrannos*; Oedipus is literally *tyrannos* because he won the throne instead of inheriting it, though in fact he is the legitimate heir. They subtly refer to Oedipus here: his violence, the threat to kill Kreon, and the disrespect for oracles, have led them to sing this song. Wealth and power beyond what is fitting (874–5) lead one to rush into sheer necessity (877), where there is no good footing (878). Oedipus has bad feet, and Oedipus rushes. In this situation, the Chorus asks a famous question: "If these deeds are honored, why should I dance?" (895–6). The question pertains to the activity it is engaged in, participating in a chorus in honor of Dionysos, and connects its activities to the religious life of the audience. Preferring order to chaos, the Chorus turns from Oedipus and hopes that the gods will make themselves visible.

The messenger goes on and tells Oedipus that Polybos and Merope were not his birth parents, at which point Jokasta begins to put the pieces together. She begs Oedipus not to go any further in his quest for self-knowledge; taking the political tack again, he accuses her of being a snob, ashamed of his presumed bastardy (1079, 1062–3). At this point, Oedipus continues on his course and calls himself the "son of Chance." Both he and Jokasta at different times say that it is best to live at random. For the ancient Greek, however, an archaic meaning of Chance would more properly have been "divine providence," not the haphazard notion that came into usage toward the later fifth century. Thus, while Jokasta and Oedipus think that depending on chance means that they are free of fate, chance is actually an aspect of the fatedness of their lives. The coincidental meeting of Oedipus and Laios, the coincidental arrival of the messenger, the fact that Oedipus just happened to be passing by the Sphinx—these are elements essential for bringing the prophecy to pass and revealing its meaning. After Oedipus' proclamation of his chancy parentage, the Chorus too swings out of balance and embraces the possibility that Oedipus is some kind of divine foundling; Mount Kithaeron, intended to be his place of death, becomes his mother, and some god was his father (1086–109).

In the end, the oracles are vindicated when Oedipus discovers not only that he is the killer of Laios, as he feared, but that the drunk was right—he did not know his own parents—and he has already fulfilled the prophecy he thought he was avoiding. He says, "Apollo, it was Apollo, accomplishing these evil, evil sufferings" (1329–30). This emphasis foregrounds the question of the relationship between the human and the divine, and knowledge. Is it, therefore, a tragedy about fate? First of all, let us remember that Oedipus' fated actions took place in the past. And he was fated to do these things not because there was anything wrong with him but because his parents gave him life. Sophocles specifically does not tell us the source of the curse. Laios might have done something to bring it on their heads, and it is possible that the audience would have had it in their minds if they knew the alternative versions of the legend. One set of questions about this play has focused on fate and free will, and their relationship to *hamartia*, error or flaw. But what was predicted was not in any case the error or fault of the unborn Oedipus.

Second, Oedipus did not have to fulfill the oracle literally for it to have been accurate, since it could have been enacted symbolically or in a dream. He has performed the fated actions through the exercise of his free will. Having heard a rumor that he does not know who his parents are, he acts as if he does know when he leaves Delphi without that crucial bit of information. If he were not so decisive, so secure in his own knowledge, he could perhaps have avoided fulfilling the terms of the prophecy. We could say that he would not have killed the man he met at the crossroads if he had not been "proud" and violent. Does that mean that Oedipus deserved his fate? Not precisely, since pride was not a bad thing for a Greek prince (indeed, for princes of any time), and he was in any case not the aggressor. Moreover, while a modern audience of *Oedipus Tyrannos* might take his action as a sign of his angry and violent personality, amply demonstrated throughout the play, Sophocles does not have any character suggest that Oedipus was excessive even in killing all the retinue. These actions may have taken place through his character, but the consequences were not a punishment for it.

Third, the play as opposed to the myth unfolds through Oedipus' character. The truth comes to light and he suffers in part because of his *virtues*. He views his people as his children (1), and he wants to hear for himself not from others (6–7). He is a "doer" (76–7) and one who feels with the people (11–13). He thinks that he suffers more for them than for himself (93–4); he is wrong, but again his empathy is praiseworthy. He is open and resists Kreon's politically astute suggestion that he might want to hear the oracle's response in private even though hearing it in public could foreclose some of his options. Throughout the rest of the play, his activity and energy are evident. The textual structure emphasizes human agency, for at each step of the way Oedipus is explicitly shown making a choice over the attempts of others to stop him—for instance, Teiresias tries to avoid telling him what he knows, and Jokasta, most famously, tells him not to go any further in his quest to find out who he is.

The play, then, is set in motion not by a mistake but by a positive trait: Oedipus is a king who cares for his people. Like Kreon in *Antigone* he might seem to start off with right on his side and develop into an angry tyrant, and surely the choral ode on *hubris* supports that interpretation, but, unlike Kreon, his only *staged* excess is the pursuit of the truth. Thus, if we blame Oedipus for his fall, we are essentially saying ignorance is bliss, or leave well enough alone. Can the moral of the story be to be like Kreon, who exercises the virtue of moderation? No: rather, there is no simple lesson to be found. Even if the gods have unfairly burdened Oedipus, the play does not attack their existence, nor does it justify the gods by indicating that Oedipus deserved what he got. It simply presents it as a fact: he has done this, and finding out leads him to *punish himself*, with the same rush to judgment that has characterized him throughout (he will regret it in *Oedipus at Kolonos*).

Finally, however, the play does not close with Oedipus' self-mutilation. Oedipus returns to his former self, in that he tries to give orders. He does not even now control his fate; rather, he is simply led inside while Kreon seeks further orders from Delphi. The Chorus takes Oedipus as a model (1193, 1525–30) for the tragic truism: call no man happy until the end of his life. In *Oedipus at Kolonos*, his unique status is recognized, and Oedipus comes to the realization that though he committed these crimes, he was not the monster that he thought he was. So it would seem that one lesson we can take is the one that the Chorus gives us: deferral of judgment.

In the Athenian context, the alternation of political and ritual dimensions, human and divine power and forms of knowledge, might have seemed to refer to the city itself. This mode of interpretation returns us to the question of ideology raised earlier (Chapter 2). Athens was in intellectual ferment, with many rationalists and secularists as well as traditionally religious citizens; the sophists were active in the city and in Perikles' circle, which Sophocles was a part of. This political atmosphere permeates the play. Some have seen Oedipus as Perikles, while others take him to be standing for Athens as a whole. He has the virtues of energy and the intellectual curiosity that characterized the city, but his tendency toward tyranny might point to the dangers of empire. Oedipus' emphasis on plots and the political would have been familiar to the Athenian audience. Jean-Pierre Vernant (Vernant and Vidal-Naquet 113–40) has pointed out two relevant Athenian institutions: ostracism (where the highest man in the city, most in danger of becoming a tyrant, is expelled for a time) and the ritual of the scapegoat (*pharmakos*). Oedipus plays both *tyrannos* and *pharmakos*. But the play is importantly set in Thebes, not Athens. How is that significant? It is possible to see Thebes as Athens' opposite; it is a place that is far away, and plays set there can allow Athenians to contemplate tragic truths at a safe distance from themselves (Zeitlin 1990b). Athens uses Thebes to work out issues of inclusion/exclusion and of bad rule (tyranny) that might be problematic at home.

Freud and others have seen universal not local significance in this play. Oedipus may be taken as "man," with all the multiple meanings of that word. If we put this play in the context of Sophocles' other plays, in particular *Antigone*'s Ode on Man, it would seem that Oedipus exemplifies human striving and conquest of adversity; he also perverts nature through the incest and parricide, which makes him, like the figure in the ode. As a result, he goes from being high in the city to being without city. As we have noticed, the play has a great deal to say about human blindness and knowledge: Teiresias is blind, yet knows, whereas Oedipus sees, but actually knows nothing. In the end he will move forward on a new basis: his character has not changed (he still tries to take control of the action), but now he knows who he is. The emphasis on the human element here takes scientific form in Claude Lévi-Strauss' reading (209–15). Taking the incest taboo as universal, he reads the Oedipus story in all its variants (including Freud's) as being about a fundamental human dilemma as to whether people derive from the earth (autochthony) or derive from two parents, and the underrating (killing) or overrating (marrying) of blood relations.

Freud has been a major influence in the long shadow cast by the Oedipus myth; in the *Interpretation of Dreams* (294–8) he hypothe-

sized that audiences still resonate to the story not because of its han-
dling of destiny and human subjectivity but because each has his own
Oedipus complex (desire to sleep with the mother and kill the father).
Of course, Oedipus does not really have a complex (Vernant and
Vidal-Naquet 85–112), and the point that Jokasta is making is that
dreams can stand in for the *enactment* of desires. Nonetheless, the
name Oedipus will conjure up the complex, and psychoanalytic readings of the play can uncover patterns of behavior (denial, displacement,
doubling) that may arise from unconscious wishes (or fears). Using
the Freudian concept of the unconscious, we have a secular version of
the oracle in which the drives of the unconscious constitute a form
of fate.

The family, according to Freud, is founded on the incest taboo,
which prevents the child from sexual intimacy with the first object of
desire and prevents hostility and/or jealousy being expressed toward
the father. For the contemporary reader, the play may also open up a
question as to who is the real parent. In the relatively primitive understanding of the incest taboo that we see activated in the play, the biological parents are *the* ones, but in modern society there are many
people who parent (even in the play there are multiple parents named—
Kithaeron and Pan, for instance). Adoption, sperm donors, and sur-
rogacy complicate the definitions; you may feel that the parents who
bring you up are the "real" parents. The emphasis on the biological
and natural in this play, then, becomes a topic of discussion, not to
be assumed as the stable ground.

But all of these interpretations rest on the assumption that Oedipus
stands for universal "man." Is there any such thing? To go back to
the male/female binary, to what extent are the story and play gendered? In her poem "Myth," Muriel Rukeyser has Oedipus come back
to the Sphinx to ask why everything worked out so badly for him, and
she points out the mistake in his solution:

> Long afterward, Oedipus, old and blinded, walked the
> roads. He smelled a familiar smell. It was
> the Sphinx. Oedipus said, "I want to ask one question.
> Why didn't I recognize my mother?" "You gave the
> wrong answer," said the Sphinx. "But that was what
> made everything possible," said Oedipus. "No," she said.
> "When I asked, What walks on four legs in the morning,
> two at noon, and three in the evening, you answered,

Man. You didn't say anything about woman."
"When you say Man," said Oedipus, "you include women
too. Everyone knows that." She said, "That's what
you think." (480)

He thought his answer was universal, or at least applicable to all human
beings; Rukeyser is pointing out that man means male human being.
Freud and Lévi-Strauss make the same mistake: Lévi-Strauss founds
the universal incest taboo on the exchange of women; Freud names
his universal complex after a boy's position in the family.

The challenge is gendered in other ways as well. The Sphinx is
Oedipus' adversary, and she is eroticized in legend; she only attacked
young men and killed them by strangling. Because of this, perhaps,
prostitutes were sometimes called sphinxes. Moreover, the sexuality of
the Sphinx is hinted at throughout the play, and though it is not
explicit, her femininity is. Feminist critics have stressed the family ties
and in particular the way in which the role of Jokasta is socially constructed. As I noted earlier, knowledge or intellectual ability gave
Oedipus dominance. His conquest of the female monster gave him his
political power, and his confidence in his knowledge is based on that
scene of domination. Thus, his confidence in his own abilities is gendered, not simply human. Moreover, only a man could have encoun-
tered the Sphinx since only a man would have been wandering the
countryside. Oedipus' fate is, of course, entirely dependent on his
masculinity in the legend. In interpretation, critics influenced by nineteenth-century ideology of separate spheres have made much of the
fact that Jokasta tries to slow him down in his quest, seeing in her a
woman who keeps the heroic man back. Then, too, performances of
this play can't avoid the gendered elements because we will see on
stage the masculine and feminine enacted, even though in antiquity
all the actors would have been men.

If we take seriously the fact that everything that happens to Oedipus
happens because he is a man, does that make the play or the story less
meaningful? I would say no, because the play presents a problem
related to power, and anyone who gains that kind of political power
may take their success to be their own and lose sight of how they
gained it, or they may take it to indicate their invulnerability. Moreover, anyone can identify with Oedipus' coming to consciousness, and
conscience, even though in the ancient audience that would not necessarily have been the primary emphasis. The plays set in Thebes work

by counterposing king and subject, male and female, city and family, gods and humans. The resulting grid yields multiple points of entry for ancient and modern viewers, and we may even respond differently at different times in our lives.

In Part II I have directed our gaze to those excluded from the democracy and seen the effects of putting them at the center of tragedy, a form staged by the city. I chose texts that dealt with war, family, and the gods and looked at them through the binary oppositions (male/female, barbarian/Greek, free/slave, mortal/immortal) that were fundamental to the ancient Greek world view. Admittedly, the structure is complicated and was made more so because of the complexity of the plays themselves. These are plays and, as a result, they express multiple points of view and internal contests. Moreover, tragedy has been receptive to many different critical methods—those attentive to cultural diversity, class, and gender, as well as those allied with anthropology, psychology, or literary theory—and these methods bring out various dimensions of the plays being studied. Throughout, we have been looking backward and forward like Janus, because while the ancient context(s) are crucial, the ancient meaning(s) are not the only ones. The present reader is significant, and we each bring with us our own ways of looking at things, which lead us to privilege elements differently. I hope I have persuaded you that reading ancient Greek tragedy can fill you not with stultifying awe but with an openness to new ways of looking. In the concluding section on modern performances, we will focus on the ways in which some modern theater practitioners have produced these ancient plays, and why.

Texts

Oxford Classical Texts. Oxford: Oxford University Press.
  Aeschylus, ed. Denys Page, 1972.
  Sophocles, ed. Hugh Lloyd-Jones and Nigel G. Wilson, 1990.
  Euripides, ed. J. Diggle, 3 vols., 1981–94.

Aris and Phillips has a series of Greek texts with commentary and translations:
Aeschylus, *Eumenides*, Anthony Podlecki (1989); *Persians*, Edith Hall (1996); *Prometheus Bound*, Anthony Podlecki (2002).
Sophocles, *Ajax*, A. F. Garvie (1998); *Antigone*, Andrew Brown (1987); *Electra*, Jennifer March (2001); *Philoctetes*, Robert G. Ussher (1990).

Euripides, *Alcestis*, D. J. Conacher (1988); *Andromache*, Michael A. Lloyd (1994); *Bacchae*, Richard Seaford (1996); *Children of Heracles*, William Allan (2001); *Electra*, Martin Cropp (1988); *Heracles*, Shirley Barlow (1996); *Hecuba*, Christopher Collard (1991); *Hippolytus*, M. Halleran (1995); *Ion*, Kevin H. Lee (1997); *Iphigeneia among the Taurians*, Martin Cropp (2001); *Orestes*, Martin L. West (1987); *Phoenician Women*, Elizabeth Craik (1988); *Trojan Women*, Shirley Barlow (1986).

Suggestions for further reading

It is very difficult to select from the vast bibliography on the plays. In addition to P. E. Easterling's *Cambridge Companion to Greek Tragedy* (Cambridge: Cambridge University Press, 1997) and Justina Gregory's *A Companion to Greek Tragedy* (Oxford: Blackwell, 2005), and the other works cited and recommended above in Part I, see Simon Goldhill, *Reading Greek Tragedy* (Cambridge: Cambridge University Pess, 1986); Laura McClure, *Spoken like a Woman: Speech and Gender in Athenian Drama* (Princeton: Princeton University Press, 1999); Victoria Pedrick and Steven M. Oberhelman, ed., *The Soul of Tragedy: Essays on Athenian Drama* (Chicago: University of Chicago Press, 2005); Charles Segal, *Interpreting Greek Tragedy: Myth, Poetry, Text* (Ithaca: Cornell University Press, 1986); M. S. Silk, ed., *Tragedy and the Tragic: Greek Theatre and Beyond* (Oxford: Clarendon Press, 1996); Victoria Wohl, *Intimate Commerce: Exchange, Gender, and Subjectivity in Greek Tragedy* (Austin: University of Texas Press, 1998).

On Aeschylus, for a general introduction, see Alan Sommerstein, *Aeschylean Tragedy* (Bari: Levante, 1996). On *Persians*, in addition to Hall, see Thomas Harrison, *The Emptiness of Asia: Aeschylus' Persians and the History of the Fifth Century* (London: Duckworth, 2000). On the *Oresteia*, see Anne Lebeck, *The Oresteia: A Study in Language and Structure* (Washington, D.C.: Center for Hellenic Studies, 1971); Simon Goldhill, *Aeschylus: The Oresteia* (Cambridge: Cambridge University Press, 1992).

On Sophocles, for a general introduction, see Bernard Knox, *The Heroic Temper* (Berkeley: University of California Press, 1964); Charles Segal, *Tragedy and Civilization: An Interpretation of Sophocles* (Cambridge, MA: Harvard University Press, 1981); R. P. Winnington-Ingram, *Sophocles: An Interpretation* (Cambridge: Cambridge University Press, 1980). Mary Blundell, *Helping Friends and Harming Enemies: A Study in Sophocles and Greek Ethics* (Cambridge: Cambridge University Press, 1989) takes a more particular tack. On Oedipus, see Bernard Knox, *Oedipus at Thebes: Sophocles' Tragic Hero and His Time* (New York: Norton, 1971 [1957]); Charles Segal, *Oedipus Tyrannus: Tragic Heroism and the Limits of Knowledge*, 2nd ed. (Oxford: Oxford University Press, 2001). There are also two collections of essays, somewhat old, but still useful, Thomas Woodard, *Sophocles: A Collection of Critical Essays* (Englewood Cliffs: Prentice-Hall, 1966) and Michael O'Brien, *Twentieth-Century Interpretations of Oedipus Rex* (Englewood Cliffs: Prentice-Hall, 1968).

On Euripides, see D. J. Conacher, *Euripidean Drama: Myth, Theme and Structure* (Toronto: University of Toronto Press, 1967) and *Euripides and the Sophists* (London: Duckworth, 1998); Anne Michelini, *Euripides and the Tragic Tradition* (Madison: University of Wisconsin Press, 1987); Philip Vellacott, *Ironic Drama: A Study of Euripides' Method and Meaning* (Cambridge: Cambridge University Press, 1975); T. B. L. Webster, *The Tragedies of Euripides* (London: Methuen, 1967). For a feminist reading, see Nancy Sorkin Rabinowitz, *Anxiety Veiled: Euripides and the Traffic in Women* (Ithaca: Cornell University Press, 1993). A recent collection by Judith Mossman, *Oxford Readings in Classical Studies: Euripides* (Oxford: Oxford University Press, 2003), gives many of the important essays on Euripides.

8

Epilogue: Modern Performances

(with Sue Blundell)

The prophets of doom and gloom, the William Bennetts and Lynne Cheneys of the U.S. culture wars that I began with, seem to have been proven wrong especially if we look at performances of tragedy. Their fears that postmodernism, multiculturalism, and feminism would be the death of classics have not been realized, and instead there has been a bumper crop of new productions of Greek tragedy at the end of the twentieth and beginning of the twenty-first centuries. We might legitimately say that those movements have revitalized Greek tragedy. While we obviously must take seriously the ancient setting, the modern versions of the plays may shed light on the possible meanings of the play and on the time of its re-production if we pay attention to the ways in which they are staged.

There are many ways as well as many reasons to produce an ancient Greek play. A basic division seems to be between "faithfulness" to the past (often pejoratively called the "museum" approach) and "relevance" to the present. To be sure, there is no way that most present-day productions can be truly faithful to the past because the setting is entirely different. While we have many venues and opportunities to see plays, the ancient Greeks were limited to a few theaters and to performances a few days a year at religious festivals. Some of the fundamental physical features (the plays took place outside, during the day) and the cultural ones (the civic and religious atmosphere) will inevitably be missing. Even when the plays are performed at a "festival" in Epidauros or Delphi today, the connotation of the word is very different.

To take one example, contemporary directors and translators are faced with many issues of interpretation. They have to decide how they will handle the convention of the chorus and its music and dance. Or how will they cast the roles: all male, mixed gender, all female (at a women's college, perhaps)? Will actors and members of the chorus be masked? What kinds of costumes will they wear? The Guthrie Theater, in its production of the *House of Atreus* in Minneapolis (1966–7), attempted not to "reconstruct the sort of impressions which an Athenian audience may have felt. . . . Rather [it] let them consider whether the archetypal situations have been re-created in a manner which makes them an interesting and vivid theatrical event" (Hartigan 71).

The performance practices of ancient tragedy can stimulate creativity in the present. As David Wiles argues, specific ancient techniques can inspire experiments in modern times: the chorus emphasizes an understanding of the world through the body that is not necessarily individual and personal; the auditorium emphasizes collectivity; and the mask "frees us from a philosophically discredited obsession with interiority. By blotting out the face, the mask paradoxically reintegrates the body and makes it an instrument capable of embodying rather than reciting a text. Greek theatre has proved to be a form that allows us to address these fundamental concerns" (2004: 263). The mask has been popularized, and not necessarily through a return to an "authentic" performance style, as it was in Peter Hall's *Oresteia* (1981) for the British National Theatre; rather, it is often part of the trend toward interculturalism, that is, an increased emphasis on the interplay among cultures. Masks are used in ritual and artistic performances in many traditional cultures, and that is part of their appeal to contemporary directors. Masking and the use of indigenous music enable a director to access ritual, also one of the roots of tragedy. At the same time, in this era of postmodernism in the theater, hybridity or cultural referents may be accepted as desirable in their own right, not for another end.

The integration of elements from different cultures can be seen in some very famous late twentieth-century productions. Between 1990 and 1993 Ariane Mnouchkine (Théâtre du Soleil) produced a tetralogy called *Atrides*, combining Euripides' *Iphigeneia at Aulis* with Aeschylus' *Oresteia*. She used Kathakali (Indian) and Noh (Japanese) forms of theater to get at the underlying ritual sense of the Greek drama. The vivid Kathakali face/masks, costumes, and gestures make an unforgettable impression that goes far beyond the linguistic. The cultural tradition of the Greeks has also been combined with Asian theater by major Japanese directors like Tadashi Suzuki and Yukio Ninagawa. Suzuki takes aspects of traditional Japanese theater, but also uses English and American actors. He employs Noh and Bunraku masks, and by doing so points up the cross-cultural nature of the Greek themes. His *Clytemnestra*, first performed in Japan in 1983, diverges from the Greek original, but it does so in order to make explicit what was implicit there: the incest of Orestes and Elektra, the fact that their mother was murderous. These elements can be read back into the text of Aeschylus, but Suzuki also sees a connection to Japanese men's relationships to their mothers. Ninagawa's *Medea* used a very famous cross-dressed Kabuki actor of female roles (*onnagata*) as Medea; the costume was replete with artificial breasts, and white face makeup that looked like a mask. As Medea came closer to killing her children, the elaborate robe with breasts was removed, and the actor was left in a close-fitting red robe that went over his head. In the end, s/he was dressed all in white when she made her exit in Ninagawa's version of the machine.

There is no single answer to the question "why do a Greek play?" The tragedies that have come down to us have been staged with contemporary relevance in every conceivable setting. It is not easy, therefore, to make clear distinctions between periods of production, but the volume *Dionysus Since 69: Greek Tragedy at the Dawn of the Third Millennium* makes a strong case for 1968 as a watershed moment. Before 1968 the productions "rarely challenged mainstream political ideology, or indeed the performance traditions of western naturalism, but there were exceptions" (Hall 2004a: 1). Since 1968 the predominant approaches have been quite radical politically and aesthetically.

Hall's assertion that "more Greek tragedy has been performed in the last thirty years than at any point in history since Graeco-Roman antiquity" (Hall 2004a: 2) seems to be borne out by a study of the U.K. theater scene. Over the last three decades there have been numerous productions of Attic tragedies in the British Isles, at venues ranging from the National Theatre in London to poky rooms over back-street pubs in Cardiff or closed woollen mills in Bradford. New York, Washington, and other locations in the U.S. have similarly seen many translations and adaptations of the tragedies on stage, to say nothing of college and university productions. Since this is occurring at a time when very few school or university students study either the Greek language or Greek literature, we naturally hunt around for reasons. There is interest in the form, as we saw above, but mostly it is the content and the fact that the plays raise questions about contentious issues (war, gender and the family, the exotic outsider) that attract attention. Instead of seeing the ancient world as statuesque and unchanging, critics now tend to see it as dysfunctional, and thus as a mirror to our own difficult times (Hall 2004a: 2).

In Europe the Greek tragedies in general have a high culture status. For Greeks, traditional performances bolster a claim to national identity based on a direct link to the ancients, and the festivals that include performances of ancient tragedy support the tourist industry. When the National Theatre of Greece brought Aeschylus' *The Persians* to New York (2006), they performed it in modern Greek with a full chorus that danced and sang to a new musical score, though without masks. The audience stood up when representatives of the Greek embassy entered, making clear the political grounding of the artistic experience. Especially in Germany after World War II, there was a tendency to return to the classics in part to establish a continuity with badly eroded humanistic values (Fischer-Lichte 342).

But also as a result of this status, the ancient plays have been employed as a way of safely questioning authority. They offer protective cover to critical writers since they have an irreproachable pedigree. In Greece, under the conditions of censorship (1967–74), staging the ancient tragedies could be a mode of subversion (Hall 2004b: 172). For instance, Antoine Vitez mounted a version of Sophocles' *Electra* in 1986 that made the connection to the situation in Greece under the generals; through simple staging devices, modern sounds and gestures, they were able to integrate the earlier time of the original play into the present (Neuschäfer 137). The distinction is drawn between Electra, who is still mourning, and others who have knuckled under to political pressure. Neuschäfer argues that in the Greek case the spectators recognized that "These events are happening under the shadow of a military dictatorship, invisible but omnipresent. . . . Electra's wretched existence is like a magnifying mirror which exposes the individual suffering experienced by a people oppressed by an unjust regime" (138). Similarly when *Electra* was staged in the North of Ireland in 1992, audience members made the connection to recent violence in which nine people had been killed. At the end of the performance, they simply stood in silence. Shaw says "They stood not for us, of course, but for themselves and for their grief" (Shaw 133).

Heiner Müller, writing under the repressive regime of the German Democratic Republic, also used Greek myth to speak the unspeakable, because of the high status of Hellenism in East Germany. His play *Medeamaterial* (1982) linked the Medea and Jason story to abuse of the environment, taking a cue from the *Argonautica*, which ends with Jason killed by a board from the Argo. According to his editor, Müller saw "Jason's story as the earliest myth of colonization in Greek legend: 'Jason is slain by his boat. . . . European history began with colonization. . . . That the vehicle of colonization strikes the colonizer dead anticipates the end of it. That's the threat of the end we're facing, the "end of growth" ' " (Weber 124). Müller is not optimistic, however, about the political efficacy of theater: "*Landscape with Argonauts* presumes the catastrophes which mankind is working toward. The theatre's contribution to their prevention can only be their representation" (126).

Even in democracies, free speech may be compromised in wartime. Director Peter Sellars sees the ancient drama as a way to mount a critique of U.S. foreign policy: "When one is working in a theater that is called the American National Theater, one begins to think of Greek drama and the idea of a popular theater that is able to discuss issues that are very serious and, in fact, would be considered in our day undiscussable" (90). Sellars was confronting a situation where the censorship was not official so much as the result of a culture that does not encourage its citizens to think: "For me the appeal of Greek drama is this insistence of those three playwrights to ask questions that our society rejects before you even ask" (93). He compares the education U.S. citizens receive from TV to the education offered to citizens in Athens by the drama.

> I do feel that Greek drama was instituted as a kind of biological survival mechanism about society, to teach people how to vote, to teach people what democracy is, and the gesture of voting for your favorite play was actually training for jury duty. . . . Right now, most American juries are very sad, because Americans' only training is *Rambo* and *Hill Street Blues*. (93)

His version of *Persians* enabled Sellars and writer Robert Auletta to present "almost an alternative information system—what can't be shown on television can be said on-stage" (Hall 2004b: 184, from Mark Pappenheim, "The Greeks Had a Word For It," *The Independent*, August 16, 1993).

The reviewers had difficulty imagining the Iraqis (in the first Gulf War) as at all sympathetic, which is what Aeschylus requires us to do when he makes the vanquished Persians the center of his play. People got up and left the performances in 1993 at the Mark Taper Forum; they believed the play was anti-American and did not want to listen to what it had to say about the U.S. as an aggressor, as potential "terrorists." In the light of the tendency to see even those critical of official policies as traitors, it is not surprising that audiences did not like being forced to imagine the U.S. as a terrorist nation.

> Applying the most charged terms in the American political imagination to the Americans themselves, making the Americans the wielders of force and garottes, probing the extreme limits of linguistic relativism, pushing the audiences to discover where the edges of their collective group loyalty and consciousness lay—these are the tasks for which Auletta and Sellars found the earliest tragedy in the western repertoire to be especially suited. (Hall 2004b: 182)

But of course, the audience can leave, as it did in this case, or the producer can be denied a stage on which to perform; there are many ways to bury information, in other words.

In the U.K., militarization has led to the increased presence of Attic tragedy on stage. War is not, of course, a recent invention, and in many ways those who lived through World War II and knew people who had survived World War I were much more deeply affected by warfare than the current generation have been so far. But war may have become more problematic to the British. In addition to violent civil conflict in Northern Ireland and the bombings and shootings as a result, Britain has also been involved in military operations that have aroused tremendous controversy, including the Gulf War of 1991, the NATO air-raids on Serbia during the Kosovo conflict of 1999, and the U.S.-led invasions of Afghanistan in 2001 and Iraq in 2003.

In the 1990s it was sometimes said that in Britain there was such a dearth of new plays addressing political issues that audiences were forced to go back to the Greeks if they wanted to reflect on the current state of the world. But this is hardly the case today: in particular, U.K. involvement in the Middle East has generated a large amount of political theatre, including David Hare's *Stuff Happens* (2004), Richard Norton-Taylor's *Justifying War* (2003), Gillian Slovo's *Guantanamo*, and Robert Soans' *Talking to Terrorists* (2005). Yet still the Greeks are with us. Conflict within the family is in fact a more prominent theme of Greek tragedy than conflict between warring states, and very few, if any, Greek plays can be judged to be unequivocally pacifist in their sentiments. However, as we have seen in previous chapters, a significant number take place against a background of military aggression, and highlight very graphically the horrors of warfare. In many of them the plot is drawn from stories surrounding the Trojan War, so that a city which for Greeks in the fifth century had already assumed a mythical status now provides us as well with an imaginary space in which to play out our never-ending versions of bitter confrontation.

As you will recall, *Agamemnon*, the first play in Aeschylus' *Oresteia*, features a returning war hero whose family history and personal exploits are steeped in violence of a horrific kind. In Katie Mitchell's 1999 production of the *Oresteia* at the National Theatre, the *Agamemnon* was re-titled *The Home Guard,* and was supplied with a Chorus of veterans whose varying degrees of disability (some were confined to wheelchairs) gave added depth to their recital of wartime hostilities: one theater critic complained that Mitchell had turned the piece into "a glib anti-war morality play" (Charles Spencer, *Daily Telegraph*, December 3, 1999). New productions of the *Agamemnon* were staged in 2004 and 2005, the latter as part of a trilogy renamed *Blood Bath.*

But the Greek play that is most readily assimilated into an anti-war position is Euripides' *Trojan Women*. Indeed, when the play is staged, Edith Hamilton's statement that it is the greatest anti-war play ever written is often quoted. It is invariably presented as that, as an anti-war play, even though we do not know whether Euripides intended it as such. Given its presentation of the suffering of the Trojan women after the Greek victory, it comes as no surprise that London saw fringe productions of this tragedy in 1991, 1999, 2001, 2002, and 2004 in the context of world conflicts in Bosnia and wars in Iraq. It was in the mid-1990s that the play's focus on the female victims of war had its strongest reverberations, at a time when the conflict in Bosnia was giving rise to widespread slaughter and rape. The composer Nigel Osborne referred to this directly in his three-part opera *Sarajevo* (1994), whose first part was closely based on Euripides' tragedy. Annie Castledine undoubtedly had the same terrible events in mind when she staged her version of *Trojan Women* at the National Theatre in 1995, while the conflict was still raging. The ragged women of Troy clambering with their pathetic bundles among heaps of rubble could not fail to remind audiences of the displaced persons and devastated cities seen every day in news footage. But Bosnia was certainly not Castledine's only reference point: the Chorus was multi-racial, and the Greeks, somewhat incongruously, were given American accents, with Helen assuming a familiar Marilyn Monroe appearance.

In the U.S. critics note that the *Trojan Women* has been taken to refer to Chechnya, Bosnia, Hiroshima, Algeria. In the program notes to a production of a version by Ellen McLaughlin (2003), Rachel Dickstein, the director, says,

> Ellen McLaughlin's new version of *The Trojan Women* infuses this elegiac embrace of a lost home into Euripides' classic tale of suffering and pain. Inspired by the experiences, memories and songs of refugee women from Serbia, Croatia, Albania and Bosnia, Ellen has offered us a lyrical, bracing and hopeful portrait of Troy and its survivors recovering from the most brutal siege of all times.

She goes on to talk about the research that members of the cast did. This use of the past as model for the present predictably bothers some writers, who think the theater of twenty-four hundred years ago does not need to be updated to make a point, and pleases others, who think that "museum pieces" miss the power of theater to make us identify. In these productions, however, modernization runs the risk of encouraging too facile associations: Troy was not a third-world country; it was a well-established and well-developed city that was not very different from the cities of Greece. And Hekabe was Queen. We lose something if we forget that the play's poignancy is in part based on loss of status. The Athenians, though living in a democracy, had a mythology based on the great doings of heroes, not on the little person.

Euripides' *Hekabe* also evokes the grim aftermath of warfare and its effect on women and children, but in the 1990s it was produced far less frequently than *Trojan Women*. If it was thought then that the horrible revenge taken by Hekabe might dilute our sympathy for the suffering women, these sensibilities had disappeared by the time of the 2003 invasion of Iraq. "How Hecuba thrives while war rages in Iraq: queen of the knives" was the headline which introduced one weekly paper's article on the crop of Hekabes arriving at that time on the English stage (*Times Literary Supplement*, September 24, 2004).

There were fringe performances of the play in 2003 and 2004, and two high-profile productions in 2004 and 2005. Revenge killings were on many people's minds during this period, and the theme was vividly brought to life in the 2004 version of *Hecuba* directed by Jonathan Kent at London's Donmar Theatre. Here the visceral language of Frank McGuiness' translation was matched by Claire Higgins' passionate performance as the ravaged and desperate queen. The horror of her situation and actions was underlined by the staging, which included a backdrop inscribed with the names of war casualties of every age, and a plastic sheet bearing the bloody remains of the boys whom Hekabe slaughters.

In an article that summer, Matthew Parris used the play as a way to think about economic issues in England (*Times*, August 7, 2004), and in the program he commented that it was a "Brutal translation of a brutal story. . . . brutalization of war. . . . This play is about the potency of the unquiet grave. How many such now yawn at us from Palestine, Israel, Ground Zero, Afghanistan or Iraq?" The Royal Shakespeare Company's version of the play was performed at Stratford-on-Avon and at London's Albery Theatre in 2005. Contemporary events were certainly significant for its translator, the poet Tony Harrison, who records that he was prompted to tackle the piece by "the recurring image of an old woman appealing to the camera that has captured her agony. . . ." These women, Harrison writes, are from many places—from "Sarajevo, Kosovo, Grozny, Gaza, Ramallah, Tbilisi, Baghdad, Falluja—women in robes and men in metal helmets as in the Trojan War" ("Bitter Tears," *The Guardian*, March 19, 2005). But Vanessa Redgrave in the title role was a bleakly calculating queen rather than a passionate one, and the full chorus of twelve women in embroidered folk dresses lent the play an air of ritual formality. For most critics this was a far less searing vision of an old woman's shocking plight than the one presented at the Donmar. The comparison of the two harmed the reception of Redgrave in the U.K.

It was Redgrave's and Boswell's interpretation of the second half which attracted the disappointed attention of the critics. . . . For anyone keen to show the corrupting horrors of conflict this is the moment: the maddened queen, transformed by loss and pain, pushes pins into eyes and blades into young boys and, in so doing, proves what war must always do for reason.

Redgrave might reasonably have been expected to take such an opportunity. Her supporters might reasonably have been disappointed when she did not. Once it was clear that she had about as much post-murder madness as Miss Marple in a vicarage, understandable dissatisfaction set in. The critics, as synchronized in this regard as the best of Greek choruses, gave her [a] full-on clobbering. (Peter Stothard, "Hit Me Here, and Here, and Here," *Times Literary Supplement*, April 15, 2005)

When this production moved to the U.S., it was changed a great deal due to its reception in London; the army tents of the set and the costumes did more than hint at the Iraqi setting. The references to the coalition and terrorists were retained. However, it suffered from comparison to the same view of Hekabe, even though audiences had not had access to the Donmar production, as the review in *The New York Times* makes clear.

But if we can admire this desperate figure's salvaged aplomb, we rarely get a visceral sense of the despair and the rage at injustice that make the character so compelling. Ms. Redgrave's perhaps intentionally remote, emotionally inarticulate performance keeps the audience at a cool distance. Ms. Redgrave's empty-hearted Hecuba represents an intellectually sound illustration of the idea that war destroys its victims' souls even more efficiently than it takes their lives. But it makes for a less than satisfying theatrical experience.

The most reliable way to tap into the power of Greek tragedy is not by larding it with topical allusions but by giving full expression to the range of emotion its formal structure so elegantly contains. In muting the display of feeling in her character, Ms. Redgrave has also limited the scope of our responses to her fate. Hecuba may exist in a permanent state of emotional shellshock, but few in the audience are likely to leave the theater in a similar state. (Charles Isherwood, "In Thrall to the Greeks," *New York Times*, June 20, 2005)

As was mentioned earlier, Euripides' *Iphigeneia at Aulis* dramatizes the buildup to a war rather than its aftermath. It is not often performed in the U.K., but, as with *Hekabe*, the situation in Iraq created a revival in interest. In Edna O'Brien's translation, staged at Sheffield's Crucible Theatre in 2003, the emphasis was on personal relationships and moral failings rather than political machinations. However, at the National Theatre in 2004 Katie Mitchell directed a version of the play that was set in a requisitioned mansion, and perfectly evoked the shabby makeshift quality of 1940s wartime life. Men in khaki bustled in and out with clipboards, while a chorus of black-frocked women beautifully conveyed the nervy and desperate atmosphere of the time. When at the end of the play, to a background noise of whirling helicopters, a bunch of officials rushed onstage to silence the frantic Clytemnestra, one could appreciate Mitchell's point about the moral turmoil induced by warfare.

In recent productions of the *Oresteia*, *Iphigeneia at Aulis* has sometimes been inserted at the beginning, as it was in Ariane Mnouchkine's *Atrides*; the Guthrie Theater's *Clytemnestra* omitted the *Eumenides* but included *Iphigeneia*. German director Christoph Schroth staged a four-play cycle comprised of *Iphigeneia in Aulis*, *Agamemnon*, *Trojan Women*, and Aristophanes' *Acharnians* (1982; see Bierl). These plays spoke to the modern condition of seemingly endless war, with their focus on violence, both intergenerational and sexual, and the place of the rule of law. In this version, the Trojan War was seen as the first colonial war because the Greek cities came together in a coalition to attack Troy. False reasons for the war are disclosed; recognizing that Helen was merely an excuse stands for the need to see through ideology. The event closed with a comedy, Aristophanes' *Acharnians*, where the "little man gets his peace." But after it was over, the cast and the audience united, as the program notes report: "The five-hours' spectacle ends with a friendly gesture of the actors: down from the stage they offer wine and cheese to the spectators as an invitation to jointly ponder on the main question of our days and to pay tribute to all those who have engaged in the struggle against war and for the preservation of peace." Greek theater, then, was used as a stimulus to thinking critically in the present.

So far, we have been for the most part examining the ways in which selected Greek tragedies have been staged in the major capitals of the west in the period since 1968. Given the objections to these canonical texts from multicultural perspectives, and given their defense by conservatives as examples of "the best that has been thought and written," it is especially interesting to note that they are often (if not always) performed now in a way that marks resistance. Their popularity in post-colonial settings is similarly striking. While the texts might seem part of the dominant order by reason of their place in elite education, and while they might seem to have been imposed on the colonized by that educational system, they have instead been used by the oppressed and colonized to express a critique of that dominant order. Edith Hall points out that the first rediscovery of Greek tragedy coincided with the discovery of the New World; the current rediscovery, surprisingly perhaps, coincides with post-colonialism (Hall 2004a: 24–5). Looking first at Africa, we can find use made of the Antigone story in the anti-apartheid struggle. After a proposed production of *Antigone* failed to come off because two actors had been imprisoned, Athol Fugard, John Kani, and Winston Ntshona wrote and performed *The Island* (1973), which depicts two inmates enacting scenes from *Antigone* for production in a prison colony. The specifics of Antigone's situation are burned away, and what is left is the person who stands up against injustice. The prisoners reenact the confrontation between Antigone and Kreon as an interrogation scene. Gender is relevant because Winston, who is to play her, objects to representing a woman (60); his partner, John, tells him that "this is Theatre. . . . they'll laugh. But who cares about that as long as they laugh in the beginning and listen at the end" (61–2). In an interesting side note, Nelson Mandela was Kreon in a performance in another jail; in his memoirs he said he spent some of his time in prison reading

classic Greek plays . . . and found them enormously elevating. What I took out of them was that character was measured by facing up to difficult situations and that a hero was a man who would not break even under the most trying circumstances. . . . [Kreon's] inflexibility and blindness ill become a leader, for a leader must temper justice with mercy. It was Antigone who symbolized our struggle; she was, in her own way, a freedom fighter, for she defied the law on the grounds that it was unjust. (Mandela 397)

Femi Osofisan's *Women of Owu* sets the *Trojan Women* of Euripides in nineteenth-century Nigeria; when it was performed in England at Chipping Norton (2004), the playbill referred to the shared importance of religion, cloth, status, and communication in both the ancient Greek and the Yoruba setting. At the same time, the new production made the point that in Iraq, and in the African context, women are still "the spoils of war." There was both a feminist and a humanist claim being made, according to director Chuck Mike: "feminine opposition movements worldwide show how undaunted the human spirit can be even when the struggle is reduced to how and where one dies."

The work of another Nigerian playwright, Ola Rotimi's *The Gods Are Not to Blame*, is a version of *Oedipus Tyrannos*. In a recent production (London 2005), humor and sensuality between Oedipus (Odewale) and his mother were played up; while telling the basic Oedipus story, Rotimi interweaves Yoruba elements through the use of chants, rituals, words, and songs. Some details were changed: when the people come to Odewale, he asks what they are doing for themselves, thereby pointing out that it is a problem if the people completely depend on their leaders to resolve difficult situations. Moreover, Laios (Adetusa) does not simply strike Odewale as he does in the original; he has tried to take Odewale's land, and he makes disparaging remarks about his people. Odewale learns not only who his father was, but more importantly, that his tribal loyalty was deadly. The universal themes (we don't know who we are really, powerful leaders can be tyrannical) dovetail with the local situation of the Biafran War, and Rotimi makes a connection between Greek ritual and Yoruba ritual. The updating was very successful; the audience sat in the round, children had pride of place instead of Athenian notables, and the drumming made one feel that one was simultaneously in an African village and watching the traditional chorus in the Athenian orchestra.

Wole Soyinka's *The Bacchae of Euripides: A Communion Rite* shows the complexity of the term "post-colonial." The work was commissioned by the National Theatre in the U.K. (1973) and takes Euripides' *Bacchai* into a Nigerian context. While the ancient Greeks drew a parallel between the Egyptian god Osiris and Dionysos, Soyinka makes the association with the Yoruba god Ogun. His work is evidence for a key tenet of Afrocentrism, that African religions had their own plays, their own tragedy, and were not dependent on the Greeks. Like Rotimi, Soyinka and other playwrights find "strong affinities between indigenous African performance and the heavily music- and dance-based idiom of early Greek tragedy" (Balme 41). Nonetheless, we can't assume that the play takes a political position. Slavery is emphasized in the cast list, but the members of the Chorus are explicitly mixed race, eliminating any easy assumptions about racial identity.

Moreover, Soyinka's status (he was educated in colonial and British institutions) and the British commission for the work show the complexity of calling this work simply "African." One might say that these post-colonial versions of Greek myth show another, intellectual, form of colonialism. Playwrights raised and educated in colonial schools go back to these materials; but they are not enslaved to them and feel free to adapt and use these models for their own purposes. The deployment of these ancient texts takes different forms in different locations depending on local contexts. It seems, for instance, that francophone Africa was not drawn to them, perhaps because they had already been reworked by modern French playwrights, making them a less attractive resource to those in resistance to French authority.

Former British colonies in the Caribbean, too, have made their own versions of the Greek plays, and Ireland has shown a pronounced affinity for them. The educational tradition in Ireland forbade the teaching of Greek and Latin in schools; as a result using these plays became a mode of resistance to, not complicity in, colonialism (Hardwick 81). Thus, there is a long Irish tradition of the study of Latin in local and nationalist "hedge" schools, and many performances of the tragedies. In England, Iraq and the issue of global terrorism have been far more notable as reference points for Greek tragedy than the situation in Northern Ireland. However, since 2003 London has seen two stagings of *The Cure at Troy*, based on Sophocles' *Philoctetes*. In the play, Achilles' son, Neoptolemus, and Odysseus come to convince Philoctetes to return with them to Troy because his bow is essential to victory. The Greeks had abandoned him to his fate on an island years before because he was injured and his wound gave off a foul smell. Seamus Heaney's translation struck a chord with the situation in Ireland in 1990, and he added some contemporary allusions that made the connection explicit:

> The innocent in gaols
> Beat on their bars together.
> A hunger-striker's father
> Stands in the graveyard dumb.
> The police widow in veils
> Faints at the funeral home
>
> History says, *Don't hope
> On this side of the grave.*
> But then, once in a lifetime
> The longed-for tidal wave
> Of justice can rise up,
> And hope and history rhyme. (Heaney 1991: 77)

What is the basis of the optimism? Is Philoctetes going to take Troy, that is, Northern Ireland? Will that be without reprisal? Or will he give up his vendetta (his wound) and will that be his cure? It is not clear.

Some critics objected to the modernizing particulars, and Heaney himself reconsidered them (his translation is sometimes performed without them) (Hardwick 92–3). Should a work of art, based very closely on an ancient text, refer so explicitly to any specific current situation? The play asks large questions that might be compelling to anyone involved in a struggle, in much the same way that *Antigone* has proven to be almost endlessly flexible as an emblem for the politically intransigent. After all, anyone can take pleasure in their suffering, can become addicted to their wounds, and flash "them around like decorations" (Heaney 1991: 2). Philoctetes' celebrated wound can be reinterpreted in the contemporary climate to refer to any illness that leads to pariah status (e.g., HIV/AIDS). The play and its original, *Philoctetes*, raise other philosophical issues that are widely applicable, such as what is one's essential nature? To what extent is it inherited from our parents? And, to what extent is such an essence constructed by the environment in which we live (in Neoptolemus' case, the warrior code of masculinity and honor)? While we can say that the play does not have to refer to Northern Ireland, we can also see that at the time and place of its first performances in Derry in 1990, it was likely to be taken in that way.

Heaney also translated *Antigone* as *The Burial at Thebes*. He was encouraged to do so because he saw that "the situation that pertains in Sophocles' play was being reenacted in our own world" (2004: 75). As the playwright's relationship to Philoctetes was complicated (poets stand in between, he says, on p. 2), he similarly complicates the response to *Antigone* and sees Kreon's suffering as a "substantial counterweight" to Antigone's. At the same time, Heaney points out that the music of the tragedy was a powerful influence on him (2004: 76–7). He saw a link between Antigone and an eighteenth-century Irish lament. We can see, therefore, that he was moved to do the play not only because he saw the parallel to his own location and to the events in the larger world, but also because the aesthetics of the form appealed to him. This combination of factors will be significant in any contemporary revision or reproduction of Greek tragedy that does justice to it. Many other modernizations have been performed in Ireland, and they are often criticized for the "liberties" they take with the ancient models; the criticism itself indicates that the ancient plays are reproduced not out of some elitist desire to "do the Greeks," but because they have continuing relevance.

To return to my observation at the beginning of this chapter, the rediscovery of the Greeks has also interestingly coincided with feminist movements. Part of the early second wave of feminism saw ancient Greek culture as misogynist, and was suspicious of the high value placed on canonical works without concern for the way women were treated in those works. Critics like Sue-Ellen Case saw the simultaneous absence of physical women and the emphasis on female characters in tragedy as paradigmatic of the way culture suppresses women, "replacing them with masks of patriarchal production" (Case 7). Nonetheless, actresses have consistently been drawn to the strong females of Greek tragedy: Clytemnestra, Elektra, Medea, Antigone, to name a few. Indeed one could argue that because of the contemporary interest in gender, modern productions of the myth of the house of Atreus tend to emphasize Clytemnestra more than the war or revenge.

In the Guthrie's 1992 production of *Iphigeneia at Aulis, Agamemnon* and *Electra* (Sophocles), actress Isabell Monk was delighted to play Clytemnestra, saying: "She has everything. Every emotion" (*Guthrie Preview*, Summer 1992, Vol. 8, no. 1, "A Conversation with Isabell Monk on Clytemnestra," 3). When questioned about the relevance of the plays and in particular the last speech in their version, Monk replied: "I don't know if all women should go out and kill their husbands if they do them wrong," but "This speech is about revenge and avenging. To stand up and empower women to take charge of their lives. The one thing that Clytemnestra does is take full responsibility for her actions. We all have to take responsibility for our actions. If that final speech puts that into anyone's mind, I think that's positive" (3).

As I have emphasized throughout, the Greek myths used in tragedy typically relate the personal (household) to the public (city) because the major characters are generally political leaders. Aeschylus' trilogy puts the sacrifice of a daughter and the Trojan War in the background to the present action in which a wife kills her husband and a son kills his mother; he concludes the trilogy with the foundation of a court to try such cases in the future and to put an end to the cycle of violence. Thus, his *Oresteia* is preeminently concerned with justice as well as gender and the family. In recent years, however, the emphasis has been more on the family dynamics. As we have seen, productions sometimes add Euripides' *Iphigeneia at Aulis* as a "first act," thus emphasizing the father–daughter dimension. In different eras different elements might be heightened. Tastes change; so, for instance, Sophocles has gone in and out of favor, and within his plays, feminism has led to an increased interest in Antigone over Oedipus, and to an emphasis on the women within the Theban cycle.

The "sexual revolution" of the sixties and seventies generated many performances of Euripides' *Bacchai*, which had not been popular before, and has not been since. With the confluence of the hippie movement and the avant-garde theater movement, there was a return to this play which celebrates or at least attests to the power of the violent god Dionysos. The transformation of Pentheus into a woman draws attention to the cross-dressing of the actors of Greek tragedy. *Dionysus in 69*, which was staged in 1968 by the Performance Group, capitalized on the potent mix of ritual and sex/gender in the original, but merged them with the avant-garde theater movement and the social atmosphere of the times. The goal was to change the audience through their participation at the play.

The Athenian use of men to perform female roles has made the Greek plays attractive to companies wanting to explore themes of sexuality. Surprisingly perhaps, playwrights interested in gender and sexuality have found *Medea* a capacious vehicle allowing for imaginative casting. Charles Ludlam's Theatre of the Ridiculous (1988) alternated male and female Medeas and Nurses, while John Eppworth's *My Deah* (2006) had Medea and the Nurse played by the same female actor and utilized a cross-dressed chorus of bourgeois matrons who were the heroine's bridge partners. The sons were played as stereotypical gay teenagers, and the Paidagogos was a flirtatious football coach. Other fringe productions, such as John Fisher's *Medea the Musical* (1996), and a production by the Greek Active group in Seattle (1992), in which Medea was played as a drag queen, have similarly used sexuality to highlight Medea's transgressive nature.

Medea's perspective on the relationship between mothers and children is also a concern of Marina Carr, a young Irish playwright whose work is frequently inspired by Greek tragedy. *By the Bog of Cats*, commissioned in 1998 by the Abbey Theatre, Dublin, and performed in San Jose in 2001 and London in 2004/5, transposes the story of Medea to a bleak bogside in contemporary Ireland, but follows the main features of the plot quite closely. Hester Swane, a woman whose origins as a traveler have made her into an outsider in her own community, was abandoned by her mother when she was a girl. When her partner, Carthage Kilbride (a significant surname), dumps her in order to marry the daughter of a local landowner, she sets fire to his farm. Her daughter, Josie, does not feature in her plan for revenge, but as she prepares to kill herself and hears Josie crying, "No Mam, stop! I'm goin' with ya!," Hester cuts her child's throat so that she will not have to live with the soul-destroying knowledge that she was deserted by her mother.

Race and gender can come together powerfully in stagings of *Medea* (Wetmore 132–204). In the original, Medea was a Colchian woman, and in myth Colchians were black. It is possible to cast Medea as a woman of color, Jason as white, to emphasize Medea's foreignness as a matter of racial difference. Medea's murder of her two sons was so legendary that a female slave who killed her children was called "Medea" in the press, and this story then provided the kernel for Toni Morrison's *Beloved* (1988). *Black Medea*, by Wesley Enoch, was staged as a commentary on contemporary black experience in Australia; his Medea was an indigenous woman (Belvoir St. Theatre, 2006). In a move that relates activism and theater, Rhodessa Jones, performance artist, activist, and co-director of *The Medea Project* for the San Francisco-based theater company Cultural Odyssey, has used the Medea story to ask women in prison to consider the ways in which they might be killing their own children, whether literally or metaphorically. At first, Jones reports, the women were not interested in the play; they were horrified by Medea's action and dismissive of her. Jones and her partner had to work hard to make the relevance clear, asking them why they were not with their own children if they were so much better than Medea. In working on the play, the actresses were learning about themselves. The Greek heroine is used to point up both the similarities and differences between the present and the past; in Euripides' *Medea*, the Chorus pointedly asks how women's stories can be told with honesty since men control the lyre (and therefore the means to produce works of art). Jones' answer is to use the play as a catalyst so that women in the present can tell their own stories. The prison project led to performances outside the jail, and there the audiences as well as the performers continued the educational process.

We have come to the end of this chapter, and to the end of this introduction to Greek tragedy. As I hope you have seen, tragedy, though from a far distant time and place, can still stimulate us to ask difficult questions. And performances of ancient Greek tragedies, whether translations or adaptations, can do that and more. Modern productions serve a variety of purposes. They can celebrate a core tradition of western theater or make the connection between that tradition and others (Yoruba, Japanese, Indian). They can also critique the dominant order, using the ancient texts in new ways. Multiculturalism and feminism have made their mark not by removing these plays from the canon but by leading to new interpretations of them. While the claim that the plays have universal meanings is dubious given the wide diversity of the human condition(s), it is clear that various other cultures have found something in them that resonated with their own experience. And while we cannot assume that there is a privileged transhistorical value in studying Greek tragedy, generations of readers and spectators have made value for themselves and have found the plays useful for thinking through thorny issues. Different perspectives from antiquity up to the present have changed the way we look at these texts; I would encourage each reader to do for him- or herself what the directors and translators mentioned here have done. That is the fun of working with the far distant past.

Suggestions for further reading

In addition to chapters in *The Cambridge Companion to Greek Tragedy*, ed. P. E. Easterling, *A Companion to Greek Tragedy*, ed. Justina Gregory, and the volumes already cited in this chapter, there are books on modern performance such as *Medea in Performance 1500–2000*, ed. Edith Hall, Fiona Macintosh and Oliver Taplin (Oxford: Legenda, 2000); *Dionysus Since 69: Greek Tragedy at the Dawn of the Third Millennium*, ed. Edith Hall, Fiona Macintosh, and Amanda Wrigley (Oxford: Oxford University Press, 2004); *Agamemnon in Performance 458 BC to AD 2004*, ed. Fiona Macintosh, Pantelis Michelakis, Edith Hall, and Oliver Taplin (Oxford: Oxford University Press, 2005); and *Rebel Women: Staging Ancient Greek Drama Today*, ed. John Dillon and S. E. Wilmer (London: Methuen, 2005).

References

Translations cited

Aeschylus. *Oresteia*. Trans. Richmond Lattimore. Vol. 1. In *The Complete Greek Tragedies*. Ed. David Grene and Richmond Lattimore. Chicago: University of Chicago Press, 1959.

Aristotle. *Poetics*. Trans. S. H. Butcher. Introduction by Francis Fergusson. New York: Hill and Wang, 1961.

Euripides. *Iphigenia at Aulis*. Ed. and trans. Mary-Kay Gamel. In *Women on the Edge: Four Plays by Euripides*. Ed. and trans. Ruby Blondell, Mary-Kay Gamel, Nancy Sorkin Rabinowitz, and Bella Zweig. New York: Routledge, 1998.

Sophocles. *Electra*. Ed. and trans. Jenny March. Warminster: Aris and Phillips, 2001.

Sophocles. *Oedipus at Colonus*. Trans. Robert Fitzgerald. Vol. II. *The Complete Greek Tragedies*. Ed. David Grene and Richmond Lattimore. Chicago: University of Chicago Press, 1959.

Thucydides. *The Peloponnesian War*. Trans. Rex Warner. Baltimore: Penguin Books, 1954.

Works cited

Bakhtin, Mikhail. 1981. *The Dialogic Imagination: Four Essays*. Ed. Michael Holquist. Trans. Caryl Emerson and Michael Holquist. Austin: University of Texas Press.

Balme, Christopher. 1999. *Decolonizing the Stage: Theatrical Syncretism and Post-Colonial Drama*. Oxford: Oxford University Press.

Bierl, Anton. 2005. "The Chorus of Aeschylus' *Agamemnon* in Modern Stage Productions: Towards the 'Performative Turn.' " In *Agamemnon in Per-*

formance 458 BC to AD 2004. Ed. Fiona Macintosh, Pantelis Michelakis, Edith Hall, and Oliver Taplin. Oxford: Oxford University Press. 291–306.

Bloch, Maurice. 1992. *Prey into Hunter: The Politics of Religious Experience.* Cambridge: Cambridge University Press.

Burkert, Walter. 1966. "Greek Tragedy and Sacrificial Ritual." *Greek, Roman, and Byzantine Studies* 7: 87–121.

Burnett, Anne P. 1998. *Revenge in Attic and Later Tragedy.* Berkeley: University of California Press.

Butler, Judith. 2000. *Antigone's Claim: Kinship between Life and Death.* New York: Columbia University Press.

Cartledge, Paul. 1997. " 'Deep Plays': Theatre as Process in Greek Civic Life." In *The Cambridge Companion to Greek Tragedy.* Ed. P. E. Easterling. Cambridge: Cambridge University Press. 3–35.

Case, Sue-Ellen. 1988. *Feminism and Theatre.* New York: Routledge.

Cheney, Lynne. 1988. *Humanities in America: A Report to the President, the Congress, and the American People.* Washington, D.C.: NEH.

Conacher, D. J. 1974. "Aeschylus' *Persae*: A Literary Commentary." In *Serta Turyniana: Studies in Greek Literature and Palaeography in Honor of Alexander Turyn.* Ed. John L. Heller. Urbana: University of Illinois Press. 143–68.

Connor, W. R. 1990. "City Dionysia and Athenian Democracy." In *Aspects of Athenian Democracy.* Ed. W. R. Connor, M. H. Hansen, K. A. Raaflaub, and B. S. Strauss. Copenhagen: Museum Tusculanum Press. 7–32.

Csapo, Eric and William J. Slater. 1995. *The Context of Ancient Drama.* Ann Arbor: University of Michigan Press.

Derrida, Jacques. 1976. *Of Grammatology.* Trans. Gayatri Spivak. Baltimore: Johns Hopkins University Press.

duBois, Page. 2003. *Slaves and Other Objects.* Chicago and London: University of Chicago Press.

Eagleton, Terry. 1976. *Marxism and Literary Theory.* Berkeley: University of California Press.

Eagleton, Terry. 1991. *Ideology: An Introduction.* London and New York: Verso.

Fischer-Lichte. 2004. "Thinking about the Origins of Theater in the 1970s." In *Dionysus Since 69: Greek Tragedy at the Dawn of the Third Millennium.* Ed. Edith Hall, Fiona Macintosh, and Amanda Wrigley. Oxford: Oxford University Press. 329–60.

Foley, Helene. 1985. *Ritual Irony: Poetry and Sacrifice in Euripides.* Ithaca: Cornell University Press.

Foley, Helene. 2001. *Female Acts in Greek Tragedy.* Princeton: Princeton University Press.

Freud, Sigmund. 1965. *The Interpretation of Dreams*. Trans. and ed. James Strachey. New York: Avon.

Fugard, Athol, John Kani, and Winston Ntshona. 1976. *Sizwe Bansi is Dead and The Island*. New York: Viking Press.

Girard, René. 1977. *Violence and the Sacred*. Trans. Patrick Gregory. Baltimore: Johns Hopkins University Press.

Goldhill, Simon. 1990. "The Great Dionysia and Civic Ideology." *Journal of Hellenic Studies* 107 (1987): 58–76; reprinted in *Nothing to Do with Dionysos? Athenian Drama in Its Social Context*. Ed. John J. Winkler and Froma Zeitlin. Princeton: Princeton University Press. 97–129.

Goldhill, Simon. 2002. *Who Needs Greek? Contests in the Cultural History of Hellenism*. Cambridge: Cambridge University Press.

Griffin, Jasper. 1998. "The Social Function of Attic Tragedy." *Classical Quarterly* 48: 39–61.

Griffin, Jasper. 1999. "Sophocles and the Democratic City." In *Sophocles Revisited: Essays Presented to Sir Hugh Lloyd-Jones*. Ed. Jasper Griffin. Oxford: Oxford University Press. 73–94.

Hall, Edith. 1989. *Inventing the Barbarian*. Oxford: Oxford University Press.

Hall, Edith, ed. and trans. 1996. *Aeschylus. Persians*. Warminster: Aris and Phillips.

Hall, Edith. 2004a. "Introduction: Why Greek Tragedy in the Late Twentieth Century?" In *Dionysus Since 69: Greek Tragedy at the Dawn of the Third Millennium*. Ed. Edith Hall, Fiona Macintosh, and Amanda Wrigley. Oxford: Oxford University Press. 1–46.

Hall, Edith. 2004b. "Aeschylus, Race, Class, and War in the 1990s." In *Dionysus Since 69: Greek Tragedy at the Dawn of the Third Millennium*. Ed. Edith Hall, Fiona Macintosh, and Amanda Wrigley. Oxford: Oxford University Press. 169–98.

Hardwick, Lorna. 2000. *Translating Worlds, Translating Cultures*. London: Duckworth.

Hartigan, Karelisa. 1995. *Greek Tragedy on the American Stage: Ancient Drama in the Commercial Theater, 1882–1994*. Westport, CT: Greenwood Press.

Heaney, Seamus. 1991. *Cure at Troy*. New York: Noonday Press.

Heaney, Seamus. 2004. *The Burial at Thebes*. New York: Farrar, Straus and Giroux.

Hegel, Friedrich. 1962. *Hegel on Tragedy*. Ed. and with an introduction by Anne Paolucci and Henry Paolucci. Garden City, NY: Anchor Books.

Irigaray, Luce. 1994. *Thinking the Difference: For a Peaceful Revolution*. Trans. Karin Montin. New York: Routledge.

Jebb, R. C. 1967. *The Electra of Sophocles*. Abridged commentary by Gilbert A. Davies. Cambridge: Cambridge University Press.

Lacan, Jacques. 1992. *Seminar VII: The Ethics of Psychoanalysis, 1959–60*. Ed. Jacques-Alain Miller; trans. Dennis Porter. New York: Norton.

Lévi-Strauss, Claude. 1967. *Structural Anthropology*. Garden City: Anchor.

Longo, Odone. 1990. "The Theater of the *Polis*." In *Nothing to Do with Dionysos? Athenian Drama in Its Social Context*. Ed. John J. Winkler and Froma Zeitlin. Princeton: Princeton University Press. 12–19.

Loraux, Nicole. 1995. *The Experiences of Tiresias: The Feminine and the Greek Man*. Princeton: Princeton University Press.

McClure, Laura. 2006. "Maternal Authority and Heroic Disgrace in Aeschylus's *Persae*." *Transactions of the American Philological Association* 136: 71–97.

Mandela, Nelson. 1994. *Long Walk to Freedom: The Autobiography of Nelson Mandela*. Boston: Little Brown.

Mee, Charles. 1998. *The History Plays*. Baltimore: Johns Hopkins University Press.

Mee, Charles. 2002. "Notes toward a Manifesto." In *Shattered and Fucked Up and Full of Wreckage: The Words and Works of Charles L. Mee*. Ed. Erin Mee. *TDR: The Drama Review* 46.3: 83–104.

Mills, Sophie. 1997. *Theseus, Tragedy, and the Athenian Empire*. Oxford: Clarendon Press.

Neuschäfer, Anne. 1996. "Antoine Vitez: The Script and the Spoken Word: Intercultural Dialogue in the Theatre." In *The Intercultural Performance Reader*. Ed. Patrice Pavis. London: Routledge. 131–9.

Nietzsche, Friedrich. 1956. *The Birth of Tragedy*. Trans. Francis Goffing. New York: Doubleday.

Nussbaum, Martha. 1986. *The Fragility of Goodness: Luck and Ethics in Greek Tragedy and Philosophy*. Cambridge: Cambridge University Press.

Page, Denys, ed. 1938. *Euripides. Medea*. Oxford: Oxford University Press.

Parke, H. W. 1977. *Festivals of the Athenians*. Ithaca: Cornell University Press.

Rabinowitz, Nancy Sorkin. 1993. *Anxiety Veiled: Euripides and the Traffic in Women*. Ithaca: Cornell University Press.

Rukeyser, Muriel. 2005. *The Collected Poems of Muriel Rukeyser*. Ed. Janet E. Kaufman and Anne F. Herzog. Pittsburgh, PA: University of Pittsburgh Press.

Said, Edward. 1978. *Orientalism*. New York: Pantheon.

Seaford, Richard. 1994. *Reciprocity and Ritual: Homer and Tragedy in the Developing City-State*. Oxford: Clarendon Press.

Sellars, Peter. 1992. "Peter Sellars' Talk at Carnuntum." In Marianne McDonald, *Ancient Sun, Modern Light: Greek Drama on the Modern Stage*. New York: Columbia University Press. 89–95.

Shaw, Fiona. 1996. "Electra Speechless." In *Sophocles' "Electra" in Performance*. Ed. Francis M. Dunn. Stuttgart: M and P. 131–8.

Sourvinou-Inwood, Christiane. 1994. "Something to Do with Athens." In *Ritual, Finance, Politics: Athenian Democratic Accounts Presented to David Lewis.* Ed. Robin Osborne and Simon Hornblower. Oxford: Clarendon Press. 269–90.

Sourvinou-Inwood, Christiane. 2003. *Tragedy and Athenian Religion.* Lanham, MD: Lexington Books.

Suzuki, Tadashi. 1986. *The Way of Acting: The Theatre Writings of Suzuki Tadashi.* Trans. J. T. Rimer. New York: Theatre Communications Group.

Taylor, Don, trans. and intro. 1990. *Euripides. The War Plays.* London: Methuen.

Thomson, George. 1946. *Aeschylus and Athens: A Study in the Social Origins of Drama.* 2nd ed. London: Lawrence and Wishart.

van Gennep, Arnold. 1960. *The Rites of Passage.* Trans. Monika B. Vizedom and Gabrielle L. Caffee. Chicago: University of Chicago Press.

Vernant, Jean-Pierre. 1980. "Théorie générale du sacrifice et mise à mort dans la *thysia* grecque." In *Le sacrifice dans l'antiquité.* Ed. Jean Rudhardt and Olivier Reverdin. Geneva: Fondation Hardt. 1–30.

Vernant, Jean-Pierre. 1991. *Mortals and Immortals: Collected Essays.* Ed. Froma Zeitlin. Princeton: Princeton University Press.

Vernant, Jean-Pierre. 1996. *Entre Mythe et politique.* Paris: Seuil.

Vernant, Jean-Pierre and Pierre Vidal-Naquet. 1988. *Myth and Tragedy in Ancient Greece.* Trans. Janet Lloyd. New York: Zone Books.

Vidal-Naquet, Pierre. 1986. *The Black Hunter: Forms of Thought and Forms of Society in the Greek World.* Trans. Andrew Szegedy-Maszak. Baltimore: Johns Hopkins University Press.

Weber, Carl, ed. and trans. 1984. *Heiner Müller: Hamletmachine and Other Texts for the Stage.* New York: Performing Arts Publications.

Wetmore, Kevin Jr. 2003. *Black Dionysus: Greek Tragedy and African American Theatre.* Jefferson, N.C.: Mcfarland.

Wiles, David. 1997. *Tragedy in Athens: Performance Space and Theatrical Meaning.* Cambridge: Cambridge University Press.

Wiles, David. 2002. *Greek Theatre Performance: An Introduction.* Cambridge: Cambridge University Press.

Wiles, David. 2004. "The Use of Masks in Modern Performances of Greek Drama." In *Dionysus Since 69: Greek Tragedy at the Dawn of the Third Millennium.* Ed. Edith Hall, Fiona Macintosh, and Amanda Wrigley. Oxford: Oxford University Press. 245–64.

Wilson, Peter. 1997. "Leading the Tragic *Khoros:* Tragic Prestige in the Democratic City." In *Greek Tragedy and the Historian.* Ed. Christopher Pelling. Oxford: Clarendon Press. 81–108.

Winkler, John J. 1990. "The Ephebes' Song: *Tragôidia* and *Polis.*" In *Nothing to Do with Dionysos? Athenian Drama in Its Social Context.* Ed. John J.

Winkler and Froma Zeitlin. Princeton: Princeton University Press. 20–62.

Zeitlin, Froma. 1965. "The Motif of Corrupted Sacrifice in Aeschylus' *Oresteia*." *Transactions and Proceedings of the American Philological Association* 96: 463–508.

Zeitlin, Froma. 1966. "Postscript to Sacrificial Imagery in the *Oresteia* (*Ag*.1235–37)." *Transactions and Proceedings of the American Philological Association* 97: 645–53.

Zeitlin, Froma. 1978. "The Dynamics of Misogyny: Myth and Mythmaking in the *Oresteia*." *Arethusa* 11: 149–84.

Zeitlin, Froma. 1990a. "Playing the Other: Theater, Theatricality, and the Feminine in Greek Drama." In *Nothing to Do with Dionysos? Athenian Drama in Its Social Context*. Ed. John J. Winkler and Froma Zeitlin. Princeton: Princeton University Press. 63–96.

Zeitlin, Froma. 1990b. "Thebes: Theater of Self and Society in Athenian Drama." In *Nothing to Do with Dionysos? Athenian Drama in Its Social Context*. Ed. John J. Winkler and Froma Zeitlin. Princeton: Princeton University Press. 130–67.

Zeitlin, Froma. 1996. *Playing the Other: Gender and Society in Classical Greek Literature*. Chicago: University of Chicago Press.

Index

Achilles, 110, 112, 113, 140–2
actors
  acting style in ancient Greece, 28
  meter and, 28
  traditional functions of, 27–8
  transformation and, 63
Aeschylus, *see also Agamemnon*;
      Eumenides; *Libation Bearers*;
      Oresteia; *Persians*; *Suppliants*
  in Aristophanes' *Frogs*, 17
  Persian Wars and, 39, 89
  surviving plays of, 11–12
Africa and tragedy, 3, 191–3
Agamemnon
  abuse of power by, 55, 95, 102
  deceitfulness of, 109, 110
  emasculation of, 100, 103, 127
  as father and husband, 118–19
  hubris and, 95
  representations in epic vs. tragedy,
      80
  unmanliness of, 100, 110, 144,
      145
Agamemnon (Aeschylus), *see also*
      Agamemnon; Clytemnestra;
      Kassandra; *Oresteia*
  chorus' role in, 27
  feminization of Aigisthos in,
      100–1

performance of, 25, 186, 195
promiscuity in, 96, 97–8, 101
psychologizing in, 29
rhetoric in, 48
use of messenger character in, 28
Ajax, 19–20, 21, 79, 159
anagnôrisis, 14, 15
Anouilh, Jean, 166
Antigone
  familial relations and, 161–2
  as freedom fighter, 191
  incest and, 161, 162
  masculinity of, 158
  as tragic hero, 156, 157, 165
  as woman, 157–8, 162
Antigone (Sophocles), *see also*
      Antigone; Kreon
  ethical decision-making in, 58
  historical context of, 155–6
  incest in, 157, 161, 162
  justice in, 191
  male vs. female in, 160
  modern interest in, 165–6
  modern performances of, 191,
      194
  odes in, 163–5
  prophecy in, 78
Aphrodite
  desire for honor by, 68–9

Aphrodite (*cont'd*)
  disruptive influence of, 69, 77,
    111, 135, 164
  sexual love and, 52, 75, 76, 77,
    113–14, 149
Apollo
  criticism of, 120–1
  maleness and, 105, 107
  matricide and, 47, 78, 102, 105
  plague and, 51
  rationality and, 64
  vengeance and, 106, 117
archon, 11, 12, 44–5, 46, 49
Argos, Athenian alliance with, 49
Aristophanes
  rhetoric and, 47
  tragedy and, 17
  use of cross–dressing by, 28
Aristotle, *see also Constitution of the
    Athenians; Poetics; Rhetoric*
  art and, 16
  definition of tragedy and, 14–15
  democracy and, 36, 37, 45
  slavery and, 57
  value of tragedy and, 16–18
arrêphoroi, 68, 71–2
Artemis, rituals associated with,
    71–2
Assembly, 36, 37, 38
Atê, 73, 93, 94, 164
Athena, as male, 107
Athens
  calendar of, 66
  map of, 22
  vs. other democracies, 33–4, 37
  as setting for plays, 48
Atossa, Queen, 89, 91, 92, 93
Atrides, 181, 190
Attica defined, 11, 33
audience
  chorus as, 34
  comparison with Assembly and
    law courts, 45

composition of, 56–7
democracy represented by, 35
original vs. modern, 21, 81, 86,
    120, 138
religious resonances in tragedy
    for, 65–6, 74, 75, 79, 82,
    83–4
responses to plays
  ancient, 48–51, 53–4, 57, 65–
    6, 119, 134, 144, 154
  modern, 117, 119, 120, 135,
    138, 154, 166, 174–5
segregation of women in, 44
slaves in, 56
Auletta, Robert, 94, 184

Bacchai (Euripides), 55, 81–4, 192,
    196
Bakhtin, Mikhail, 53–4
barbarians defined, 40; *see also*
    binary oppositions, barbarian
    vs. Greek
barbaros, 40, 90
Bennett, William, 2–3, 5, 180
binary oppositions, *see also* self and
    "the other"
  barbarian vs. Greek, 99, 111,
    137–8, 145–6, 147, 151–2,
    153
  complexity of, 177
  East vs. West, 115, 147
  male vs. female
    in *Antigone,* 160
    in *Elektra* (Euripides),
      118–19
    in *Hekabe,* 140–1, 142,
      143
    in *Iphigeneia at Aulis,* 109–11
    in *Medea,* 151–2
    in *Oedipus Tyrannos,* 175–6
    in *Oresteia,* 96–101, 103, 105–
      6, 107–8
    in *Persians,* 90–2

in *Trojan Women,* 133, 136
mortal vs. immortal, 99, 153, 154, 156, 158–9, 172
nature vs. nurture, 126, 143, 168, 194
polis vs. *oikos,* 86–7, 101 (*see also* binary oppositions, state vs. family)
politics vs. religion, 168–70
public vs. private, 97–8, 111, 140–1, 160, 168
slave vs. free, 40, 91, 110, 136, 141, 143
state vs. family, 156, 157, 159–60, 164, 168, 195–6 (*see also* binary oppositions, *polis* vs. *oikos*)
structuralism and, 4, 5, 85–6 (*see also* structuralism)
war vs. family, 101, 103, 105, 109, 195
woman vs. Greek, 110–11
words vs. deeds, 123–4, 126, 128–9
Blondell, Ruby, 110, 111
Burkert, Walter, 69, 70
Burnett, Anne, 144
Butler, Judith, 166

Carr, Marina, 196
Case, Sue-Ellen, 195
Castledine, Annie, 186–7
Cheney, Lynne, 2, 5, 180
chorêgos, 11, 44, 45
chorus
  composition of, 20
  meter and, 26
  in modern performances, 181
  political symbolism of, 34–5
  theatrical importance and functions of, 25–7, 29
Christian values, inappropriate use of, 15

citizenship, Athenian, *see also* democracy; *dêmos*
  choral participation and, 35
  classes within, 36
  inclusion vs. exclusion, 38–9, 43
  participation in public life, 37–8
city (as political entity), *see polis*
City Dionysia, *see also* processions
  as context for tragedy, 33, 35
  described, 11
  empire and, 46–7
  ideological conflict and resolution in, 54–5
  inequalities in, 55–6
Classics
  criticism of, 3
  importance to western civilization of, 2, 3
  origins of, 1
close reading, 3–4
cloth/clothing
  cultural importance of, 36, 92, 98, 143, 191
  Elektra and, 117, 119, 125, 129
  tearing, 89, 91, 142 (*see also* lamentations/funeral speeches)
Clytemnestra, *see also Oresteia*
  masculinity of, 96, 100, 101, 118
  as mother, 103, 106, 121, 127
  performance of rituals by, 73
  promiscuity of, 96, 97–8, 119
  rhetoric and, 48
  as shameless, 126–7
  as wife, 119, 127
colonization, *see* post-colonialism
conservatism, educational, 2, 33, 58, 190
Constitution of the Athenians, 36, 37
contexts for studying tragedy, 1
costumes, performances in, 29–30

cross-dressing, 27, 56, 65, 72–3, 82, 83, 182, 196; *see also* gender fluidity
Csapo, Eric, 56
cults
  observances by, 61, 63, 65, 66–7
  rites of passage and, 75, 121–2
culture wars, 1–3, 5–6, 180

Darius, 39, 89, 92, 93, 94
deconstructive criticism, 5
deinos, nature of man and, 163
Delian League, 41, 42, 46
democracy, *see also* citizenship, Athenian; *dêmos;* empire, democratic; freedom
  Athenian, development of, 36–9
  censorship in, 184–5
  ideology of, as represented in tragedy, 52–5
  theaters and, 23, 37
  tragedy's relevance to, 33–5, 184
  war and, 42
  wealth and, 37
demos, see also citizenship, Athenian; democracy
  defined, 36, 38
  elites vs., 156
  empire and, 42
  power given to, 37
Derrida, Jacques, 5
deus ex machina, 25, 152, 182
Dickstein, Rachel, 187
Dionysos, *see also* maenads; satyrs
  connections with tragedy, 64–5
  death and, 62
  Dionysian vs. Apollonian, 64
  Eleuthereus, 11, 35, 60, 81
  festivals for, 61–3 (*see also* City Dionysia)
  liminality of, 62, 65, 83
  madness and, 64, 81–3, 165
  of the Marshes, 62, 83

  as outsider, 65, 81, 83
  rebirth of, 63
  representation in tragedy, 81–4
  resistance to, 61, 63–4, 81–3
  sacrifices and, 69
  satyrs and, *12*
  wine in Dionysian myth, 63–4
Dionysos, Theater of, *23, 24,* 84
dithyramb, 11, 18, 61

Eagleton, Terry, 51
ekkyklêma, 25, 104
Electra, see Elektra
Elektra
  excessive mourning by, 119–20, 124–7
  as loving sister, 130
  marriage of, 117–18, 120, 121
  masculinity of, 128–9
  overidentification with father by, 5
  similarities to Clytemnestra, 119, 126–7
  as slave, 80, 103, 120
Elektra (Euripides), *see also* Elektra; Jason; Orestes
  costumes in, 30
  historical context of, 116
  justice in, 119, 120, 121
  male vs. female in, 118–19
Elektra (Sophocles), *see also* Elektra; Jason; Orestes
  epic tone of, 123, 128
  historical context of, 116
  Homeric references in, 123, 124
  justice in, 123, 126, 127
  modern performances of, 183, 195
  modern/political interpretations of, 131–2
  open-endedness of, 131
emotions, tragic, *see* pity and fear (tragic emotions)

empire, *see also* Delian League
  Athenian ideal of, 39, 53
  City Dionysia and, 46
  dangers of, 93, 137–8, 174
  democratic, 34, 42, 85, 138
  Persian, 39, 91, 93, 94
  war and, 94, 133
  wealth and, 40–1, 46–7, 91, 93,
    94
Enoch, Wesley, 197
Eppworth, John, 196
ethical criticism, 58–9
Eumenides (Aeschylus), *see also*
    Apollo; Furies; *Oresteia*;
    Orestes
  references to Athenian politics in,
    48–9
Euripides, *see also Bacchai*; *Elektra*;
    Hekabe; *Iphigeneia at Aulis*;
    Medea; *Trojan Women*
  as reformer of tragedy, 122
  rhetoric and, 48
  surviving plays of, 11–12
  use of chorus by, 26

family, *see* binary oppositions, *polis*
    vs. *oikos;* binary oppositions,
    state vs. family; binary
    oppositions, war vs. family
fate
  as element of tragedy, 6, 102,
    104, 112, 171–2
  Greek concept of, 78–9, 135
  Moirai, 78, 104, 165
feminism
  criticism/theory, 9, 34, 85, 154,
    166, 176
  influence on performances, 191,
    195–6
festivals, 61–3; *see also* City Dionysia
  political nature of, 66
Fisher, John, 196
Foley, Helene, 58, 70

formalism in Greek tragedy
  conventions of, 30
  and lack of realism, 8, 23–4, 28,
    29, 30
free will, 110, 172; *see also* fate
freedom, *see also* binary oppositions,
    slave vs. free
  vs. barbarism, 40
  vs. empire, 42
  of speech, 53
  from tyranny, 35, 53, 142
  from work, 38, 41
Freud, Sigmund, 5, 7, 174–6; *see
    also* psychological criticism
Fugard, Athol, 191
funeral speeches, *see* lamentations/
    funeral speeches
Furies, *see also* vengeance, Furies as
    agents of
  Athens and, 107–8
  Oedipus and, 77
  Orestes and, 74, 78, 102, 104

Gamel, Mary-Kay, 110, 111, 114
gender fluidity, *see also*
    cross-dressing
  actors and, 27–8, 29
  Clytemnestra and, 96–8
  Dionysos and, 82, 83
  in rituals, 65, 72–3, 83
Gernet, Louis, 4
Girard, René, 69–70
gods
  described, 76–7
  hubris against, 15
  relations with humans, 77–9,
    134–5
  temples to, 37, 43
  worship/sacrifices and, 68–9,
    134–5
Goldhill, Simon, 1, 53, 65
Great Dionysia, *see* City Dionysia
Griffin, Jasper, 58

guest-friendship, *see xenia*; Zeus,
    Xenios (guardian of
    hospitality)

Hall, Edith, 90, 92, 182, 183, 185,
    190
Hall, Peter, 181
hamartia, 15, 172
Hamilton, Edith, 186
Hare, David, 185
Harrison, Tony, 188
Hartigan, Karelisa, 181
Heaney, Seamus, 193–4
Hecuba, *see Hekabe*
Hegel, Georg W. F., 157
hegemony, *see* empire
Hekabe
    as barbarian, 141, 144, 146
    as mother, 139, 140
    as powerful woman, 139, 141,
        143–5
    rationality of, 141
Hekabe (Euripides), *see also* Hekabe
    as an anti-war play, 139, 187–9
    historical context of, 139
    justice in, 141, 144
    male vs. female in, 140–1, 142,
        143
    marginal setting of, 139
    modern performances of, 187–9
    rhetoric in, 48
Helen
    as greedy, 135
    as promiscuous, 74, 80, 96, 110,
        114
    rape and, 80, 109
    seductive power of, 135
    as victim, 80, 111, 113–14, 135
Herakles, *12*
Herodotus, 18, 38, 87, 151
heroism
    ancient ideal of, 72, 112, 113,
        128, 143, 150

critiques of, 110, 118, 120, 123,
    132, 144, 151, 153, 156–7
Dionysos and, 65
female, 120, 132, 144, 150–1,
    158
hubris and, 95
Hestia, 66, 77
Higgins, Claire, 188
Hippolytos (Euripides)
    binary oppositions in, 4
    gods in, 68–9, 153
    misogyny in, 149
    rites of passage in, 75
    sexuality in, 5
    tyrants in, 29, 55
historical/social mode of study,
    58–9
hospitality, *see xenia*; Zeus, Xenios
    (guardian of hospitality)
House of Atreus, 80, 95, 108, 116,
    117, 147, 168, 195
House of Atreus, 181
household, *see* binary oppositions,
    polis vs. *oikos*
hubris
    concept of, 15
    East vs. West and, 90, 95
    godly anger and, 136
    tyranny and, 55, 171, 173
    Xerxes and, 93–4

ideology, *see also* democracy;
        freedom; post-colonialism,
        tragedy as subverting or
        supporting; war, values
        and
    modern conceptions of, 51–2
    tragedies as affirmations of, 55,
        92, 106–7
    tragedies as challenges to, 53,
        92–3, 114–15, 122 (*see also*
        performances, modern,
        subversiveness of)

Iliad (Homer), 23, 51, 64, 77, 96
infanticide, 147, 153, 154; *see also*
    Medea, infanticide and
initiation rituals, *see also* rites of
    passage
    affirmation of Athenian ideology
      and, 55
    cross-dressing in, 56
    personal transformation through,
      56, 58, 63
    references to, in specific tragedies,
      92, 96, 114
Iphigeneia
    patriotism of, 114
    sacrifices and, 69, 72, 74
    transformation from private to
      public figure, 112
    virginity of, 96
    willing sacrifice of, 112–13
Iphigeneia among the Taurians
    (Euripides), 80, 108
Iphigeneia at Aulis (Euripides)
    Agamemnon in, 80
    gods in, 113–14
    male vs. female in, 109–11
    modern performances of, 189–90,
      195
    psychologizing in, 29
    rhetoric in, 48
    war in, 109, 189–90
Ireland, tragedy's popularity in,
    131–2, 183, 193–4, 196–7
Irigaray, Luce, 166
Isherwood, Charles, 189

Jason
    Golden Fleece myth and, 147
    misogyny of, 149
    as rational Greek male, 151–2
    rhetoric and, 47
Jebb, R. C., 123
Jones, Rhodessa, 197
Jung, Carl Gustav, 5

kakos, 110, 150, 169
Kani, John, 191
Kassandra
    as barbarian, 100, 101
    marriage and, 74, 118–19, 136
    revenge of, 136–7
    as victim, 134, 136
katharsis, role in tragedy of, 15, 16–
    17, 64–5; *see also* pity and
    fear (tragic emotions)
Kent, Jonathan, 188
Kindly Ones, *see* Furies
Kleisthenes, 37, 67
kommos, 27, 124, 162; *see also*
    lamentations/funeral
    speeches
Kreon
    destruction of, 165
    mortal vs. divine and, 157, 158–
      9, 161, 163
    rhetoric and, 47–8
    state vs. family and, 156, 160–1,
      164
    as tragic hero, 156–7, 158–9, 194
    as tyrannical ruler, 158–9, 160–1,
      162–3, 164, 191

Lacan, Jacques, 5, 165
lamentations/funeral speeches; *see*
    also kommos; mourning
    speech/action vs., 128, 141, 143
    state control of, 56, 91, 156
    in tragedies, 27, 94, 194
    tragedy's roots in, 75–6, 124
    women and, 91, 119, 126
Laws (Plato), 35, 45
lênai, *see* maenads
Lévi-Strauss, Claude, 4, 174, 176
Libation Bearers (Aeschylus), *see also*
    Clytemnestra; Elektra; Furies;
    Oresteia; Orestes
    chorus' role in, 27
    plot summary of, 102

Libation Bearers (Aeschylus) (*cont'd*)
   rituals in, 73–4, 124
   sexual double-standard in, 148
   vengeance in, 102, 104
libations, 61, 62, 67; *see also*
   sacrifices
literary theory, 34, 177
Loraux, Nicole, 56
Ludlam, Charles, 196

McClure, Laura, 92
McGuiness, Frank, 188
McLaughlin, Ellen, 187
maenads; *see also* Dionysos;
    sparagmos
   defined, 61, 82
   in Euripides' *Bacchai*, 81–2
   rites of, 62, 63, 83
Mandela, Nelson, 191
marriage
   death and, 74, 110–11, 118, 120,
     136–7, 143, 162
   for material gain, 151
   purpose of, 55–6
   rape/slavery and, 136, 137
   women's misery in, 148
marshes, *see* Dionysos, of the
   Marshes
Marxist analysis, 9, 34, 51–2
masks, use of, 20, 29, 62, 181–2,
   195
Medea
   as an imitation woman, 150, 154
   as barbarian, 147, 151–2, 153
   as goddess, 152, 153
   infanticide and, 150–1, 153, 154
   masculinity of, 149–51, 152
   as mother, 151, 196–7
   multiple identities of, 147
   rhetoric and, 47–8, 152
   as wife, 148–51
Medea (Euripides), *see also* Jason;
   Kreon; Medea
   Athenian ideology in, 52
   historical context of, 146
   justice in, 150, 151, 152
   male vs. female in, 151–2
   performance of, 25, 182, 196–7
   role of messenger character in, 29
   use of speeches/rhetoric in, 28,
    47–8
Mee, Charles, tragedy and, 7–8
Meineck, Peter, 30, 99
Melian massacre, 49–50
men
   as public entities, 87
   and rites of passage in tragedies,
    74–5
messenger character, role of the,
   28–9
metics, 44, 55, 66
Mike, Chuck, 191
Mills, Sophie, 53
misogyny in Greek culture, 145,
   148, 149, 154, 195
Mitchell, Katie, 186, 189
Mnouchkine, Ariane, 108, 181,
   190
Monk, Isabell, 195
Morrison, Toni, 197
mourning, *see also* lamentations/
   funeral speeches
   excessive, 76, 119, 124–7
   as feminine act, 76, 91, 124, 157
   state restrictions on, 36, 75–6,
    126, 156
   in tragedy, 26, 28
   tragedy's roots in (*see*
    lamentations/funeral
    speeches, tragedy's roots in)
Müller, Heiner, 183–4
multiculturalism, 6, 33, 66, 85,
   180, 190, 198
music
   role in education, 26–7
   use of, 26–7
myth
   Dionysiac, 56, 63–4, 65

use in tragedies, 4, 30, 60, 70, 72, 78–81, 117, 195

nationalism, 46–7, 112, 113, 115
Neoptolemus, 75, 137, 193–4
Neuschäfer, Anne, 183
New Criticism, 3–4
Nietzsche, Friedrich, 64
Norton-Taylor, Richard, 185
nostalgia, 6, 7
Ntshona, Winston, 191

O'Brien, Edna, 189
Odyssey (Homer), 95–6, 100, 106
Oedipus
    blindness of, 169, 174
    endogamy/exogamy and, 4
    self-recognition and, 14, 167, 169, 176
    as symbol of Athens, 173–4
    as tyrannical ruler, 168–9, 170, 173
    as "universal man," 174–6
    as virtuous man, 172–3
Oedipus at Kolonos (Sophocles), 48, 52, 53, 77, 80, 173; *see also* Oedipus
Oedipus complex, 7, 175
Oedipus Tyrannos (Sophocles); *see also* Kreon; Oedipus
    free will/agency in, 170, 172
    historical context of, 166–7
    male vs. female in, 175–6
    modern performances of, 191–2
    politics vs. religion in (*see* binary oppositions, politics vs. religion)
    prophecy in, 78, 167, 169, 170
    typical interpretations of, 166–7
Oresteia (Aeschylus), *see also* *Agamemnon*; *Eumenides*; *Libation Bearers*
    chorus' role in, 26
    demands of the gods in, 78

hubris in, 95
justice in, 95, 102, 104, 107, 195
male vs. female in, 96–101, 103, 105–6, 107–8
messenger character, role in, 29
modern performances of, 181, 182, 186, 190
rituals in, 73–5
Orestes
    ambiguous motives of, 104, 123
    doubts about murder and, 120–1, 125
    false death of, 127–8, 129–30
    libations to, 62
    rites of passage and, 74–5, 104–5
orientalism, 40, 90, 99; *see also* self and "the other"
Osborne, Nigel, 186
Osofisan, Femi, 191
ostracism, 37, 174
other, the, *see* self and "the other"
outsiders, social
    in Athenian society, 86–7
    chorus as, 34
    Dionysos and, 81, 83
    hospitality toward, 52 (*see also* Zeus, Xenios (guardian of hospitality))
    representation in modern tragedies, 183, 196
    tyrants as, 36, 168

Page, Denys, 147
pan-Hellenism, *see* nationalism
Pappenheim, Mark, 184
Paris school, 8
Parris, Matthew, 188
patriotism, *see* nationalism
Peisistratus, 35, 36, 39
Peloponnesian War
    described, 41–2
    ideology of, 42–3
    influence on tragic plays, 49–50, 116–17, 133

Pentheus, *see Bacchai*
performances
  ancient (*see also* theaters, ancient)
    compared to contemporary
      performance events, 30–1
    as social force, 58–9
    traditional elements of, 20–1
  modern
    abundance of, 180, 182–3
    by the American National
      Theater, 184
    anti-war-themed (*see* war,
      modern tragedies critical of)
    avant-garde theater and, 196
    by the British National Theatre,
      181, 186–7, 189, 192
    by the Crucible Theatre, 189
    by Cultural Odyssey, 197
    by the Donmar Theatre, 188
    "faithful" vs. "relevant"
      productions, 180–1, 187,
      194
    feminist-themed (*see* feminism,
      influence on performances)
    by the Greek Active group, 196
    by the Guthrie Theater, 181,
      190, 195
    intercultural productions of,
      181–2, 191–4
    by the Mark Taper Forum, 185
    by the National Theatre of
      Greece, 183
    by the Performance Group,
      196
    post-colonial–themed (*see*
      post-colonialism)
    in prisons, 191, 197
    racial issues in, 197
    by the Royal Shakespeare
      Company, 188
    sexuality explorations in, 196
    subversiveness of, 182, 183,
      190

    by the Theatre of the
      Ridiculous, 196
Perikles
  death of, 43
  democracy and, 39, 45, 53
  influence on Athenian culture,
    39–40, 75, 155–6, 164, 174
  Oedipus, parallels with, 51, 167,
    174
  in *The Peloponnesian War*, 42
  rise to power, 37
peripeteia, 14, 15
Persian Wars
  Athenian democracy and, 39
  East vs. West in, 57, 133, 137
  Greek identity and, 39–40
  Peloponnesian War vs., 42
  Trojan War vs., 133
Persians (Aeschylus)
  Athenian ideology in, 52, 55,
    90–3
  as cautionary tale, 92–3, 94
  male vs. female in, 90–2
  modern performances of, 184–5
  parallels with Gulf War and Iraq
    War, 93, 94–5
Philoctetes, 75, 80, 193–4
Pindar, 151
pity and fear (tragic emotions), 14,
    15, 16, 17; *see also katharsis*
Plato
  art and, 16–18, 35
  democracy and, 45
  theater audiences and, 56
Plutarch, 19, 45
Poetics (Aristotle), 14, 16, 18, 26,
    61, 112
polis
  defined, 11, 33
  inequities within, 55–6
  vs. *oikos* (*see* binary oppositions,
    polis vs. *oikos*)
  and religious events, 66

politicians, dishonorable, 110, 141, 153
pompê, 61, 71; *see also* processions
post-colonialism
    Anglophone, 193–4
    Francophone, 33, 193
    Nigeria and, 191–2
    tragedy as subverting or
        supporting, 184, 190, 192
postmodernism, 2, 48, 180, 181
poststructuralism, 5
pride, role in tragedy, 14, 15
processions
    as public events, 36, 44
    as religious events, 60–1, 62, 65,
        71, 72, 74
Prometheus, 69, 76, 163
prophecy
    ambiguity of, 78
    and animal sacrifices, 69
    and fate vs. character, 93
psychoanalytic theories, *see*
        psychological criticism
psychological criticism
    ancient performance and, 29, 30
    described, 4–5
    family and, 105
    Freud and, 174–6
    in specific plays, 82, 108, 117,
        120, 128, 165, 167
Pythagorean table of opposites, *see*
        binary oppositions
Pythia, 78, 105–6

rape
    Helen and, 80, 109
    marriage and, 136
    in myth, 100
    representation in performance, 29
    war and, 112, 133, 136, 137,
        138–9, 186
realism, lack of, *see* formalism in
        Greek tragedy

Redgrave, Vanessa, 188–9
religion, *see* cults; gods; *polis;*
        processions; rituals
revenge, *see* vengeance
rhetoric and speeches
    examples of, 98, 107, 118–19,
        121, 123–5, 127–8, 135,
        136, 141–2, 143
    mistrust of, 47–8, 53, 147, 152
    performance of, 28
    use in tragedies, 47–8
Rhetoric (Aristotle), 17, 45
rites of passage, 62, 63, 70–3, 92;
        see also initiation rituals
rituals, *see also* sacrifices
    defined, 67
    depiction in tragedies, 73–6, 108,
        114
    gender fluidity in, 72–3
    holiday calendar and, 66
    household, 66–7
    initiation, murder as, 83, 123,
        131
    marriage (*see* marriage)
    rites of passage (*see* rites of
        passage)
    supplication, 28, 52–3, 74, 140,
        142, 144, 168
Rotimi, Ola, 191
Rukeyser, Muriel, 175–6

sacrifices, *see also* libations; rituals
    animal, 68–9
    City Dionysia and, 45, 60, 61
    examples of, 67–8
    human, 70, 72, 74, 140–1,
        142–3
    marriage and, 110–11
    murder vs., 69, 114
    at public events, 62, 66
    structuralist analysis of, 86
    tragedy's relationship to, 56, 69
Said, Edward, 90

satyr drama, 11–12, 18, 27, 29, 61
satyrs, 11, *12*, 61
Schroth, Christoph, 190
Seaford, Richard, 55, 65, 66, 83
self and "the other," 56, 64–5, 86–7, 90, 154; *see also* binary oppositions; orientalism
Sellars, Peter, 184
settings
  ancient vs. modern, 180–1, 189, 190, 191
  foreign, 53–4
  Thebes as, 54, 80, 81, 174, 176–7
  Thrace as, 139
  Troy as, 133
Shaw, Fiona, 131
Slater, William, 56
slavery, *see also* binary oppositions, slave vs. free
  Athenian dependence on, 3, 38, 41, 87
  defined, 40
  democracy and, 38
  fear of, 87, 146
  marriage and, 136, 137
  Marxist analysis and, 34
  tragedy and, 55, 56, 57
  war and, 49, 87, 133, 136, 137, 138–9
  women and (*see* binary oppositions, male vs. female; rape, war and; women, as slaves)
Slovo, Gillian, 185
Soans, Robert, 186
Socrates, 17, 47, 50, 85
Solon, 36, 37, 66, 75
sophists, 47, 152, 174
Sophocles, *see also Antigone*; *Oedipus at Kolonos*; *Oedipus Tyrannos*
  as an actor, 21
  painted scenery and, 21

Perikles and, 174
piety of, 131
popularity of, 196
surviving plays of, 11–12
war and, 39, 49
Sourvinou-Inwood, Christiane, 65, 70
Soyinka, Wole, 192
sparagmos, 63, 82, 83; *see also* Dionysos
Sparta
  Athens
    ties between, 37, 42, 156
    war with, 41–3, 49, 109, 133, 146
  education in, 35
  marriage practices in, 73
  rites of passage in, 72
speeches, *see* rhetoric and speeches
Spencer, Charles, 186
spondai, *see* libations
structuralism, *see also* binary oppositions
  axial analysis of *Agamemnon*, 101
  Classics and, 4–5, 85–6
  masculinity and, 71
  ritual analysis and, 68
suffering
  as dramatic element, 15, 55, 79
  learning through, 17, 102, 121, 122
  pleasure in, 125, 194
  purification and, 64–5, 121
Suppliants (Aeschylus)
  role of chorus in, 26
  violence depicted in, 29
Suppliants (Euripides)
  Athenian events depicted in, 49
  Athenian ideology in, 52–3
  lamentation in, 76
  setting of, 80
supplication, *see* rituals, supplication

Talthybios, 29, 136, 137
Taylor, Don, 113
terrorism, 52, 146, 185–6, 189, 193
theaters, ancient, *see also* audience; *deus ex machina*
    deme theater at Thorikos, 21–3, 25
    location amidst other state institutions, 43–4
    segregation within, 44
    Theater of Dionysos, 21–5, *23*, *24*, 25
    ticket stipend for, 45
Thebes, *see* settings, Thebes as
Theseus, *see also Hippolytos; Oedipus at Kolonos; Suppliants* (Euripides)
    arrogance and abuse of power by, 29, 55
    Athenian ideology and, 52, 53
    lamentation and, 76
    rites of passage and, 72–3
Thespis, 18, 35
Thomson, George, 66, 107
Thucydides, 39, 41–2, 43, 49, 53, 116
tragedy, Attic
    defined, 11, 13–15
    epic poetry vs., 14
    humanistic learning and, 2
    modern vs. classic, 6–7
    origins of, 18–19
    possibility in modern times, 6–7
    role in education, 16, 17–18, 35
    as stimulus to consider current issues, 197–8
tragôidia, 18, 69; *see also* tragedy, Attic
transformation, *see* initiation rituals
transvestism, *see* cross-dressing; gender fluidity
Trojan War
    gods' involvement in, 77

    as subject of tragedy, 80, 186
Trojan Women (Euripides)
    as anti-war play, 134, 186–7
    Athenian ideology in, 52
    historical context of, 133–4
    justice in, 134
    male vs. female in, 133, 136
    Melian massacre and, 49–50
    post-colonialist version of, 191
Troy, *see* settings, Troy as
tyranny, *see* tyrants
tyrants
    in Athenian history, 35–7, 39, 174
    Athenians as, 42–3, 55
    characteristics of, 29, 55
    Clytemnestra and Aigisthos as, 103
    vs. freedom, 35, 53, 142
    hubris and, 55, 171, 173
    Kreon as, 158–9, 160–1, 162–3, 164, 191
    Oedipus as, 168–9, 170, 173
    as outsiders, 36, 168
    Theseus as, 29, 53, 55

van Gennep, Arnold, 71–2
vengeance
    Furies as agents of, 102, 107
    in Greek history, 116–17
    infanticide as, 147
    interpretation by modern audiences, 117, 188, 193
    as justifiable act, 123, 127, 130–1, 144
    trial by jury vs., 107, 108
    women as agents of, 121, 144–5, 152, 195
Vernant, Jean-Pierre and Pierre Vidal-Naquet
    democracy, tragedy's role in, 33–4
    Dionysos, theater and, 65
    ideology and, 51, 53

Vernant, Jean-Pierre and Pierre
    Vidal-Naquet (*cont'd*)
  rituals and, 69, 71, 168, 174
Vitez, Antoine, 183

war
  Bosnian War, modern tragedies
    referring to, 186–7
  costs of, 46, 94, 96, 112, 113,
    134, 140, 146
  effects on language of, 116
  Gulf War of 1991, modern
    tragedies referring to, 93, 94,
    184–5
  Iraq War, tragic references to, 52,
    93, 94, 186, 187, 189
  modern tragedies critical of,
    184–90
  rape during (*see* rape, war and;
    women, as slaves)
  sexual double standard and, 103,
    119, 148
  slavery and (*see* slavery, war
    and)
  values and, 116–17, 139–40,
    141–2, 153–4, 183
wealth
  Athenian politics and, 37–8
  funding of tragedies and, 45, 66
  and happiness, 93
  and *hubris*, 94, 95, 98–9, 100
  social status and, 36, 45
  and virtue, 117–18
Wiles, David, 23, 34, 181
Winkler, John, 34
women. *see also* misogyny in Greek
    culture
  as evil, 103, 104, 105–6, 107–8,
    145, 154, 176
  literary tradition and, 148–9
  marriage and (*see* marriage)

modesty/restraint and, 97, 110,
    111, 125, 126, 127
  nationalism and, 112, 113
  outsider status of, 87
  revenge and (*see* vengeance,
    women as agents of)
  as slaves, 55, 87, 136, 137
  strong (*see* Clytemnestra,
    masculinity of; Hekabe, as
    powerful woman; Medea,
    masculinity of)
  as tragic characters, 57–8
  weak, 125, 129, 130
women, Athenian, *see also* misogyny
    in Greek culture
  attendance at theater, 44, 56–7
  Clytemnestra and, 97
  exclusion from political/public
    life, 38–9
  family loyalty and, 157–8
  Iphigeneia and, 74
  Ismene as ideal, 157, 158
  Khrysothemis as ideal, 125–6,
    129
  laws concerning, 36
  outsider status of, 87
  private sphere and, 87
  rituals involving, 71–2
  social status of, 55–6

xenia, 67, 140
Xerxes
  empire and, 91
  hubris and, 93–4
  unmanliness of, 91–2, 94

Zeitlin, Froma, 54, 55, 57, 73, 108
Zeus
  deception of, 69
  Xenios (guardian of hospitality),
    66–7, 96, 102